Active Labor Market
Policies in Europe

Jochen Kluve, David Card, Michael Fertig, Marek Góra,
Lena Jacobi, Peter Jensen, Reelika Leetmaa,
Leonhard Nima, Eleonora Patacchini,
Sandra Schaffner, Christoph M. Schmidt,
Bas van der Klaauw and Andrea Weber

Active Labor Market Policies in Europe

Performance and Perspectives

With 30 Figures and 28 Tables

 Springer

Dr. Jochen Kluve
RWI Essen
Rheinisch-Westfälisches Institut für Wirtschaftsforschung
Hohenzollernstraße 1-3
45128 Essen
Germany
jochen.kluve@rwi-essen.de

Library of Congress Control Number: 2006938715

ISBN 978-3-540-48557-5 Springer Berlin Heidelberg New York

Springer is part of Springer Science+Business Media

springer.com

© Springer-Verlag Berlin Heidelberg 2007

Production: LE-TEX Jelonek, Schmidt & Vöckler GbR, Leipzig
Cover-design: Erich Kirchner, Heidelberg

SPIN 11920052   42/3100YL - 5 4 3 2 1 0   Printed on acid-free paper

Foreword

This book is based on a "Study on the effectiveness of ALMPs" which the authors conducted for the European Commission, Directorate-General Employment, Social Affairs and Equal Opportunities, between November 2004 and December 2005 (Contract No. VC/2004/0133). We thank Fabien Dell (French Embassy in Germany, Berlin), Laura Larsson (IFAU, Uppsala, Sweden), and Alissa Goodman and Andrew Shephard (both IFS, London, UK) for very helpful comments. We also thank Africa Melis at Eurostat for excellent assistance with the data on labor market policy expenditure and participants, members of the DG Employment, Social Affairs and Equal Opportunities for valuable comments at several working meetings in Brussels, Eva Schulte and Peggy David (both RWI Essen) for their research assistance, Claudia Lohkamp (RWI Essen) for invaluable help with administrative matters, and Anette Hermanowski and Joachim Schmidt (RWI Essen) for preparing the manuscript. The opinions expressed in this book are those of the authors only and do not represent the Commission's official position.

The authors: Jochen Kluve (RWI Essen, Germany), David Card (University of California, Berkeley, USA), Michael Fertig (RWI Essen, Germany), Marek Góra (Warsaw School of Economics, Poland), Lena Jacobi (RWI Essen, Germany), Peter Jensen (Aarhus School of Business, Denmark), Reelika Leetmaa (PRAXIS Tallinn, Estonia), Leonhard Nima (RWI Essen, Germany), Eleonora Patacchini (University of Rome, Italy), Sandra Schaffner (RWI Essen, Germany), Christoph M. Schmidt (RWI Essen, Germany), Bas van der Klaauw (Free University Amsterdam, Netherlands), Andrea Weber (Institute for Advanced Studies Vienna, Austria).

Essen, September 2006   RWI Essen

Jochen Kluve

Contents

X   Contents

Executive summary

Against the background of at least two decades of unsatisfactory European labor market performance, at the Luxembourg Jobs summit in November 1997 the European Commission initiated what has become known as the Luxembourg Process. The Amsterdam Treaty introduced a new Employment Title, which for the first time raised employment issues to the same status as other key goals in the formulation of European Union economic policy. The Treaty represents a critical step in the development of the European Employment Strategy. Article 2, for instance, states that "member states [...] shall regard promoting employment as a matter of common concern and shall co-ordinate their actions". Article 3 formally recognizes that high employment should be an explicit goal "in the formulation and implementation of Community policies and activities".

The Lisbon European Council in the year 2000 updated the European Employment Strategy, specifying that by 2010 the Union should regain conditions for full employment and strengthen cohesion. In particular, by 2010 the overall EU employment rate should be raised to 70%, and the average female employment rate to more than 60%. The Stockholm Council in 2001 stated intermediate targets (67% average employment rate by 2005, and 57% for women). The Barcelona Council in 2002 confirmed that full employment was the overarching objective and called for a reinforced Employment Strategy to underpin the Lisbon targets in an enlarged European Union.

Active Labor Market Policies – including measures such as job search assistance, labor market training, wage subsidies to the private sector, and direct job creation in the public sector – are an important element of this European Employment Strategy. While such policies have been in use for many years in most countries, there is a growing awareness of the need to develop scientifically-justified measures of the effectiveness of different Active Labor Market Policies (ALMPs). Indeed, concerns about the effectiveness of ALMPs have become an increasingly important feature of the EU's Broad Economic Policy Guidelines, the Employment Guidelines, and the Recommendations for Member States' employment policies.

A substantial number of evaluations of ALMP effectiveness has been conducted in Member States, by independent researchers, by researchers commissioned by government bodies, as part of ESF programs, or as national studies contributing to the European Employment Strategy evaluation. In most cases, the focus of these evaluations has been on the short term employment effects of active measures, disregarding the possibility of positive or negative interactions between ALMP participants and other employed and unemployed workers (so-called "general equilibrium" effects). But even within this narrow focus the evidence from existing evaluations remains inconclusive: there is little consensus on whether Active Labor Market Policies actually reduce unemployment or raise the number of employed workers, and which type of program seems most promising. It is also not evident what any one country can learn from ALMP experiences in another country. Few overview studies exist, and their largely descriptive nature precludes any firm policy conclusions.

It is the objective of this study to overcome this deficit, by utilizing an appropriate conceptual framework that allows drawing systematic conclusions and deriving policy recommendations from the available cross-country evidence on ALMP effectiveness. The main part of the analysis is set against the backdrop of three frames. First, we discuss the role of the European Employment Strategy in shaping member states' labor market policies, and describe the current situation on European labor markets regarding core indicators such as the unemployment rate and GDP growth. The second frame is given by a discussion and definition of active labor market program types, and program expenditure by country and type of measure. The most important ALMP categories across European countries are (i) training programs, which essentially comprise all human capital enhancing measures, (ii) private sector incentive schemes, such as wage subsidies to private firms and start-up grants, (iii) direct employment programs, taking place in the public sector, and (iv) Services and Sanctions, a category comprising all measures aimed at increasing job search efficiency, such as counseling and monitoring, job search assistance, and corresponding sanctions in case of noncompliance. It is important to note that many active labor market programs in European countries specifically target the young workers (25 years of age and younger) among the unemployed. Whereas several countries also have specific active labor market programs for the disabled, very few evaluations of these measures exist.

The third frame regards the methodology of program evaluation. Since the cross-European analysis of ALMP effectiveness must necessarily rely on credible evaluation studies from all countries involved, appropriate outcome variables and cost measures, as well as feasible identification strategies that can help solve the so-called "evaluation problem" (i.e. the inherent unobservability of the counterfactual no-program situation) must be discussed and properly specified.

Logically building on these three frames as a backdrop, our subsequent analysis of ALMP effectiveness concentrates on two focal points. The first focus regards a set of country studies from selected EU member states. Specifically, we discuss Austria, Denmark, Estonia, France, Germany, Italy, The Netherlands, Poland, Spain, Sweden, and the UK. While taking into account idiosyncrasies of each country, for purposes of comparability the studies follow a homogeneous structure to the extent possible, discussing (a) the economic context, (b) labor market institutions, (c) ALMP practice, and (d) ALMP evaluations. Unsurprisingly, both the economic background and the institutional set-up vary substantially across countries, from currently well-performing (e.g. Denmark, Estonia) to rather sluggish economies (e.g.

Germany), and from fairly flexible (e.g. the UK) to rather heavily regulated labor markets (e.g. France, Germany). Substantial differences exist with respect to ALMP practice, too. Some countries spend a substantial share of GDP on active measures (e.g. The Netherlands, Denmark, Sweden) and run a comprehensive set of various types of ALMP (e.g. Germany), while other countries spend considerably less (e.g. the UK, Italy) and run a relatively narrow set of programs (e.g. Estonia, Spain). Denmark certainly has the most comprehensive ALMP strategy with substantial effort to activate all unemployed persons.

Similar to differences in the implementation of ALMP, also the evaluation practice varies across countries. Sweden is well-known to have a long tradition of running and thoroughly evaluating ALMP, possible also because of a correspondingly comprehensive collection of data. The Netherlands and the UK, along with the one existing study from Hungary – stand out as countries implementing some evaluations based on randomized experiments. These experimental studies analyze the effects of job search assistance programs. On the other hand, in Spain and Italy, for instance, an "evaluation culture" hardly exists, which is probably in line with a limited ALMP practice that is only just emerging. Germany is an example of a country in which – despite a fairly long tradition of running ALMPs – program evaluations were almost nonexistent until few years ago, and in which a practice of evaluating labor market policies has developed very rapidly. It is true for all countries that almost every evaluation study exclusively discusses microeconomic treatment effects, and that only very few macroeconomic studies exist.

Succeeding the country studies, the second and main focus of our analysis regards the appropriate summarizing of the available evidence. In this regard, we first review the experiences from the country studies and other evaluations from the remaining member states (as well as Norway and Switzerland) in a descriptive manner, and then concentrate on a meta-analysis of the available evidence. Before turning to a summary of that quantitative analysis, the following paragraphs present an overall assessment of the cross-country evidence.

Training programs are the most widely used active labor market measure in Europe. The assessment of their effectiveness shows rather mixed results; treatment effect estimates are negative in a few cases, and often insignificant or modestly positive. Still, there are several indications that training programs do increase participants' post-treatment employment probability, in particular for participants with better labor market prospects and for women. However, this pattern does not hold for all studies. Locking-in effects of training are frequently reported, though it remains unclear to what extent these are really entirely undesirable, and not rather a necessary element of this type of program.

The more recent literature on the evaluation of training emphasizes the need to consider long-run impacts. Such an assessment has become increasingly possible due to extended data. There are indeed indications from these studies that positive treatment effects of training exist in the long-run. Moreover, if negative locking-in effects were to matter, these would be outweighed by the long-run benefits of program participation. The existence and direction of a relation between the business cycle and the effectiveness of training programs is not clear from the evidence: Some studies report a pro-cyclical pattern, while others report the opposite.

Private sector incentive programs entail wage subsidies and start-up loans. Whereas the latter have rarely been evaluated in European countries, several evaluations of wage subsidy schemes exist. The findings are generally positive. Virtually all studies that evaluate private sector wage subsidy programs – such as several studies from Denmark, but also evidence from Sweden, Norway, Italy, etc – assert beneficial impacts on individual employment probability. These encouraging findings, however, have to be qualified to some extent, since the studies usually disregard potential displacement and substitution effects or deadweight loss that may be associated with wage subsidy schemes.

In contrast to the positive results for private sector incentive programs, direct employment in the public sector rarely shows positive effects. The evidence across countries suggests that treatment effects of public sector job creation on individual employment probabilities are often insignificant, and frequently negative. Some studies identify positive effects for certain socio-de-mographic groups, but no clear general pattern emerges from these findings. Potentially negative general-equilibrium effects are usually not taken into account. Though these measures may therefore not be justified for efficiency reasons, they may be justified for equity reasons, possibly exerting positive social impacts by avoiding discouragement and social exclusion among partic-ipants. Corresponding outcome measures, however, are difficult to assess em-pirically, such that the literature has focused on treatment impacts on actual employment.

A general assessment of Services and Sanctions across countries indicates that these measures can be an effective means to reduce unemployment. The results appear even more promising given that these measures are generally the least expensive type of ALMP. Moreover, several experimental studies exist for this program type, producing particularly robust evaluation results. There are some indications that services such as job search assistance or coun-seling and monitoring mainly work for individuals with sufficient skills and better labor market prospects, but less so for the more disadvantaged indi-viduals. This pattern, however, is not entirely clear, since some studies conclude that the opposite is the case.

Whereas in many countries some type of sanction for non-compliance with job search requirements exists, only few sanction regimes have been evaluated. The studies generally find a positive effect on re-employment rates, both for actually imposing sanctions and for having a benefit system including sanctions. The "New Deal" programs in the UK appear to be a particularly well-balanced system of job search services and sanctions, combined with a set of other active measures such as training and employment subsidies. This points to the conjecture that the interplay between the services provided by the PES, the requirements demanded from the unemployed individual, and the portfolio of active measures plays an important role regarding ALMP ef-fectiveness. The comprehensive activation approach implemented in Denmark, for instance, also appears promising, even though it clearly requires substantial effort.

For youth programs, no clear pattern arises from the cross-country summary of studies. There are some indications that wage subsidies work for young unemployed individuals, especially the ones with a more advantaged background. However, some studies do not find this effect, and again potential general-equilibrium effects are disregarded. Youth training programs sometimes display positive treatment effects on employment probability, but negative results are also reported. Whereas the extensive "New Deal" in the UK illustrates the potential effectiveness of Services and Sanctions for youths, this result is not found in evaluations from other countries (e.g. Portugal).

Regarding programs for the disabled, due to a lack of evaluation studies no conclusive evidence exists. The results of the limited empirical evidence available are rather disappointing. Vocational rehabilitation programs seem to have no positive and significant impact on the employment rates of disabled unemployed.

The limited set of available macroeconomic evaluation studies also does not point to a consistent pattern. There are some indications for positive effects on net employment for training programs in general and also for youth, while other results indicate that these programs only reduce unemployment but do not enhance employment, or have no net employment impact due to crowding out effects. Several macro studies, however, underline the dismal performance of direct job creation schemes in the public sector. Rather mixed results are reported for wage subsidies in the private sector. Some studies reveal an overall positive net employment effect, but substitution effects may outweigh a positive employment effect. Finally, job search assistance and counseling exert positive direct effects on the employment rate, but may have negative effects through shifts in wages and job search behavior as well. Monitoring and sanctions have the potential to improve welfare. These results underline the importance of collecting further empirical evidence on an aggregate level, since some macroeconomic results confirm corresponding microeconomic evidence, whereas other results indicate reinforced or even reversed effects. The number of macro studies is quite small relative to the set of microeconomic program evaluations in Europe.

In summary, looking at the overall assessment of the available evidence, it is difficult to detect consistent patterns, even though some tentative findings emerge: Services and Sanctions may be a promising measure, direct job creation in the public sector often seems to produce negative employment effects, training measures show mixed and modestly positive effects.

On the basis of these tentative findings, it is the objective of the meta analysis to draw systematic lessons from the more than 100 evaluations that have been conducted on ALMPs in Europe, and to complement the more descriptive analyses and country-level summaries in the preceding parts of our study. Most of the evaluation studies considered have been conducted on programs that were in operation in the period after 1990. This reflects the fact that the past 15 years have seen an increasing use of ALMPs in Europe, and some improvement in the methodologies used to evaluate these programs. Thus, we believe that lessons drawn from our meta-analysis are highly relevant to the current policy discussions throughout Europe on the appropriate design of ALMPs.

The picture that emerges from the quantitative analysis is surprisingly clear-cut. Once the type of the program is taken into account, the analysis shows that there is little systematic relationship between program effectiveness and a host of other contextual factors, including the country or time period when it was implemented, the macroeconomic environment, and a variety of indicators for institutional features of the labor market. The only institutional factor that appears to have an important systematic effect on program effectiveness is the presence of more restrictive dismissal regulations. But even this effect is small relative to the effect of the program type.

Traditional training programs are found to have a modest likelihood of recording a positive impact on post-program employment rates. Relative to these programs, private sector incentive programs and Services and Sanctions show a significantly better performance. Indeed, we find that evaluations of these types of programs are 40–50 percent more likely to report a positive impact than traditional training programs. By comparison, evaluations of ALMPs that are based on direct employment in the public sector are 30–40 percent less likely to show a positive impact on post-program employment outcomes. Also the target group seems to matter, as programs aimed specifically at young workers fare significantly worse than programs targeted at adults, displaying a 40–60 percentage points lower probability of reporting a positive effect.

The general policy implications that follow from these findings are rather straightforward. Decision makers should clearly focus on the type of program in developing their ALMP portfolio, and the European Commission should spell out similar recommendations to member states within the European Employment Strategy: Training programs should be continued, and private sector incentive schemes should be fostered. Particular attention should be paid to Services and Sanctions, which turns out to be a particularly promising and, due to its rather inexpensive nature, cost-effective type of measure. A well-balanced design of basic services such as job search assistance and counseling and monitoring, along with appropriate sanctions for non-compliance, seems to be able to go a long way in enhancing job search effectiveness. If further combined with other active measures such as training and employment subsidies, this effectiveness could be increased, even for youths, as promising results from the UK's "New Deal" show.

Direct employment programs in the public sector, on the other hand, are rarely effective and frequently detrimental regarding participants' employment prospects. On this account they should be discontinued, unless other justifications such as equity reasons can be found. Some countries have already resorted to redefining the objective of direct employment programs such that they should increase "employability" rather than actual employment, an outcome that is notoriously difficult to assess empirically.

Young people appear to be particularly hard to assist. It is not clear if it follows from this disappointing result that youth programs should be abolished, or rather that such programs should be re-designed and given particular attention. It might also be the case that Active Labor Market Policies are not at all the appropriate policy for this group, and public policy should therefore focus on measures that prevent the very young from becoming dis-advantaged on the labor market in the first place.

The development of an "evaluation culture" has been positive in basically all member states, though different countries clearly find themselves at different stages of that development. One evident conclusion of this study is that evaluation efforts should be continued and extended. An ever-refined meta-analysis of an ever-extended set of European evaluation studies would continue to produce important insight into the effectiveness of ALMPs, in particular as data quality and methodology will likely continue to improve. The substantial advances in non-experimental program evaluation notwith-standing, more member states' governments interested in the effectiveness of their policies should consider implementing randomized experiments, in light of the strength of the evidence they produce.

Introduction and overview

Against the background of at least two decades of unsatisfactory European labor market performance, at the Luxembourg Jobs summit in November 1997 the *European Commission* initiated what has become known as the *Luxembourg Process*. The *Amsterdam Treaty* introduced a new *Employment Title* and thus for the first time raised employment issues to the same status as other key goals in the formulation of European Union economic policy. The Treaty represents a critical step in the development of the *European Employment Strategy* (*EES*). Article 2, for instance, states that "member states [...] shall regard promoting employment as a matter of common concern and shall co-ordinate their actions" (Article 2). Article 3 formally recognizes that high employment should be an explicit goal „in the formulation and implementation of Community policies and activities".

The Lisbon European Council (March 2000) updated the European Employment Strategy, specifying that by 2010 the Union should regain conditions for full employment and strengthen cohesion. In particular, by 2010 the overall EU employment rate should be raised to 70%, and the average female employment rate to more than 60%. The Stockholm Council (March 2001) stated intermediate targets (67% average employment rate by 2005, and 57% for women). The Barcelona Council (March 2002) confirmed that full employment was the overarching objective and called for a reinforced Employment Strategy to underpin the Lisbon targets in an enlarged European Union.[1]

Active Labor Market Policies – including measures such as job search assistance, labor market training, wage subsidies to the private sector, and direct job creation in the public sector – are an important element of this European Employment Strategy. While such policies have been in use for many years in most countries, there is a growing awareness of the need to develop scientifically-justified measures of the effectiveness of different Active Labor Market Policies (ALMPs). Indeed, concerns about the effectiveness of ALMPs have become an increasingly important feature of the EU's Broad Economic Policy Guidelines, the Employment Guidelines, and the Recommendations for Member States' employment policies.

A substantial number of evaluations of ALMP effectiveness has been conducted in Member States, by independent researchers, by researchers commissioned by government bodies, as part of ESF programs, or as national

---

[1] See http://europa.eu.int/comm/employment_social/employment_strategy/index_en.htm for further details on the European Employment Strategy.

studies contributing to the European Employment Strategy evaluation. In most cases, the focus of these evaluations has been on the short term employment effects of active measures, disregarding the possibility of positive or negative interactions between ALMP participants and other employed and unemployed workers (so-called "general-equilibrium" effects). Even within this narrow focus, however, the evidence from existing evaluations remains inconclusive: there is little consensus on whether Active Labor Market Policies actually reduce unemployment or raise the number of employed workers, and which type of program appears most promising in achieving these goals. It is also not evident what any one country can learn from ALMP experiences in another country. Few overview studies exist, and their largely descriptive nature renders the drawing of firm policy conclusions difficult.

For policy purposes, thus, the conceptual framework underlying most of the existing evaluations is limited. A substantially broader conceptual framework is required, that allows inference on ALMP effectiveness across countries, taking into account idiosyncrasies of a given country's ALMP strategy and evaluation practice, as well as institutional setting and macroeconomic background. This study constitutes an effort to take a step forward in analyzing the effectiveness of ALMPs in Europe against the backdrop of such a framework.

The main objective of the study is to review the experiences with ALMP practice and ALMP evaluations across European countries. Ideally, this amounts to assessing the question "which program works for what target group under what circumstances?", the word "circumstances" describing the situation against which a program is implemented in a specific country, given by the institutional context and the state of the economy. We aim to get at this core objective by following a structure that is set against three frames. The first frame for the analysis of the effectiveness of ALMP in Europe is given by the European Employment Strategy. The European Employment Strategy has a fundamental impact on how member states' governments shape their (active) labor market policy, and in particular how program evaluation efforts in particular countries have developed recently.

The second frame is given by the Active Labor Markct Policies themselves. It is essential to define and classify the types of program that exist, to assess the role they play in terms of governmental expenditure, and to discuss the economic rationale behind running active measures. Finally, the third frame for the analysis is given by the methodological requirements for program evaluation. Since the cross-European analysis of ALMP effectiveness must necessarily rely on credible evaluation studies from specific countries, appropriate outcome variables and cost measures, as well as feasible identification strategies that can help solve the so-called "evaluation problem" (i.e. the inherent unobservability of the counterfactual no-program situation) must be discussed and properly specified.

Logically succeeding these three frames – (i) EES, (ii) ALMPs, (iii) evaluation methodology – is the main part of the analysis. This main part, in turn, consists of two focal points. The first focus is a set of reports from member states, in which for each country the particular ALMP practice and ALMP evaluation practice is discussed, in relation to the institutional setting and economic situation. For comparability, these country studies follow a common structure, yet do not disregard idiosyncratic features of the country's ALMP strategy, ALMP practice, and evaluation customs.

The second focus regards the appropriate summarizing of the available evidence: First, the analysis contains an extensive list of all recent evaluation studies and their core features and findings, both for microeconomic and macroeconomic evaluation studies. Moreover, a summary section reviews the main findings from the country reports. Finally, complementing these descriptive and comprehensive overviews, we summarize the evidence using a meta-analytical approach. This final step concludes the assessment of the effectiveness of European ALMPs, and potentially provides quantitative evidence that would allow deriving clear implications and policy recommendations.

In order to attain the objectives of the analysis as described, and present the three crucial frames as the backdrop before concentrating on the two focal points of the study, this book is structured as follows. Chapter 1 presents an overview of the European Employment Strategy. We discuss the historical development, including the impact evaluation in 2002, and describe the current situation on European labor markets. Chapter 2 continues with an overview of Active Labor Market Policies, focusing on the types of programs that exist, their suitable classification, and the money that is being spent on them. Chapter 3 reflects the methodology of program evaluation. It discusses the core elements of any evaluation endeavor, formulates the evaluation problem, and details empirical solutions based on experimental and, as is much more common in Europe, non-experimental or observational data. In Chapter 4 we present reports from a selected set of EU25 member states, each focusing on the economic background, the institutional context on the labor market, the role that ALMPs play in the policy strategy, and the evaluations of these measures that have been conducted. The list of countries comprises the Netherlands, Sweden, Austria, Germany, Italy, Denmark, Estonia, Poland, Spain, France, and the UK. Chapter 5 discusses the findings that emerge from evaluation research. After presenting an overview of previous evidence and summarizing the results available from recent micro- and macroeconomic evaluation studies in Europe, the core of chapter 5 lies in conducting a quantitative analysis that correlates program effectiveness with program type, research design, timing, and indicators for the institutional context on the labor market as well as the economic situation. Chapter 6 concludes and infers policy recommendations arising from the available evidence.

Chapter 1: The European Employment Strategy

1   Historical development[1]

Employment policies officially became one of the main priorities of the European Union with the launch of the European Employment Strategy (EES) at the Luxembourg Jobs Summit in 1997, while the process of integrating employment objectives into EU economic policy already started in the beginning of the 1990s. During this period, European countries began facing high and persistent unemployment rates, along with an increasing risk of long-term unemployment, possibly indicating structural problems in the labor markets. The European Union as a whole appeared to have no promising tools and strategies to tackle severe macroeconomic shocks and these high levels of unemployment. Increased interest about European solutions through co-ordination and convergence came up with the negotiation of macroeconomic policies through the Maastricht treaty in 1992, which finally resulted in a commitment to the Economic and Monetary Union (EMU). Member states agreed to pool their monetary sovereignty and to comply with certain targets set in the Stability and Growth Pact.

However, there was rather little attention yet towards a "soft" co-ordination of economic policies, which sets joint targets for each country, but also leaves space open for national policies and processes. Inspired by the economic coordination procedures a new debate about European structural policies emerged. The EU Member States decided to tackle the unemployment problems during the 1990s with the implementation of a soft policy coordination, which had to be in line with the economic policies. Therefore, member states decided to engage in concerted action and to mimic the economic policy coordination through the implementation of Broad Economic Policy Guidelines (BEPGs). Nevertheless, since there has been no formal sanction system associated with the case of deviations from these guidelines, the Council could only adopt non-binding recommendations for the member states (cf. e.g. De la Porte, Pochet 2003).

The important initial impulse for the launch of the EES was made by the Delors Commission with the development and publication of the "White Paper on Growth, Competitiveness and Employment" in 1993. In this paper

---

[1] See also the website of the European Commission at http://europa.eu.int/comm/employment_social/employment_strategy/develop_en.htm for further details and, in particular, for full documentation of Joint Employment Reports, National Action Plans, and Employment Guidelines.

the Commission suggests several solutions and policy guidelines to tackle the economic downturn and structural problems of the European economy. Furthermore, is highlights the importance to develop active and more flexible employment measures (cf. e.g. Arnold 2001).

Influenced by the Delors White Paper, the EES began to take shape at the Essen European Council in December 1994, which played an important role in the development of the EES. The European Council emphasized "the fight against unemployment as a long-term and paramount policy aim for the Union" (De la Porte, Pochet 2003), and set five key objectives, which had already been elaborated by the Delors White Paper:

- Improvement of employment by investing in education and vocational training.
- Increase of employment intensive growth through more flexible work organizations and working time.
- Reduction of non-wage labor costs to foster the hiring of low-skilled workers.
- Further development of Active Labor Market Policies through the reform of Public Employment Services (PES).
- Fight against youth and long-term unemployment.

The Essen summit introduced a new policy tool, by urging member states to translate the recommendations into long-term programs and to submit annual reports about their progress on the labor market to the European Council (cf. e.g. Goetschy 1999). Nevertheless, since employment policies still remained under the exclusive responsibilities of the member states, the conclusions by the Essen summit were non-binding mainly due to a missing legal base.

Following the meeting at Essen, another two important European Council summits took place in Madrid in December 1995 and in Dublin in 1996. The summit in Madrid identified job creation as the main social, economic and political objective, whereas the European Council in Dublin once again emphasized the fight against unemployment as a priority task for the EU and its member states. This was declared as the "Dublin Declaration on Employment – The Jobs challenge" which stressed the importance of a macroeconomic policy favorable to growth and employment (cf. Arnold, Cameron 2001).

A significant turning point in the development of the EES was determined by the Luxembourg jobs summit in November 1997. The objective of a *high level of employment* became an explicit priority for the EU in the Amsterdam Treaty, attaining an importance equal to the macroeconomic objectives of growth and stability. Furthermore, an employment chapter was included in the treaty, which considered employment as a separate policy field and introduced a much stronger role for the European institutions, the Council and the Commission.

The new employment chapter consists of six articles. Article 126 urges the EU and the member states to consider employment as a matter of common concern. Articles 127 and 128 authorize the Commission to propose Employment Guidelines, which are adopted by the Council and recommended to the member states. Although these guidelines are not binding, the member states have become obliged to participate (cf. Arnold 2001). On the basis of these yearly guidelines, member states are asked to develop annual *National Action Plans* (NAPs, relabeled "National Reform Programmes" starting with 2005, cf. section 1.2 of this chapter) for employment, which describe the employment policies and document the annual progress and planned measures and actions by the countries[2]. The Commission and the Council examine the implementation of these employment policies and publish their results in a *Joint Employment Report* (JER). Moreover, this document is the foundation for reshaping the Guidelines and elaborating specific and individual Employment Recommendations for the member states' employment policies (cf. e.g. Ardy, Umbach 2004). The Employment chapter of the treaty became fully operational at the Luxembourg Jobs Summit in 1997, and was ratified by the member states in 1999.

With the Amsterdam Treaty the Luxembourg Jobs Summit started what has become known as the Luxembourg Process and finally implemented the European Employment Strategy in November 1997 as a framework to promote employment. Moreover, the Summit launched the "Open Method of Coordination" (OMC) as a new system of governance. The OMC seeks to encourage member states to develop and to co-ordinate their social policies and to exchange best practices to achieve greater convergence towards the EU goals (cf. De la Porte, Pochet 2003). Finally, the Summit endorsed the first set of *Employment Guidelines* (EGs), which are the central policy document dealing specifically with labor market issues and which shall coordinate the employment policies of the member states (Arnold, Cameron 2001). Moreover, these Employment Guidelines are required to be consistent with the Broad Economic Policy Guidelines (BEPGs). The EGs were structured into the four pillars of employability, entrepreneurship, adaptability and equal opportunities:

- *Improving employability*: member states should enable every young person a new start within the first six months and every adult within the first twelve months of unemployment, giving them an opportunity to participate in training, work experience or employment schemes;
- *Developing a new culture of entrepreneurship and job creation*: the main objective of this pillar was to encourage member states to foster self employment and job creation. They should simplify the process of starting a business and also reduce the impediments of tax pressure and indirect labor costs;
- *Encouraging adaptability of business and their employees*: the aim is to foster the modernization of work organizations and to make firms more competitive, but also to keep a balance between flexibility and security for workers;
- *Strengthening equal opportunities for women and men*: This aims at reducing the discrimination against women in the labor market and halving the gender gap within the next five years; (cf. Goetschy 1999).

---

[2] The ten countries that became member states on May 1st 2004 prepared their first NAPs for employment in 2004.

Overall, the main objective behind these four pillars was to foster the shift to a more active and preventive approach of reintegrating the unemployed into the labor market.

Though the European Employment Guidelines have been reviewed on a yearly basis, the four pillars remained the underlying foundation of the EES until 2003. Moreover, employability became the central pillar of the EES, despite rather disappointing results reported from the impact of active measures in the OECD countries, which indicated that these measures only had negligible impacts on employment. In 1999, a "peer review guide" was established in the framework of the EES to identify and evaluate good practice in Active Labor Market Policies. This can be characterized as the qualitative component of the EES to assess the suitability of transferring good practice in one country to other member states (De la Porte, Pochet 2003).

The development of the EES reached a pinnacle at the Lisbon European Council in March 2000, when the summit set the new strategic goal to make Europe the world's most competitive and dynamic knowledge-based economy, capable of sustainable economic growth, more and better jobs and greater social cohesion. Further, as part of the *Lisbon Strategy* the Council set full employment as the main long-term objective. Therefore it was decided to implement a ten-year strategy until 2010, which comprises quantitative targets of an overall employment rate of 70% and an employment rate of 60% for women. Furthermore, the first session of the Spring European Council in Stockholm in 2001 set intermediate targets until 2005 with an overall employment rate of 67% and an employment rate of 57% for women. They set an additional target of increasing the employment rates for older workers aged 55–64 to 50% in 2010 (e.g. De la Porte, Pochet 2003).

A Mid-term review of the EES was conducted in 2000, but the period of only three years was too short to examine the impact on employment. Therefore, the Nice European Council in 2000 endorsed to complete the review and impact assessment of the EES in 2002, which was then conducted by the Commission and member states (cf. below). Furthermore, the Council highlighted the importance of quality of work as an important objective of the strategy.

In addition to the employment targets, six horizontal objectives were added to the Employment Guidelines in 2001: to increase the employment rate, to improve the quality of employment, to define a coherent and global strategy for lifelong learning, to involve the social partners in all stages of the process, to have a balanced implementation of all four pillars, and to develop relevant social indicators (De la Porte, Pochet 2003). Moreover, the Barcelona European Council in 2002 called for a reinforced Employment Strategy and highlighted the importance of "Active policies towards employment: more and better jobs" deserving more attention (European Commission 2002b).

1.1   The 2002 impact evaluation of the EES

This section provides a concise review of the impact evaluation of the first five years of the EES after its launch at the Luxembourg Job Summit. The impact evaluation comprises eight thematic chapters based on national impact evaluation studies conducted by the member states, an overall policy review and an aggregate assessment of the EU-wide employment performances conducted by the Commission.[3] The results of this evaluation were additionally laid down in a Communication adopted in July 2002, which provides first orientations for future policies and changes of the EES.

The results of the impact evaluation highlight clear structural employment improvements in the EU labor market over the first five years, with an increasing job creation of slightly more than 10 million jobs, of which 6 million were created for women. In addition, the results report a substantial decline of unemployment by more than 4 million, while labor force participation increased by almost 5 million. Furthermore, the Commission emphasizes that the EES has given a stronger priority for employment at the national level and significant changes in national employment policies with a clear convergence towards the objectives and guidelines defined under the EES. The open method of co-ordination has proved to be successful in fostering partnerships and new working methods across member states (cf. European Commission 2002b).

Nevertheless, important and substantial structural problems and large differences between member states remain. The evaluation highlights that in 2001 almost 13 million people are still unemployed, with a relatively large share of 42% being long-term unemployed (although this rate decreased from nearly 50%). Therefore, strong and sustained efforts are needed to achieve the 2010 Lisbon employment targets. There are also concerns about the increasing productivity gap between the EU and the US and persistent substantial regional differences among member states, especially in terms of unemployment.

In addition, it is also emphasized that some member states[4] had implemented main employment policies in line with the key principles already prior to the launch of the EES. Therefore the EES had contributed relatively little to the policy formulation in these countries. Moreover, Denmark, Finland, Sweden, the Netherlands and the UK already implemented specific active policies in line with the active labor market principles and a focus towards the prevention of long-term unemployment. Nevertheless, for the remaining countries the implementation of the EES fostered clear convergence towards the key principles, although this happened at a differing pace. The activation target, which claims that 20% of the unemployed shall benefit from active measures, has been globally reached.

It is also stressed that the EES affected more policy fields than just the traditional labor market policies. The EES had a strong influence on social inclusion especially in countries with low unemployment rates, such as Denmark and the Netherlands. Positive impacts on lifelong learning and education were found especially in Portugal, Ireland and Italy. Further, the EES had a strong influence on the pillar "equal opportunities", with increased

---

[3] The results of the chapter "Unemployment Prevention and Active Labor Market Policies" of the impact evaluation are presented in chapter 5.1.

[4] This was the case for Denmark, Finland, Sweden and the Netherlands.

efforts of gender mainstreaming and tackling gender gaps. Nevertheless, there are still differences on the degree of implementation across member states.

Overall, the Commission concludes that "the EES shifted its priority from a predominant focus on long term unemployment towards a long-term approach of employment creation and access to employment" (European Commission 2002a) and points out a clear convergence towards the key principles of activation and prevention.

1.2   The 2003 revision and the 2005 revamp of the EES

Following the 2002 evaluation and a decision on the streamlining of the annual economic and employment policy coordination cycles at the Barcelona Council (March 2002), the Commission adopted a Communication on the future of the EES in January 2003. In accordance with the results of the Impact Evaluation, the Communication identified four major issues for the reform of the EES: clear objectives in response to policy changes, simplified policy guidelines, improved partnership and governance, and greater consistency with other EU processes and guidelines (e.g. the BEPGs). Most importantly, in this Communication, the Commission outlined the revision of the strategy with concrete objectives and targets, highlighting three overarching objectives: (i) Full employment, (ii) Improving quality and productivity at work, (iii) Strengthening social cohesion and inclusion. Subsequently, the European Council adopted the new set of corresponding Employment Guidelines and Recommendations in July 2003 (cf. Council of the European Union 2003a, 2003b).

Most recently, in light of a decline in economic performance, in February 2005 the European Commission formulated a proposal for a revamp of the Lisbon strategy to focus on delivering stronger, lasting growth and more and better jobs. This process led to a complete revision of the EES, the guidelines of which will from now on be presented as *integrated guidelines* in conjunction with the macroeconomic and microeconomic guidelines, and will be fully reviewed only once every three years. Accordingly, in July 2005, the Council of the European Union (2005) formulated the integrated guidelines for growth and jobs for the time period 2005 to 2008 as follows:

- Guideline No 17: Implement employment policies aiming at achieving full employment, improving quality and productivity at work, and strengthening social and territorial cohesion.
- Guideline No 18: Promote a lifecycle approach to work.
- Guideline No 19: Ensure inclusive labor markets, enhance work attractiveness, and make work pay for job-seekers, including disadvantaged people, and the inactive.
- Guideline No 20: Improve matching of labor market needs.
- Guideline No 21: Promote flexibility combined with employment security and reduce labor market segmentation, having due regard to the role of the social partners.

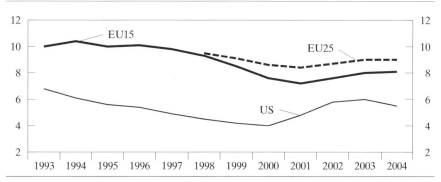

Figure 1. Total unemployment rates in the EU15, EU25 and the US; 1993 to
2004; in % of labor force
Source: Eurostat.

• Guideline No 22: Ensure employment-friendly labor cost developments
  and wage-setting mechanisms.
• Guideline No 23: Expand and improve investment in human capital.

The three overarching objectives mentioned above retain their importance.
Also, the targets and benchmarks set for the EES in 2003 continue to hold (cf.
Council of the European Union 2005).

2 The current situation on European labor markets

Over the past years there have been not only substantial differences between
the unemployment rates of the EU and the US, but also large differences
across the European member states.

Figure 1 depicts the development of the total unemployment rates in the
EU15 and EU25 compared to the US. Following a period of a high and persistent average unemployment rate of around 10 percent in the EU15 over the
years 1993 to 1996, average unemployment subsequently decreased and
dropped to a rate of just over 7 percent in 2001. It then increased again and
reached around 8 percent in 2004. The average unemployment rate for the
EU25 did not decrease as strongly after 1998 and currently amounts to
9 percent. In contrast, the US unemployment rate declined from around
7 percent in 1993 to approximately 4 percent in 2000, with an average gap to
the EU15 of almost 4 percentage points over that time period. However, US
unemployment increased to an average rate of 5.5 percent in 2004, reducing
the gap to the EU15 to 2.5 percentage points.

Figure 2 shows the large heterogeneity of unemployment rates across
member states in 2004. The range goes from relatively low unemployment
rates of around 4–5% for Austria, Ireland, Luxembourg, the Netherlands, the
United Kingdom, and Cyprus up to rather high unemployment rates for
Poland and the Slovak Republic of 18% and more. The remaining countries lie

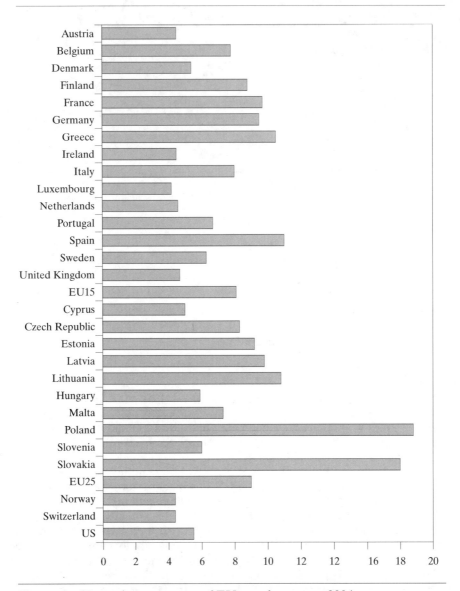

Figure 2. Unemployment rates of EU member states; 2004
            Source: Eurostat.

in between these bounds; some large member states such as France, Germany,
and Spain average around an unemployment rate of 10%.

Regarding the situation for unemployed youths under 25 years, Table 1
shows a wide disparity of unemployment rates among member states for the
year 2004, ranging from around 8.0% for the Netherlands and Denmark to up

Table 1. Youth unemployment rates in the EU and US, 15-24 years of age; 1998 to 2004

	1998	1999	2000	2001	2002	2003	2004
Austria	6.4	5.4	5.3	5.8	6.7	8.1	9.7
Belgium	22.1	22.7	17.0	17.5	18.5	21.0	19.8
Denmark	7.3	8.8	7.0	8.4	7.9	9.9	8.2
Finland	23.5	21.4	21.4	19.8	21.0	21.8	20.7
France	25.6	23.4	20.1	19.4	20.0	21.1	22.0
Germany	15.0	12.7	10.6	12.8	14.2	14.7	15.1
Greece	30.1	31.9	29.2	28.2	26.8	26.8	26.9
Ireland	11.3	8.4	6.7	6.7	8.0	8.3	8.3
Italy	29.9	28.7	27.0	24.1	23.1	23.7	23.6
Luxembourg	6.9	6.9	7.2	7.3	8.3	11.4	12.9
Netherlands	7.6	6.8	5.7	4.5	5.0	6.3	8.0
Portugal	10.6	9.1	8.9	9.4	11.6	14.4	15.4
Spain	31.3	25.8	22.9	21.7	22.3	22.7	22.1
Sweden	16.1	12.3	10.5	10.9	11.9	13.4	16.3
United Kingdom	13.1	12.8	12.3	11.9	12.1	12.3	12.1
EU15	**19.0**	**17.1**	**15.3**	**15.1**	**15.6**	**16.3**	**16.6**
Cyprus	.	.	11.5	10.3	9.7	10.7	10.6
Czech Republic	12.8	17.7	17.8	17.3	16.9	18.6	21.1
Estonia	15.2	22.0	23.6	23.5	19.3	23.4	21.0
Latvia	26.8	23.6	21.4	23.1	23.9	17.9	19.0
Lithuania	25.5	26.4	30.6	30.8	23.8	26.9	19.9
Hungary	15.0	12.7	12.1	11.1	12.0	13.5	14.8
Malta	.	.	13.7	19.0	18.3	19.1	16.7
Poland	22.5	30.1	36.3	39.8	41.8	41.2	39.5
Slovenia	17.8	17.9	16.2	16.0	15.3	15.7	14.3
Slovak Republic	.	34.2	37.1	39.0	37.6	33.8	32.3
EU25	.	.	**17.4**	**17.6**	**18.1**	**18.6**	**18.7**
Norway	9.1	9.4	9.9	10.3	11.1	11.6	11.4
US	10.4	9.9	9.3	10.6	12.0	12.4	11.8

Source: Eurostat.

to 32.3% for the Slovak Republic and 39.5% for Poland. Furthermore, quite a few countries – including Belgium, Finland, France, Greece, Italy, Spain, the Czech Republic, Estonia and Lithuania – have youth unemployment rates around 20% and more.

The importance of tackling long-term unemployment as one of the key objectives of the EES is underlined by the data presented in Table 2, which depicts the incidence of long-term unemployment as a percentage of the total active population. The proportion of individuals in the labor force who are unemployed for more than 12 months has persisted on a rather high level for the EU15 over the last years, and currently (2004) amounts to 3.4% in the EU15, and 4.1% in the EU25. Although countries like Austria, Denmark, Finland, Sweden and the United Kingdom have a below-average long-term unemployment rate, Greece and Germany are clearly above this average, with 5.6% and 5.4%, respectively, of the labor force being out of work for more than

Table 2. Long-term unemployment in the EU and US; 1993 to 2004; in % of total active population

	1993	1994	1995	1996	1997	1998	1999	2000	2001	2002	2003	2004
EU 25	:	:	:	:	:	4.4	4.1	3.9	3.8	3.9	4.0	4.1
EU 15	:	5.0	4.9	4.9	4.8	4.4	3.9	3.4	3.1	3.1	3.3	3.4
Belgium	4.5	5.6	5.8	5.7	5.4	5.6	4.9	3.7	3.2	3.6	3.6	3.9
Czech Republic	:	:	:	:	:	2.0	3.2	4.2	4.2	3.7	3.8	4.2
Denmark	2.6	2.5	2.0	1.8	1.5	1.3	1.0	1.0	0.9	0.9	1.1	1.2
Germany	3.1	3.7	3.9	4.1	4.6	4.5	4.1	3.7	3.7	3.9	4.5	5.4
Estonia	:	:	:	:	:	4.2	5.0	5.7	5.7	5.0	4.7	4.8
Greece	4.2	4.4	4.6	5.2	5.3	5.8	6.5	6.2	5.5	5.3	5.3	5.6
Spain	9.2	11.0	10.5	9.6	8.9	7.7	5.9	4.8	3.9	3.9	3.9	3.5
France	3.9	4.5	4.4	4.5	4.7	4.5	4.1	3.5	3.0	3.1	3.7	3.9
Ireland	9.5	9.2	7.6	7.0	5.6	3.9	2.4	1.6	1.3	1.3	1.5	1.6
Italy	5.7	6.5	7.1	7.3	7.3	6.8	6.7	6.3	5.7	5.1	4.9	4.0
Cyprus	:	:	:	:	:	:	:	1.3	1.0	0.8	1.1	1.4
Latvia	:	:	:	:	:	7.9	7.6	7.9	7.2	5.7	4.3	4.3
Lithuania	:	:	:	:	:	7.5	5.3	8.0	9.2	7.2	6.1	5.6
Luxembourg	0.8	0.9	0.7	0.8	0.9	0.9	0.7	0.6	0.6	0.8	0.9	1.1
Hungary	:	:	:	5.2	4.5	4.2	3.3	3.0	2.5	2.4	2.4	2.6
Malta	:	:	:	:	:	:	:	4.4	3.7	3.4	3.3	3.5
Netherlands	3.3	3.3	3.1	3.0	2.3	1.5	1.2	0.8	0.6	0.7	1.0	1.6
Austria	:	1.1	1.0	1.2	1.3	1.3	1.2	1.0	0.9	1.1	1.1	1.3[b]
Poland	:	:	:	:	5.0	4.7	5.8	7.6	9.3	10.8	10.8	10.2
Portugal	1.8	2.6	3.1	3.3	3.2	2.2[b]	1.8	1.7	1.5	1.7	2.2	3.0
Slovenia	:	:	:	3.4	3.4	3.3	3.2	4.0	3.5	3.4	3.4	3.1
Slovakia	:	:	:	:	:	6.6	8.0	10.2	11.4	12.2	11.4	11.8
Finland	:	:	:	:	4.9	4.1	3.0	2.8	2.5	2.3	2.3	2.1
Sweden	1.4	2.3	2.3	2.7	3.1	2.6	1.9	1.4	1.0	1.0	1.0	1.2
UK	4.3	4.1	3.5	3.1	2.5	1.9	1.7	1.4	1.3	1.1	1.1	1.0
Bulgaria	:	:	:	:	:	:	:	9.4	11.9	11.7	8.9	7.0
Croatia	:	:	:	:	:	:	:	:	:	8.9	8.4	7.3
Romania	:	:	:	:	2.5	2.3	2.8	3.5	3.2	4.0	4.2	4.5
Turkey	:	:	:	:	:	:	:	1.4	1.8	3.1	2.5	4.0
Iceland	:	:	:	:	:	:	:	:	:	:	0.2	0.3
Norway	:	:	:	:	:	:	:	0.3	0.4	0.5	0.6	0.8
United States	0.8	0.7	0.5	0.5	0.4	0.4	0.3	0.2	0.3	0.5	0.7	0.7
Japan	0.4	0.5	0.6	0.6	0.7	0.8	1.0	1.2	1.3	1.7	1.8	1.6

Source: Eurostat, "Eurostat Structural Indicators", Long-term unemployment rate (12 months and more) as a percentage of the total active population. – (:) not available, (b) break in series. Data lack comparability due to changes in certain survey characteristics: between 1997 and 1998 for PT, and between 2003 and 2004 for AT. TR-data source: national Labor Force Survey. JP, US-data source: national Labor Force Survey (OECD)

12 months. Both countries perform even worse than most of the new member states, which, in turn, frequently have long-term unemployment rates above the EU15 average (Poland and the Slovak Republic being particularly bad examples, each having more than 10% of their labor force in long-term unem-

work experience programs etc. The type of guidance depends largely on the characteristics of the unemployed worker. At the start of unemployment, both unemployment insurance recipients and welfare recipients are profiled into 4 types. Type I should have sufficient skills to find work (75–80% in the inflow into unemployment insurance). Type II and Type III require assistance such as training and schooling. Type IV are most often not obliged to search for work.

The responsibility for assigning individuals to programs lies with the nationwide public insurance administration for unemployment insurance and disability insurance recipients and with the municipalities for welfare recipients. However, recently there has been a shift from public provision of Active Labor Market Policies to private provision. The nationwide public insurance administration and the municipalities do not offer active labor market programs, but instead contract commercial agencies. The underlying idea is that competition between these commercial agencies should lead to better programs and more efficient spending of resources. An essential problem is that contracts hardly depend on success and that there is much room for cherry-picking to meet minimal targets. Since the commercial agencies offer different programs, there hardly exist nationwide training and schooling programs for unemployed workers.

Below we give a short discussion of recent labor market policies.

Private and public incentive schemes

Earned income tax credit: In the Netherlands, each employed worker is entitled to an earned income tax credit. The amount of the earned income tax credit is about 1200 euros for workers until 57 years old with a full-time job and higher for older workers. The amount of the earned income tax credit is increased for individuals with children.

Private and public employment programs

Subsidized employment: In the recent past there were some relatively large programs for subsidized employment in the Netherlands. In 2003, subsidies to employers for low income jobs (*SPAK*) have been abolished. These were lump-sum payments to the employer in the form of payroll tax deductions for workers earning less than 115% of the minimum wage. And since 2004 employers cannot apply anymore for subsidies for hiring long-term unemployed low-skilled workers (*ID-banen*).

Services and sanctions

Counseling and monitoring: The first Active Labor Market Policies in the Netherlands involved advising unemployed workers in the search for work and checking their actual search behavior. These policies started in the late eighties and were implemented somewhat ad hoc by the public insurance administration. During the nineties counseling and monitoring became nationwide standard practice in the treatment of unemployed workers. However, the content of the policy and the target population changed regularly.

Sanctions: If an unemployed worker does not comply with the rules of the unemployment insurance agency or the welfare agency, then the worker can be punished with a sanction. Reasons for giving a sanction are insufficient job search effort, unnecessary job loss, fraud or a lack of willingness to participate in training or schooling programs. The key element of a sanction is a temporary benefit reduction. However, if a sanction has been imposed, the individual gets a detailed explanation on the reasons for the sanction and which behavior is expected to avoid future sanctions. Furthermore, the sanctioned worker enters a stricter monitoring regime.

The length of the sanction period and the size of the benefit reduction depend on the reason why the sanction is imposed. For unemployment insurance recipients a sanction can vary from a 5% reduction during 4 weeks to a 25 to 30% reduction during 13 weeks. For welfare recipients sanctions are almost always 1 or 2 months and the benefit reduction is 5, 10 or 20%. Only in case of fraud the sanction can be more severe.

Sanctions to unemployment insurance recipients exist since the introduction of the Unemployment Law in 1987. The rate at which sanctions are imposed to unemployment insurance recipients increased enormously in the beginning of the nineties. Sanctions to welfare recipients have been frequently imposed since 1992.

Other policy measures

Screening: Each benefit program has a screening procedure for checking eligibility criteria. Eligibility to collecting unemployment insurance benefits depends on the employment history of the worker. If the worker meets the required work history, the individual will receive unemployment insurance benefits. Only in case of unnecessary job loss the individual might get punished with a reduced benefits level during the first few months of unemployment insurance.

Eligibility for disability insurance depends on the medical conditions of the individual. The degree of disability depends on the potential earnings loss as a consequence of the condition that caused disability. However, recently the disability insurance agency also started checking if the applicant and the employer devoted sufficient effort in getting the worker back to his job during the period of sickness absenteeism.

Welfare benefits are means-tested and the level of welfare benefits depends on the household composition. Therefore, screening of eligibility focuses on potential eligibility for other benefits programs, the income and wealth of the applicant and other household members.

1.4   Evaluation studies

On September 7, 2001, the Minister of Social affairs wrote to the parliament that *supported by the economic growth, eight years of (active) labor market policies caused an increase of 1.2 million jobs.* To support this claim a report was sent along with a summary of all available evaluation studies of Active Labor Market Policies. The list of evaluation studies only contains two studies that account for selectivity in the treatment assignment (and in the report both studies are criticized for their lack of observed individual character-istics).

Most evaluation research is done by commercial bureaus. These com-mercial bureaus lack the econometric skills for high quality quantitative eval-uation research. The Netherlands does not have a tradition in which policies are evaluated at the start. Many large-scale programs have never been evaluated. Policy evaluation in the Netherlands suffers from the lack of suitable high quality data and the unwillingness to have well designed experi-ments. More striking is that many policies do not have a clearly defined and well motivated goal. Goals like spending all resources or minimizing the dropout of participants are not seldom. This limits the impact of the evaluation research on actual policy.

Currently active labor market programs are provided by many commercial agencies, which each have there own programs or treatment. This implies that it is difficult to distinguish general programs and that there is not much public knowledge about the effectiveness of programs. In this section we focus on specific policies that have been evaluated empirically. In particular, we focus attention on microeconometric studies in which serious attention has been paid to selective participation in the program.

Counseling and monitoring

In the Netherlands there have been two social experiments that investigated the effect of counseling and monitoring of unemployed workers. In both studies the target population consists of individuals collecting unemployment insurance benefits. Counseling and monitoring implies regular meetings between the case worker of the unemployment insurance administration and the unemployed workers. During these meetings recent job search effort is evaluated (monitoring) and the unemployed workers are advised in their future job search (counseling). An important element in the monitoring is that if the case worker detects a lack of job search effort, the unemployed worker can be punished with a temporary reduction of the unemployment insurance benefits.

The first social experiment described in Gorter/Kalb (1996) discusses the introduction of a more intensified version of counseling and monitoring. For the individuals in the treatment group the time spent between the case worker and the unemployed worker was increased compared to the standard practice. Van den Berg/Van der Klaauw (2006) discuss a social experiment in which the individuals in the treatment group received the common practice and the indi-viduals in the control group did not receive any counseling and monitoring at all. Therefore, the treatment population in Van den Berg and Van der Klaauw (2006) and the control population in Gorter/Kalb (1996) received roughly the same counseling and monitoring.

Gorter/Kalb (1996): This social experiment took place in 1989/1990 in seven Dutch regions. In total the experiment involved 1631 unemployment insurance recipients, who were randomly assigned to the treatment and control group. However, due to item non-response the empirical analyses only considered 722 individuals. The individuals who were randomized into the treatment group received extended counseling and monitoring meetings compared to the individuals in the control group.

The key outcome variable of interest is the duration of unemployment, although Gorter/Kalb (1996) also investigate the effect of counseling and monitoring on the number of job applications. Gorter/Kalb (1996) find that the effect of counseling and monitoring on the job finding hazard is modest and insignificant for individuals who previously had a permanent contract and significantly negative for individuals who previously had a temporary contract. They explain this big difference by stating that the aim of counseling and monitoring is to provide unemployed workers with a permanent contract, which might be difficult to obtain for individuals who were previously in temporary employment. Furthermore, they find that counseling and monitoring significantly increases the job application rate.

Van den Berg/Van der Klaauw (2006): The social experiment in this study was conducted in 1998/1999 in two cities and involved around 400 type I unemployed workers collecting unemployment insurance benefits. Randomization occurred at the level of the individual and for those individuals who were randomized into the program, counseling and monitoring started with an intake meeting immediately after inflow into unemployment. After that the program continued until 6 months after becoming unemployed with meetings every 4 weeks.

The main goal of the program was to reduce the entitlement period to unemployment insurance benefits. Therefore, the duration of unemployment is the key outcome variable of interest. The empirical results show a very small and insignificant positive effect of counseling and monitoring on the probability of finding work. Since counseling and monitoring is a relatively inexpensive policy, the benefits in terms of unpaid unemployment insurance benefits are 6 months after inflow into unemployment approximately the same as the costs of providing counseling and monitoring.

There exist some differences between the study by Gorter/Kalb (1996) and Van den Berg/Van der Klaauw (2006). First, the actual treatment differs as Van den Berg/Van der Klaauw (2006) investigate the effectiveness of the regular counseling and monitoring program and Gorter/Kalb (1996) study the effectiveness of intensifying the regular program. Second, the study by Gorter/Kalb was conducted in a period of recession, while Van den Berg/Van der Klaauw (2006) investigate a period with very favorable business cycle and labor market conditions. Third, the target population in Van den Berg/Van der Klaauw (2006) is restricted to type I unemployed workers, while the population in Gorter/Kalb (1996) also includes type II, III and IV unemployed workers. This implies that on average the target population in Gorter/Kalb (1996) is more disadvantaged.

Sanctions

In the Netherlands there have been two studies on the effect of imposing sanctions to unemployed workers. Both studies only focus on the effect of actually imposing a sanction (the ex-post effect). One could argue that this gives a lower bound to the effects of sanctions, as sanctions also have a preventive effect. The threat of having a benefits system with sanctions most likely induces unemployed workers to spend more effort on job search (ex-ante effect).

Abbring/Van den Berg/Van Ours (2005) focus on unemployment insurance recipients and Van den Berg/Van der Klaauw/Van Ours (2004) study welfare recipients. In the empirical analyses the unanticipated nature of imposing sanctions is exploited. This implies that the process towards finding work is jointly modeled with the probability of imposing sanctions. This approach takes account of unobserved differences between individuals who have been punished with a sanction and those who did not get a sanction.

Abbring/Van den Berg/Van Ours (2005): This study uses administrative data from the records of the unemployment insurance agency. The data describe individuals who became unemployed in 1992 and these individuals are followed until finding work, or September 1993. The full data set contains 182,239 unemployment spells. In 2.9% of these spells a sanction was imposed and 43.5% of these spells have not ended in employment before the end of the observation period.

For the empirical analyses smaller samples are constructed. In particular, the study focuses on 7,758 unemployment spells of individuals who were previously employed in the metal industry and 32,331 spells of individuals who were previously employed in the banking sector. The empirical results indicate that the sanction probability increases during the first 16 weeks of collecting unemployment insurance and remains constant afterwards. The effects of imposing a sanction on the transition rate from unemployment to employment are in both sectors substantial and significant. Imposing a sanction increases the re-employment probabilities of the sanctioned worker. Sanctions seem to have a somewhat larger effect on the re-employment probabilities of females than of males.

Van den Berg/Van der Klaauw/Van Ours (2004): The data used in this study consists of all job losers who applied for welfare benefits in the city of Rotterdam in 1994. This is a sample of 7,978 individuals, who were followed until stopping collecting welfare benefits or until October 1996. About 14% of these individuals had a sanction imposed before October 1996, while only 39% had left welfare benefits.

The empirical results show that the sanction rate is highest between 6 and 12 months of collecting welfare benefits, which coincides with the time period in which the first thorough investigation of files occurs. The effect of imposing a sanction on the transition rate from welfare to work is both substantial and significant. A sanction raises the exit rate to work by about 140%.

Screening

Screening focuses on checking eligibility criteria for a benefits program. The intensity of this screening can be seen as a policy measure. De Jong/Lindeboom/Van der Klaauw (2005) discuss the results from an experiment, where in two Dutch regions a stricter screening regime for disability insurance applications was implemented. The case workers in these two regions have spent on average 9.4% additional time on each disability insurance application. To control for existing differences between regions, difference-in-difference estimation is used. It should be noted that an insufficient rehabilitation activity report cannot be a reason for a denial of a disability insurance application. It can only lead to a sanction to the employer of the worker. A sanction to the employer implies that the waiting period of sickness absenteeism before entering disability insurance is extended by a few months. During this period, the employer has to continue paying the salary of the sick worker. If the sanction is given to the worker, the worker receives only reduced benefits during the first few months of disability insurance.

De Jong/Lindeboom/Van der Klaauw (2005): A worker should apply for collecting disability insurance benefits between 35 and 39 weeks of sickness absenteeism. During the period of sickness absenteeism the worker has a joint responsibility with the employer to try to get back to work. The application for disability insurance benefits should be accompanied with a detailed report on the rehabilitation activities of the worker during the period of sickness absenteeism. This study discusses the results from an experiment, where in two Dutch regions the screening regime was stricter than in the rest of the Netherlands. The case workers in these regions were instructed to devote more time on screening the re-employment activity report and to regularly visit employers and have face-to-face contacts with disability insurance applicants.

The empirical results show that this regime of stricter screening reduces the number of disability insurance applications. In particular, due to the stricter screening significantly less workers report sickness absenteeism. If stricter screening would be applied nationwide, the number of sickness absenteeism reports and disability insurance applications would be reduced substantially. A cost-benefit analysis shows that the costs of additional screening are ignorable compared to reduction in disability insurance benefits payments due to the lower inflow into disability insurance. It should be noted that the reduction in disability insurance applications did not increase the inflow into unemployment insurance.

1.5   Summary

The programs of counseling and monitoring that have been evaluated in the Netherlands have not been very effective. Comparing the results from these studies with the results from other countries suggests that the more intensive the job search assistance, the higher the exit rate to work. Also, the worse the labor market prospects (individual or macro-economic), the larger the effect of monitoring on the exit rate to work.

Sanctions are always found to be a powerful policy measure. Targeting of sanctions is a crucial element. Unemployed workers with low re-employment rates benefit most from having a sanction imposed. A stricter sanction policy that punishes more unemployed workers will therefore have smaller effects of imposing sanctions. The success of sanctions does not straightforwardly imply that more sanctions should be imposed.

There seems to be a substantial moral hazard in the Dutch social insurance programs. It is shown that policies such as screening and experience rating reduce moral hazard in the disability insurance program and thereby reduces the size of the program. There is some (anecdotal) evidence that also welfare and unemployment insurance suffer from similar moral hazard problems at the inflow.

2 Active Labor Market Policies in Sweden

2.1 General economic situation

Between 1960 and 1990, Sweden experienced very low unemployment rates remaining virtually unchanged at around 2 percent. A deep and sudden depression in the beginning of the 1990s, when GDP declined by 5 percent between 1990 and 1993, lead to a dramatic change for the exemplary "Swedish Model". Whereas in 1990 the average unemployment rate was about 1.6 percent, this rate increased to 10.3 percent in 1994 (Andrén, Andrén 2002). This has lead to a new perspective on labor market policy, where the justification of high expenditures on such policy (about 3 percent of GDP e.g. in the year 1994) hinges on producing evidence of its effectiveness.

Sweden has not fully recovered from the depression in the early 1990s, but it underwent an economic revival in the second half of the 1990s. Today the labor market is still affected by an economic slump between 2001 and 2003. A cutback in adult education was one reason that the unemployment rate rose to 5.5 percent in 2004.

2.2 Labor market institutions

Middle- and long-term goals of the Swedish government's economic policy are an employment rate of 80 percent of those aged 20–64 years, and full employment, respectively. During 2004 the economy expanded and exports rose sharply. Remarkable is the structure in today's unemployed individuals, a large proportion of which have a university-level degree. This seems to be a result of the crisis in the IT and telecommunications sectors in recent years. An indication of the leading role of Sweden in the evaluation of ALMP is the existence of the Institute for Labor Market Policy Evaluation (IFAU), a research institute under the Ministry of Industry, Employment and Communication, situated in Uppsala. By its own account, IFAU's objective is to promote, support, and carry out evaluations of the effects of labor market

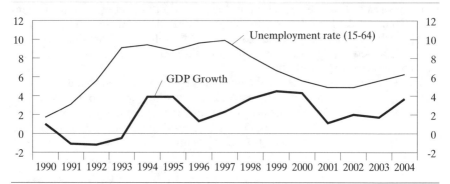

Figure 7. GDP growth and unemployment rate in Sweden; 1990 to 2004; in %
Source: Eurostat and Statistics Sweden.

policies, studies on the functioning of the labor market and evaluations of the labor market effects of measures within the educational system (cf. ifau.se).

An important point in the examination of ALMP in Sweden is to take into account the relative generosity of passive benefits such as unemployment insurance, as part of which unemployed individuals receive around 80 percent (with some variation over time) of the former wage for 60 calendar weeks. An institutional feature worth noting used to be that eligibility to receive unemployment compensation could be renewed by participating in a labor market program. On this account, one potential reason for taking part in ALMP could be to hold up eligibility.

2.3   Measures of Active Labor Market Policy[1]

Training programs

In the beginning of the 1960s training for the unemployed was started in Sweden. *Labor market training* (AMU) has been targeted at unemployed persons, as well as employed individuals running the risk of getting unemployed. The purpose of the program is to improve the chances for job seekers of obtaining a job. Two types of AMU exist: Vocational and non-vocational labor market training. Vocational training takes place in educational companies, universities and municipal consultancy operations, while non-vocational training takes place in the regular education system. In the 1980s, 40,000 individuals participated each month. This increased up to 85,000 in the

---

[1]   Some of the ALMP measures in Sweden do not fit exactly into the categories used throughout all country studies. For comparability this chapter follows the same classification.

early 1990s and decreased after 1992 to about 30,000 to 40,000 (1 percent of the labor force; AMU 2001). The AMU is the most expensive type of ALMP and has now existed for several decades in Sweden.

Trainee replacement schemes were introduced in 1991, and consist of an unemployed person replacing an employed worker who is on leave for education. This measure has advantages for both the unemployed individual and the firm, because the skill of the latter's employees gets updated. The goal is to raise the qualification of the employees and to help the employment office to find temporary jobs. This measure mostly takes part in the public sector and, in particular, in health and related community services.

The program *subsidized career breaks/sabbatical year*, which was introduced as a pilot in 2002, eventually started in 2005. Employees obtain the opportunity for recreation, starting an own business or education, while an unemployed individual gets the chance to take part in the labor market as a substitute.

Private sector incentive schemes

In 1993 relief work (cf. below) was almost completely replaced by *work experience schemes* (ALU). Participants of this measure perform tasks that otherwise would not have been taken care of. In contrast to relief work, displacement should be avoided. Participants in work experience schemes are primarily unemployed persons whose benefits are about to expire. The program lasts for up to six months and often takes place in non-profit private sector firms.

Employment subsidies replaced relief work, recruitment subsidies and trainee replacement schemes. The target groups are long-term unemployed. The subsidy was initially 50 percent of the wage costs for a maximum period of six months. In 1999 an extended employment subsidy was introduced, which has stricter regulations and a more generous subsidy.

Start-up grants are subsidies for job seekers who start their own business. The target group consists of unemployed individuals, people at risk of losing their job and individuals of regional development areas.

Public sector employment schemes

The oldest measure aiming at creating employment is *relief work*, which has existed since at least the 1930s and aims at counteracting cyclical and seasonal unemployment fluctuations. Most of the occupations are in the local public service sector. The duration is about six months and 50 percent of the wage costs are subsidized. This program was used up to 1998 as ALMPs were reformed and replaced by new types and measures. *Workplace introduction* (API) replaced a number of older job-experience programs and offers the unemployed a period of workplace training. The participant should only carry out work in the public or private sector that would otherwise not have been done.

Services and sanctions

Since the 1970s each municipality has had the responsibility to offer education for adults. This program is called *KOMVUX* and contains education at compulsory or upper level. Originally vocational training programs were common, but courses like Swedish for immigrants have become part of adult education. In the 1990s computer activity centers and IT programs were established. The *Adult Education Initiative* (AEI) was established in July 1997 for the duration of five years. All municipalities in Sweden participated. It was the largest skill-raising program ever started in Sweden. The objective was to halve unemployment by the year 2000. This measure is a continuation of KOMVUX and is often called *Knowledge Lift*. The target group of this program covers employees and unemployed individuals with low levels of education. Everyone who had not attained the proficiency equivalent to a high school degree, who had reached 20 years of age, and lived in Sweden, was entitled to take part.

The focus of the program lies in general skills like Swedish, English and mathematics. The education is organized in half-year terms supplied by each municipality, who is responsible for the availability and supply of courses. Participation is free of charge for pupils. For financing, the municipalities receive subsidies which depend on the unemployment rate and the distribution of skill groups in the municipality. The amount of subsidies spent is roughly about 300 Mio. € p.a.

2.4   Evaluation studies

The depression in the beginning of the 1990's has lead to a more critical view on labor market policy in Sweden. Therefore, policy evaluation received particular attention at the end of the 1990s and the beginning of the new millennium. Most of the available studies distinguish the time before, between and after the depression. The large number of different measures for unemployed individuals existing in Sweden in the present and the past leads to a wide array of possibilities of evaluating the Swedish active labor market programs. The relative effectiveness of different types of programs is examined in most studies by comparing two different measures and their outcomes.

A few main databases are used for evaluation studies in Sweden. Contrary to most European States datasets of all unemployed, employed and participants in ALMPs are available. Therefore nearly all studies are based on these comprehensive, high-quality datasets:

- Data from *Statistics Sweden (SCB):* Data are collected from different registers and are merged at SCB. All people living in Sweden are kept in this database. Total population register, the register of income and wealth (RAMS) and the register of adult education (KOMVUX) are registers merged together. RAMS is the official Swedish register of income and wealth. It is obtained from yearly income declarations. KOMVUX contains individual records on participation in any adult education program.

- *HÄNDEL*: An event history database collected by the National Swedish Labor Market Board (AMS) covers all registered unemployed persons. It is possible to identify if an individual is openly unemployed or if he/she takes part in some labor market program such as AMU. Participation in the AEI is not registered. It is a part of the KOMVUX database.
- *AKSTAT*: The data come from the unemployment insurance fund and provide information on the wage level and working hours before individuals became unemployed. All recipients of compensations by the unemployment insurance are included.

In what follows a set of studies concerning the evaluation of ALMPs in Sweden will be discussed. Because of the amount of such studies available for Sweden, this overview has to remain selective. Most Swedish studies of evaluating ALMPs consider labor market training. Like Calmfors et al. (2002) notice, studies on programs of the 1980s find positive effects of AMU participation on earnings and employment. This can be seen e.g. in the study of Andrén/Gustafsson (2002) that covers the years 1984 and 1985. In contrast to the findings of Calmfors et al. (2002) not all studies considering the 1990s find negative or only insignificant effects. Rather, it appears to be the case that studies considering the great depression in the beginning of the 1990s like Regnér (1997; 2002) do not find any positive effects. Later studies considering the end of the 1990s often establish small positive or insignificant effects on earnings and employment.

Training programs

The study by Richardson/van den Berg (2001) investigates the impact of labor market training, AMU. They report a substantial and significant effect on the transition rate from unemployment to employment for vocational training after participation. This effect diminishes with time. Nevertheless, taking the time from the beginning of the program into account, the resulting net impact is about zero, which indicates the presence of locking-in effects during participation. The considered period is 1993–2000 and data of HÄNDEL and AKSTAT are used.

Andrén/Andrén (2002) distinguish between Swedish-born and Foreign-born participants in AMU in the years 1993–1997. Regarding Swedish-born, they generally find small positive rewards of employment on participation in AMU. The rewards for Foreign-born are negative in the first year, but positive for the following years. In contrast to these findings stands the study of Fredriksson/Johansson (2003), who investigate whether job creation programs and training programs increase employment probability and mobility in the longer run. The authors use panel data from a dataset named LINDA which covers three percent of the Swedish population and consists of income registers, censuses and unemployment registers. The time period considered in the analysis is 1993–1997, which is the time with a continuous high unemployment rate after the peak in summer 1993. They estimate an outflow to employment for participants of training programs that is reduced by around 40 percent. Moreover, participation was associated with locking-in effects reducing the regional mobility and therefore the job chances outside the home region.

Similar to many other countries, also in Sweden special attention is paid to the problem of youth unemployment, and special active measures for youths exist. Larsson (2002) examines youth practice and AMU and their impact on employment and earnings for youths aged 20–24 participate at one of these measures. With data from HÄNDEL and an IFAU database she finds that participation in youth practice or labor market training has negative short-term (one year after program start) effects on employment and earnings. These coefficients get insignificant regarding the long-term effects after two years of the program start. In summary, the author concludes that youth practice is "less harmful" than AMU, because the negative coefficients are smaller and the comparison of both programs leads to positive effects for participation in youth practice.

In conclusion, the most frequently used and most expensive measure in Sweden, the labor market training AMU, does not seem to be a very effective program. In periods with low unemployment like the 1980s it appears to have worked well, while in periods of high unemployment the effects for participants on their earnings performance and employment probability are negative. A study by Calmfors et al. (2002) surveys empirical studies of the effects of ALMPs in Sweden. The results for analyses of Labor Market Training (AMU) vary substantially, but the authors observe differences between studies considering the 1980s or the 1990s. In the 1980s, positive effects on income and/or employment of participants can be established, while the coefficients on treatment effects from studies regarding the 1990s are insignificant and/or negative.

Private sector incentive schemes

In their examination of job creation programs like work experience schemes and recruitment subsidies, Calmfors et al. (2002) observe that the findings are a sign of improved performance of those programs which are closer to a regular employment relation like self-employment grants and recruitment subsidies. Furthermore, the best job-creation programs seem to work better than AMU. The estimated effects of programs for young people vary, and the results remain inconclusive.

In the 1990s the participation in self-employment programs increased very sharply, while participation in employment subsidy programs remained stable. Carling/Gustafson (1999) investigate if there is a correlation of the development in participation rates and the success of these measures regarding inflows into programs in June 1995 to December 1996. The empirical analysis based on HÄNDEL and AKSTAT data shows that the probability of getting unemployed after the end of program is twice as high for participants of employment subsidies programs as for individuals who received self-employment grants.

Public employment schemes

Since the 1990s relief work has become less important and evaluations of this program exist only for the time before, such as the one by Korpi (1994), who finds significant positive effects on the duration of employment of youth in the first half of the 1980s. Recent studies evaluate relief work only in comparison to other measures. For instance, Sianesi (2002) finds that recruitment subsidies and trainee replacement schemes generate significantly better results as relief work. Carling/Richardson (2001) compare, among other things, relief work and the workplace introduction, API. The unemployment duration is significantly lower for API as for relief work participants.

Services and sanctions

The Adult Education Initiative was a large alternative to AMU in the 1990s, and many studies comparing these measures have been conducted. One example, Stenberg (2005), investigates the impact of AEI on unemployment incidence and duration, both measured immediately after completion of the program, relative to the vocational part of AMU. The data used in this study consist of all individuals who were registered in adult education at KOMVUX in the autumn semester of 1997 and the participants of AMU on 15 October 1997 (HÄNDEL). The author reports a decreasing incidence of unemployment for AEI participants, but an increase of the unemployment duration compared to participation in AMU. Stenberg (2002; 2003) compare AEI and AMU with regard to earnings effects and also find negative treatment effects for AEI participants compared to AMU participants. Albrecht et al. (2005) examine the influence of participation in the AEI on income and the employment probability compared to non-participation. The period of examination is 1991–2000 and the data used are from HÄNDEL, KOMVUX, RAMS and AKSTAT. They report positive employment effects for young men, but no significant impact on their average income. The results for women are insignificant for both outcomes. Finally, they stress that the participants among young men are on average more disadvantaged than the non-participants.

2.5 Summary

A large literature in evaluating ALMPs in Sweden exists. Many of the recent studies compare different measures and do not regard the effect of different measures relative to non-participation. The great depression in the beginning of the 1990s led to reforms of the active labor market policy, and a fairly wide range of measures is now in use. The evaluation studies that compare measures show that recruitment subsidies, trainee replacement schemes and work placement schemes work better than AMU and relief work. While relief work is an old measure and has been almost irrelevant in the last years, AMU is the most expensive measure with a large group of participants. The alternative to AMU is KOMVUX and AEI, respectively. However, the evaluation results do not show that the output is better for participants in those programs. The bottom line is that programs in which the participants obtain subsidized work experience provided by firms work better than training and adult education.

3 Active Labor Market Policies in Austria

3.1 General economic situation

After years of high GDP growth during the late 1990's, the Austrian economy slowed down considerably in 2001 and growth almost stagnated in the following 2 years. Supported by a more dynamic international economic environment, economic activity accelerated again in 2004 with a GDP growth rate of 2%. Unemployment has been traditionally low in Austria, the unemployment rate is on average 4%. Low unemployment is seen as a consequence of the early retirement programs run in the past, and strong supply reactions to fluctuations in labor demand. Nevertheless the unemployment rate has been continually rising during the 1980's and 1990's, with the only decline occurring during 2000–2001. As a consequence of slow economic development unemployment has, however, increased again during the last years up to a rate of 4.8% in 2004. Employment growth usually follows the business cycle. The number of employees in active employment has risen during 2003 and 2004, after a reduction in 2002. Figure 8 shows the development of real GDP growth, employment growth and the unemployment rate since 1993.

The average number of individuals in active employment during 2003 was 3,184,759 (Table 4). The average number of unemployed individuals was 240,079. These numbers hide, however, the strong labor turnover in the Austrian economy. The number of individuals at least one day unemployed in this year was 774,242. The turnover phenomenon is to a large extent the result of strong seasonal fluctuations in employment in Austria. The number of individuals ever enrolled in an ALMP program in 2003 was 253,133, almost one third of the unemployed.

3.2 Labor market institutions

The labor market institutions worth discussing in connection with ALMP are the unemployment insurance system and the centralized wage bargaining system. Other specifics of the Austrian labor market are early retirement regulations and the recent pension reform, the apprenticeship education system, and the strong component of seasonality in demand for labor.

The system of unemployment insurance in Austria is almost universal, that is to say compulsory for all except the self-employed. It is articulated in the administration of unemployment benefits (Arbeitslosengeld) and, after these expire, unemployment assistance (Notstandshilfe). In order to qualify for unemployment benefits a worker has to have been employed and insured under the scheme for at least 52 weeks in the past two years. This requirement is

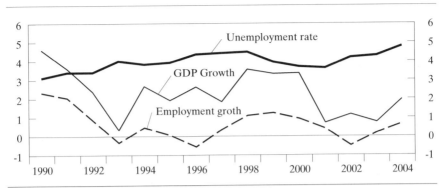

Figure 8. GDP growth and unemployment rate in Austria; 1990 to 2004; in %

Table 4. Labor market indicators in Austria; 2003

Labor market participation rate, in %	72.7
Average active employment	3,184,759
Average unemployment	240,079
Individuals ever unemployed	774,242
Individuals ever in ALMP program	253,133

lowered to only 26 weeks within the past year for young people below 25 and for those repeatedly unemployed. The duration of the period of unemployment benefits can be up to 30 weeks, depending on the duration of the employment period preceding the spell of unemployment. The replacement ratio is about 55 percent of net income, which is low by European standards, but becomes substantially higher once family allowances are taken into account. According to OECD figures for 1994, for example, the net replacement ratio for a single-earner household earning two-thirds of the average wage of blue collar workers was between 58 and 74 percent, depending on the presence of children (OECD 1997).

After unemployment benefits are exhausted, the worker can apply to receive unemployment assistance. The duration of this program is potentially indefinite and under this scheme the worker receives up to 92 percent of the amount of the previous unemployment benefits. The main difference with the previous scheme consists of the fact that unemployment assistance is means tested and therefore depends on the presence and the economic condition of the partner. To give an example of the incidence of means testing Lalive et al. (2004) estimate that in 1990 the unemployment assistance payment was about 70 percent of the median unemployment benefit check.

In Austria wages are set by collective agreements stipulated between employer, employee representatives, unions and government officials. It is often argued that this centralized wage bargaining process increases real wage flexibility at the macro level but at the same time decreases the single firm's

ability to react to idiosyncratic shocks. The consequence are quantity adjustments in the form of relatively high job turnover rates. Stiglbauer et al. (2003)
find that yearly job creation and destruction rates in Austria are comparable
to the US. Fischer/Pichelmann (1991) show that in Austria about one-third of
all unemployment spells per year and almost one-fourth of total unemployment can be ascribed to seasonal fluctuations, similarly to the USA or
Canada. Collective agreements fix minimum wages at the industry level, but
employers are of course free to negotiate higher wages with individual
workers.

Early retirement regulations used to be very generous in Austria, leading to
a low average entry age into retirement of 58. This system is often mentioned
as one of the reasons for low unemployment rates in Austria, compared to
similar European economies. The demographic development, however,
threatens the sustainability of this retirement system. A first pension reform,
implemented in 2003, has the objective to raise the effective retirement age
and impose pension cuts depending on retirement entry age.

Another factor reducing, primarily, youth unemployment in Austria is the
apprenticeship system as an alternative way of secondary schooling. Apprentices receive training in a particular occupation in a firm. In addition, the apprentices attend a part-time vocational school, for one or two days a week.
About 40 percent of a cohort complete apprenticeship in Austria.

A feature which sets Austria apart from its neighboring countries are the
high seasonal fluctuations in employment. The variation in aggregate employment over the year is about 5 percentage points from peak to trough. In
magnitude this is similar to the fluctuations observed in Canada or Scandi-
navian countries. Seasonal fluctuations can be explained by the big share the
construction and tourism sector have in the economy. Among the institutional
features, which promote seasonal employment fluctuations, we note the role
of the unemployment insurance system which does not have an element of experience rating, and the relatively mild and industry-specific regulations on
hiring and firing for blue collar workers.

3.3   Measures of Active Labor Market Policy

Active labor market policy includes counseling, placement and a broad range
of active labor market programs. To be eligible for ALMP participation in
Austria a person must be unemployed, or face the risk of becoming unemployed. Since the Austrian Ministry of Social Affairs does not specify the eligibility criteria more narrowly, this leaves a great deal of discretion to the
program administrators. The guidelines instruct the employment office
advisors actively to offer training to the unemployed who lack specific skills,
and in particular to individuals with placement disadvantages (school
dropouts, long-term unemployed, disabled, women with long work interrup-
tions). During training participation, individuals receive compensation which
amounts to the level of unemployment benefits.

Among ALMP programs in Austria a formal distinction is made between
training programs, employment subsidies, and support programs. (Support

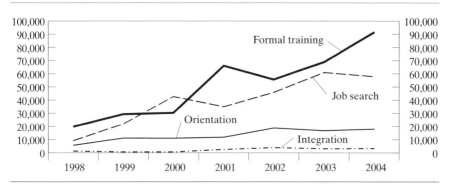

Figure 9. Number of program participants in Austria by program type; 1998 to 2004; in 1,000

programs are programs to facilitate the start up of an enterprise of child care for jobseekers with kids.) The main strategy of ALMP in Austria aims at improving individual skills. In 2003 83% of treated individuals were enrolled in a training program, 18% received an employment subsidy, and 12% received a support measure (BMWA 2004). Because of repeated program participation, these numbers do not sum up to 100%.

Training programs can be further classified into formal training, job search assistance, orientation, and integration programs. Training programs focus on education and on qualification enhancement of participants. Courses offered are vocational training courses which result in a certified education equivalent to an apprenticeship degree. Other courses train specific skills like languages or computer abilities. Course durations vary from 4 weeks to one year according to the course type. For the participants training courses are time intensive and participation may reduce their search effort and attachment to the labor market.

Job search assistance programs aim at the activation of unemployed individuals at an early stage. The programs are not focused on specific target groups but should be available for the majority of the unemployed. Job search assistance programs are designed to increase search effort and search efficiency by motivating and encouraging participants. The programs should lead to immediate transitions into employment either during the course or shortly afterwards. During the course job application practices (writing application letters, behavior in job talks) are trained. Course durations are 6–7 weeks, but not full time: three course days during the first week and one day during each of the following weeks. In contrast to formal training programs participation in job search courses is mandatory and noncompliance is subject to benefit sanctions (cf. also Scherhammer, Adam 2002). The aim was that every new entrant into unemployment should enroll in a course before completing the first 4 months of unemployment. In practice these entry regulations were, however, difficult to enforce.

Orientation programs should prepare participants for participation in a formal training course or for taking up a job immediately. During this orientation phase decisions on occupational opportunities and a future career plan should be supported.

Integration programs deal with social problems like those arising as a consequence of long term unemployment. Their aim is a psychological and social stabilization of participants in order to reintegrate them into the labor market. During integration the participant is supposed to work in a sheltered workplace for at least 50% of the course duration.

ALMP participation

Figure 9 shows the development of participation for the 4 types of training programs over time. The two most important programs are formal training and job search. For those we also see a rapid increase in participants over time. Orientation and integration programs play a minor role. A major change in the composition of programs occurred when job search assistance programs were extended beginning with 1999 and 2000, following the recommendation of the guidelines in the European Employment Strategy.

Figure 10 shows the monthly ratio of program participants to unemployed persons. Even this graph displays some seasonality, as fewer programs seem to be run in July and August. We see a sharp increase in the share of program participants from about 10% of the unemployed to almost 20% in 1999. This break is a consequence of two factors. First, the development of program participation did not follow the business cycle: while unemployment declined in 2000 and 2001, the number of program participants was still rising. Second, an additional increase in the number of program participants results from the expansion of job search assistance programs from 1999 onwards. Job search assistance programs are relatively cheap compared to formal training.

ALMP expenditures

The share of total expenditures for passive and Active Labor Market Policies in GDP has risen from about 1% in the early 1990s to 1.5% in 2004. The share of spending on Active Labor Market Policies is about 0.5% of GDP. Figure 11 shows the development of labor market policy expenditures for unemployment insurance, unemployment assistance and ALMP over time. The largest part of these is spent for unemployment insurance. The costs for this system have particularly risen during the late 80's and early 90's. Thereafter they follow the business cycle. The expenditures for Active Labor Market Policies show higher growth rates from 1999 onwards, which is in line with the increase in the number of program participants during that period.

Splitting up ALMP expenditures by program types allows a comparison of program costs per trainee. Table 5 lists yearly expenditures for course participation in the four types of training programs. These are only the training costs paid to course providers; UI benefits for participants, extra allowances for travel expenses, or course materials are not considered. On average a course participation costs about 1,500 € per participant. There are huge differences in course types. By far the cheapest measures are job search programs, which are

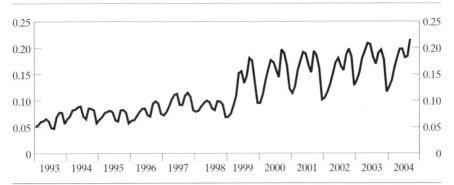

Figure 10. Monthly ratio of program participants to unemployed individuals in Austria; 1993 to 2004; in %

only 500 € per participant. These courses have shorter durations and are only part time. The costs for a formal training slot are almost 4 times higher.

Data used for ALMP evaluations

The most accurate information on ALMP participation can be found in administrative records in the database of the Austrian employment office (AMS). These data include individual information on entry and exit dates into and out of a program, a program identifier, and the reason for exiting from the program. From 2001 onwards also a strict classification of the program type is available. For earlier years this information is incomplete.

From 2001 onward the AMS also releases monthly information on the number of program participants, by program type, region, sex, and other characteristics. In addition, yearly program expenditures by program type are available. This information should make it possible to calculate average program costs per participant.

In a separate database the AMS also keeps records of assignments or invitations to programs. This information can be compared with actual program participation to evaluate the incentive or threat effects of program assignment. This data source has not been investigated so far and needs to be checked for consistency with the standard records.

3.4 Evaluation studies

A large part of evaluation studies on Austrian ALMP focuses on surveying participants. During the so called "massnahmenbegleitende Evaluierung" (i.e. program-accompanying evaluation) participants are typically asked to give their opinion on the program and its potential use for them. Although these surveys collect detailed subjective information they neglect any economic objective. For example program participants are not asked questions con-

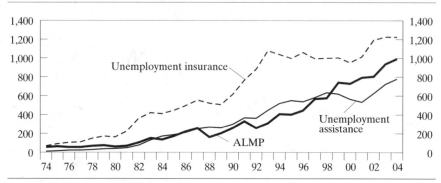

Figure 11. Yearly expenditures for active and passive labor market policies in
Austria; 1974 to 2004; in %

Table 5.   Course costs per participant in Austria

	Yearly expenditure in €	Number of participants	Average cost per participant
Job search	30,491,288	57,756	528
Formal training	193,744,933	91,564	2,116
Orientation	20,280,479	17,945	1,130
Integration	10,729,729	3,332	3,220
Total	255,246,429	170,597	1,496

cerning their wages, or labor market careers. This kind of evaluation study
mainly serves the purpose of controlling program providers. But no effort is
made to evaluate the effects on the participants.

Further, the Austrian employment office (AMS) engages in the evaluation
of single programs for specific target groups, e.g. for single mothers or long
term unemployed. The evaluation method used is usually to compare labor
market outcomes for program participants before and after the program.
Again this method completely abstracts from any effects of program selection.

Training programs

There are few scientifically rigorous evaluation studies on ALMP in Austria.
In an early study Zweimüller/Winter-Ebmer (1996) focus on public training
programs in the 1980's. They evaluate the effect of training on job stability in a
sample of unemployed who enter employment in 1986. Program participation
and a binary indicator for 12 months employment stability are jointly modeled
using a bivariate probit model. The results indicate positive treatment effects
on employment stability once selection is controlled for.

Winter-Ebmer (2001) evaluates a special training scheme which was
offered to workers affected by large-scale downsizing during privatization and
restructuring of the national steel firms in the late 1980s. One special feature of

these "Steel Foundations" is that they were financed jointly by the unemployment insurance funds and the steel firms themselves. The other feature is that the long-term program was composed of orientation, re-training and placement assistance elements. The program resulted in considerable wage gains and improved employment prospects for the participants.

Services and sanctions

In a more recent project, funded by the Austrian National Bank, Weber/Hofer (2003) evaluate the effects of different types of ALMP measures on the exit rate into employment for individuals entering unemployment in 1999. They use the timing-of-events method which estimates the program effect as a shift in the transition rate from unemployment to jobs at the moment of program entry. They find that the immediate employment effects differ substantially by program type. Job search assistance programs increase the transition rate into jobs considerably. The probability of finding a job within four months is increased by 15% for job search participants. Training programs, on the other hand, have a small but negative effect on transitions into employment. Investigating the dynamics of the treatment effect they find that the negative effect from training programs is due to a lock-in period of 60 days. After that training programs have a positive effect on the employment probability. Program effects differ for women and men. Women benefit from participation in all types of programs. There is even a positive overall program effect for women from training programs. These results also indicate that after controlling for all observable information, selection into programs by unobservable characteristics still occurs.

A second study investigates the dependence of the program effect on varying entry times for job-search assistance programs in Austria (Weber, Hofer 2004). The Austrian targeting policy is to admit every unemployed to a job-search program before the fourth month. The program effect is measured by a shift in the transition rate into employment upon program entry, using the timing-of-events method. The main findings are that the program effect is positive and does not vary significantly for program entries during the first year of unemployment, but it drops drastically thereafter. Project extensions focus on the evaluation of long term program effects on employment durations, the effects of repeated program participation, and the threat effects of program assignment among others.

A major project still in progress is the evaluation of employment subsidies co-financed by the European Structural Funds. According to the mid-term project report the authors use propensity score matching to evaluate the program effects.

3.5   Summary

The importance of ALMP has clearly been rising during the last 10 years in Austria, with public expenditures now amounting to about 0.5% of GDP. The most common programs in Austria are training programs. Only during the last years the focus has shifted from pure educational programs to job search assistance programs as well.

With the rising importance of ALMP spending in Austria, also the necessity of scientific evaluation studies has been recognized by public authorities. Whereas positive effects of training programs were found in early evaluations during the 1980s, more recent studies find that these programs increase unemployment durations. The effects are more negative for men than for women. Job search assistance programs, on the other hand, help to significantly reduce unemployment durations.

4   Active Labor Market Policies in Germany

4.1   General economic situation

Since unification, Germany has suffered from a slow growth dynamic. Between 1991 and 2003, GDP grew by only 18% (Figure 12), which is only half the growth rate of the United Kingdom (35%) or the Netherlands (34%) over that time period. The German labor market, especially in the Eastern part of the country, has suffered severely from this poor performance. Despite of high spending on active labor market policy, employment decreased by 0.4% since 1991, while unemployment has been rising constantly. Today, unemployment rates are higher than ever, ranging between 9.6% in the West and 18.6% in the East. In these days, the government's ability to reduce unemployment is viewed as the key criteria for its success. Therefore, labor market policy has become one of the central German policy fields and politicians have started to recognize the need for a thorough evaluation of measures to assess their effectiveness in bringing down German unemployment.

However, despite increasing numbers of unemployed persons, the number of participants in active labor market measures has been declining since unification (Figure 13). This development might reflect a tightening of the budget in Germany as well as the attempt to target measures more specifically to certain problem groups. The share of participants has always been higher in East Germany compared to West Germany, especially shortly after unification, but has been converging in recent years.

In what follows we will first describe the measures of German active labor market policy and then review results of existing evaluation studies.

4.2   Labor market institutions

In Germany, active labor market policy has a long tradition. Both active and passive policy measures are financed by the unemployment insurance system, which was founded in 1927. The legal basis for active measures was the *work support act* (Arbeitsförderungsgesetz, AFG) for the time period 1969 to 1998, and has been the *Book of Social Law III* (Sozialgesetzbuch, SGB III) since then. Especially after unification, when the abrupt transition from a centrally planned to a market economy came as a shock to the East German labor

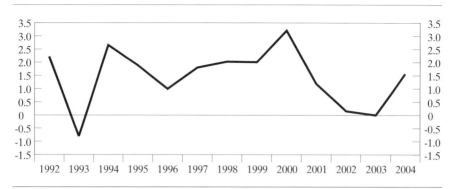

Figure 12. GDP growth in Germany; 1992 to 2004; in %

market, active labor market measures played a central role in the attempt of policy makers to alleviate the consequences of transition, and adjust East German workers' skill composition.

By international standards, the institutional setting of ALMP in Germany has been particularly generous, complex and rather unspecific for many years. Recent reforms however point towards higher efficiency and higher self-responsibility of the unemployed (the so-called principle of "rights and duties"), while essentially maintaining the system's relative generosity.

The government implemented two important reforms, the "JobAcqtiv" law in 2002, and the so-called "Hartz Reforms" (four extensive laws with the objective "to improve the public services provided on the labor market") between 2003 and 2005. The reforms aim at ameliorating the labor market's mechanisms by reducing employment protection, promoting flexible forms of work and providing labor supply incentives for low wage earners. Furthermore, a re-organization of local employment agencies and the introduction of quasi markets into some programs are expected to raise the efficiency of job seekers placement. Additionally, some new policy measures have been introduced, for instance the so-called "Ich-AG" subsidies to promote business start-ups of unemployed persons.[2]

Most importantly, the Hartz Reforms changed the general institutional setting in which Active Labor Market Policies is imbedded. Before 2005, unemployment benefit payments and ALMP participation were conditional on unemployment insurance contributions. Both benefit payments and ALMP measures were implemented by the federal employment agency and its local agencies. The monthly benefit of up to 67% of last net income was paid for up to 6 to 32 months. People with no or insufficient contributions to the unemployment insurance system received means tested social assistance from the local authorities and had no access to ALMP measures. Since 2005, in contrast, unemployment benefit payments and ALMP participation are conditional on

---

[2] Fertig/Kluve (2004) and Fertig et al. (2004) contain a detailed description of the set of Hartz Reforms I-III along with a comprehensive concept to evaluate their effectiveness.

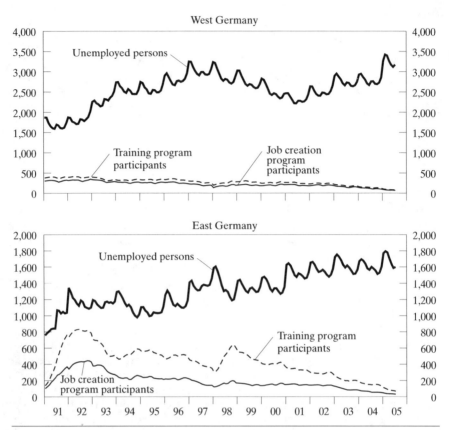

Figure 13. Unemployment and ALMP participation in Germany; 1991 to
2005; in 1,000
Source: IAB Nürnberg.

a person's ability to work. Those capable of working are assigned to the employment agencies while only those who are not capable of working due to
sickness, disability or care responsibilities, receive means tested social assistance from the local authorities. Now, an unemployed person capable of
working receives a so-called benefit type I, which is now paid for a reduced
period of 6 to 18 months. Thereafter, the unemployed receives a means tested
benefit type II, same as any other employable person who never made contribution payments. ALMP measures are now open for any person capable of
working. Program participation does not restore eligibility for benefit
payments.

Besides the reduction in benefit payments and duration, there are some
further elements in the institutional setting that realize the reform's principle
of "rights and duties" (or, as it is called, "supporting and demanding",
"Fördern und Fordern"). Since 2005, every person who enters unemployment

has to undergo a so called profiling by the case-worker. Based on this, a personalized placement strategy is set out in a binding integration agreement, which specifies both the services that will be provided to the job seeker as well as the job seekers obligation regarding job search activities and ALMP participation, where required. Although assignment to ALMP measures is regulated by law, which states eligibility conditions and priority target groups, there still seems to be a wide scope for case worker's discretion. If the unemployed deviates from the integration agreement or does not cooperate appropriately, benefit payments may be reduced as a sanction.

4.3 Measures of Active Labor Market Policy

Active Labor Market Policies are generally perceived as important policy tools in Germany, a fact that is reflected in ALMP expenditure clearly above the EU15 average (Figure 4 and Table 27 in the appendix). This perception is also reinforced by the huge set of different active labor market programs that are used in practice. The remainder of the chapter describes the various measures of German active labor market policy in more detail. Although some evaluation studies refer to earlier years, the description will focus exclusively on the period after 1998, when the SGB III was introduced. Modifications of the law will be made explicit as far as possible.

4.3.1 Training programs

Training is the most important ALMP measure in Germany. Programs are intensive, long and generous by international standards. After unification, they were utilized extensively to (re-)qualify the labor force in East Germany, to adjust their skills for the demands of the market economy. Only recently, in 2003, the Hartz reforms changed the set up of training programs considerably by cutting back financial support, tightening eligibility rules and introducing quasi markets onto training provision.

General target groups of training programs supported by the SGB III are the unemployed as well as persons directly threatened by unemployment, vocational apprentices, re-entrants to the labor market and immigrants. The federal employment agency (FEA) may pay subsistence allowances and bear training costs, as well as indirect costs like traveling expenses, costs of childcare, etc. Individuals who fail eligibility criteria set by the SGB III may receive support by the means of the European Social Fund (ESF). The main types of training programs are the following (1998–2005):

Vocational training

The FEA may support participants of training courses that award a first professional degree. Subsistence allowances are granted for trainees when financial difficulties prove to be an obstacle to qualification. Payments are therefore means tested taking into account the trainee's living and training expenses as well as his/her income and the income of parents and the spouse. Other programs aim at preparing hard-to-place young people who lack basic skills for vocational training. Direct costs of preparatory training measures are generally paid by the FEA. There is a wide variety of preparatory measures, some of which may last up to one year. Furthermore, there are programs providing support for vocational training for those with learning difficulties or social disadvantages.

Further vocational training and retraining

Further vocational training and retraining programs are measures that assess, maintain or extend vocational knowledge and skills, and adapt them to technical developments. They enable the participants to work in other employment (retraining) or may even provide a vocational qualification when missing. Since 1998, further training subsumes both further vocational training and retraining. As a prerequisite for participation, the caseworker has to deem the training measure "necessary" for integrating the participant in the labor market or for preventing future unemployment in the case that the participant is still employed.

Before the Hartz reforms, subsistence allowance levels for further training were equal to unemployment benefits (63% or 60% of the previous net income). If the person was not currently receiving unemployment benefits, he/she must previously have been in contributory employment for a given period. Apart from costs of training, participants may also receive reimbursements of transportation and childcare costs (up to 130 € per month).

The Hartz-Reform cut down support for further training substantially and increased competition in the market of training provision. The local employment office issues a training voucher to the employee confirming his/her eligibility. The employee is then free to choose any course provided by a list of approved bodies. Furthermore, receiving support for further vocational training reduces the duration of eligibility for unemployment benefits (two days of training reduce eligibility by one day). Furthermore, in 2005 subsistence allowance was abolished for those who are not unemployed, while unemployed participants just continue to receive their unemployment benefit. As before, participants who do not receive grants by the SGB III (mainly female re-entrants to the labor market) may receive support by means of the ESF-BA program.

Measures to improve prospects of integration

These measures comprise rather short term training courses or practical activities aiming at (i) assessing skills and willingness to work, (ii) supporting job search, e.g. by job-application training, counseling on job search possibilities and (iii) providing knowledge and abilities to facilitate a placement in work or the completion of a training measure. Recipients of unemployment benefits continue to receive their payments. Non-recipients of unemployment benefits or assistance are allowed to participate since 1999. They can apply for reimbursement of costs of the program as well as transportation and childcare costs and may receive subsistence allowance by means of the EFS.

Subsidies towards measures included in social plans and short time working allowance

These measures are available for workers who, because of working hours lost unavoidably, temporarily or for economic reasons, are directly threatened by unemployment. Both measures may but need not come along with training measures as long as the employer provides an appropriate financial contribution. Eligibility rules refer to the firm rather than the individual. In 2004, eligibility rules were loosened to some extent and recipients of short time working allowance are forced to undertake a profiling by the FEA before participating at a training measure.

Training through job rotation

This program came into force in 2002. It aims both at supporting small and middle sized companies in the further training of their employees, and at helping unemployed individuals integrate into working life. While the employee is undergoing training, an unemployed individual can temporarily fill his/her vacant position. The FEA subsidizes up to 100% of the wage costs of the unemployed for a maximum period of one year.

4.3.2 (Financial) Incentive schemes

The SGB III makes use of a wide variety of incentives in order to influence the behavior of employers and workers: there are monetary subsidies on wages and social security contributions, as well as suspensions or reductions of benefit payments and exemptions from employment protection rules. Incentives on the demand side of the labor market aim at inducing employers to create jobs and employ certain types of workers they would not have employed otherwise. On the supply side, incentives are utilized to make workers put efforts in job search and training, increase their labor supply and flexibility. Moreover, financial subsidies are available that help the unemployed (or persons threatened by unemployment) starting their own business.

Employer related incentives

Integration subsidies
Integration subsidies are a form of wage subsidies ("Eingliederungszuschüsse") that can be paid when the firm employs a certain type of workers. The idea is to compensate the firm for the presumably lower productivity of this type of worker. Integration subsidies are available for

• Time of familiarization ("Einarbeitungszeit") with the new activity
• Hard-to-place persons (mainly long-term unemployed and disabled persons)

- Workers aged 55 and older
- Re-entrants (mainly women)
- Unemployed person when employer is a start-up business.

The law allows for a considerable scope of discretion with respect to duration and the amount of payments. Generally, maximum duration varies between 6 and 24 months, depending on the target group and, as a rule, the maximum rate of subsidy should not exceed 50% of the calculable remuneration. In order to avoid substitution effects and free riding, payments are not available when the employer apparently dismissed a worker in order to receive the benefit or when he had already employed the respective worker within the previous four years.

Social security contribution subsidies for older workers
Since 2003, this subsidy is available for promoting employment prospects of the old among the unemployed. A firm who employs a worker of age 55 or older is exempt from contributing to the unemployment security system for this worker. However, it should be mentioned that the contribution amounts to only 3.25% of the gross wage.

Other, non-financial forms of incentives
Loosening employment protection rules is another way to provide an incentive for employment creation. In Germany, exemptions from the rather restrictive regulation of fixed term contracts are given for establishments with up to 10 employees (before 2003: 5 employees) and for contracts with employees aged 52 (before 2003: aged 58) and older[3]. In these cases, firms are exempt from the rule that fixed term contracts may not last longer than two years *without justification* ("sachgrundlos").

Staff Services agencies (PSA)
Since 2003, every local employment office sets up a Staff Service agency (PSA) that acts like a temporary work agency for the unemployed. To this end, the local employment office either may contract a private temporary work agency or, if no provider is available, may run a PSA by itself. The local employment office delegates unemployed persons to the PSA, which in turn receives a lump sum fee for each worker. The PSA may lend the worker temporarily to other firms or provide a permanent placement. During periods of inactivity, the PSA should provide training measures to the worker. Therefore, PSAs encompass aspects of training measures and job search assistance, too.

Employee related incentives

Social security contribution subsidy
("Minijobs" and "Midijobs"; since 2003) Employees with low working

---

[3]   In fact, this regulation has recently (November 2005) been ruled null and void on equity grounds by the European Court of Justice. An adjustment of the regulation is pending.

incomes receive a full subsidy for social security contributions. The income threshold for full subsidies changed several times over the past years and is 400 € at present. Since 2003, further social security subsidies are paid at a decreasing rate for incomes between 400 and 800 €. The aim of the subsidy is to make work pay for low wage workers and to foster employment in the respective segments of the labor market.

"Mainzer Modell"
This program was implemented for a short period between 2000 and 2003. It was set up as an experimental program in 2000 in the federal state of Rheinland-Pfalz. In 2002, it was implemented throughout Germany and finally ended in 2003. It aimed at providing work incentives to the long-term unemployed and persons with lower level qualification. The program offered a social security contribution subsidy for persons with incomes of up to 810 € as well as a top-up to the child benefit for parents of underage children. The level of payments depended on the number of underage children, the gross working income, as well as total household income. The program became obsolete by the introduction of Mini- and Midijobs (see above).

Wage protection for older employees
Since 2003, unemployed persons of age 50 and older may receive a wage subsidy when they accept a job offer that pays less than their previous job. The wage subsidy amounts to 50% of the difference between the previous wage and the actual wage. It is paid for the same duration as the unemployment benefit would have been paid if the person had remained unemployed.

Mobility allowance
In order to improve the matching process in the labor market and reduce unemployment, the FEA may provide financial support for persons who take up employment at a long distance from their place of residence. Mobility allowances may reimburse expenses for traveling, moving and maintaining a second household for up to 6 months. Moreover, workers can apply for an interest-free loan to remove financial obstacles to take up a job.

Sanctions
Reduction or suspension of benefit payments may be imposed when it appears that an unemployed person puts too little effort into job search activities, turns down job offers, or refuses to participate in training measures deemed necessary for a successful placement. Furthermore, if the unemployed person lost the previous job on his/her own fault, the employment agency can suspend benefit payments. Since 2003, activities expected by the jobseeker are set in a binding agreement between the employment agency and the jobseeker and the unemployed person has to be able to give proof of her job search activities.

Start-up subsidies – "Bridging allowance"
Unemployed persons and those threatened by unemployment can receive a grant on entering self-employment. The benefit is paid for 6 months and is equal to the unemployment benefit that the recipient had previously received

or could have received plus a lump-sum social security contribution. In order to receive the grant, the FEA has to approve the business plan of the new entrepreneur.

Start-up subsidies – " Ich-AG" subsidy
Since 2003, new entrepreneurs have the choice between the bridging allowance and the so-called Ich-AG subsidy. The Ich-AG subsidy is the same for every claimant, that is to say it is independent of prior social security contributions. It is paid for a maximum period of three years as long as the claimant's income does not exceed 25,000 € per year. It amounts to 600 € per month in the first year, 360 € per month in the second and 240 € per month in the third year. There are no special conditions regarding the business plan.

4.3.3 Direct job creation schemes

Direct job creation schemes have played an important role over the last one or two decades, especially in Eastern Germany, where they were implemented on a large scale to compensate for the large reduction in employment after unification. They aim at activating, maintaining and adapting the person's professional capacities for later integration in the regular labor market. Job creation works through a wage subsidy paid by the FEA. Public and, under certain circumstances, even private firms can apply for participation at the local employment agency. They must give proof that the activity is of value for society and that it is additional in nature, that is to say, without the subsidy the activity would either be delayed substantially into the future or not be performed at all. Before 2002, participation required being unemployed for more than one year and being eligible for unemployment benefits. Selection gave priority to the most disadvantaged, mainly the long-term unemployed and the elderly. Since 2002, the scale of the program has been reduced substantially, and at the same time, local employment agencies were given a wider scope of discretion, and eligibility criteria became less restrictive. There are four types of direct job creation schemes:

Active measures promoting the creation of jobs (ABM)

These measures are usually carried out by private firms or non-profit institutions. They typically last for one year, but may be shorter or longer under special conditions. Since 2003, duration can last up to three years for older workers. Until 2003, the participant received the regular wage in contributory employment, which entitled to a new round of unemployment benefit payments after completing the measure. As a rule, the wage was subsidized by the FEA at a rate of 50 to 75% and could be increased to up to 100%. Since 2003, the subsidy is a lump sum transfer that varies by qualification level. Until 2003, private firms had to provide a minimum amount of training to the participant, but this is no longer required at present.

Structural adjustment measure (SAM)

Structural adjustment measures originally were a policy for the eastern part of Germany after unification, and were extended to the western part in 1998. In 2003, SAM was subsumed under ABM in 2003. Such measures included environmental conservation, social services, cultural activity etc. The main difference to ABM is the fact that employers received a lump sum subsidy equal to the average amount of unemployment benefit or assistance saved by the specific measure.

Employment generating promotion of the infrastructure

Public institutions can apply for financial support by the FEA for activities that improve the infrastructure. The support requires that a private firm carries out the activity and employs a certain number of unemployed persons assigned by the FEA. These persons may not make up more than 35% of the total number of employees of the firm and the entire subsidy must not exceed 25% of total costs of the measure.

"1-Euro-Jobs"

Since 2005, unemployed persons receiving unemployment benefits type II (ALG II) may be assigned to additional activities created by public institutions even when these activities are not supported by the AMB scheme. Such activities do not constitute regular employment. Participants continue to receive the unemployment benefit plus 1 € per working hour.

4.3.4 Job search assistance

The local employment agencies offer job search assistance to the unemployed. Recent reforms aimed at enhancing efficiency in job placement as well as introducing quasi markets through placement vouchers. Provision was decentralized giving a wider scope of discretion on the local level with respect to spending and implementation of Active Labor Market Policies. Moreover, local agencies will have more caseworkers, changing figures from 400 unemployed people per caseworker to 150 (75 for young people) per caseworker. Assistance is implemented as case-management, meaning that the same caseworker will be responsible for one unemployed person. While prior to the reforms job search assistance was the main activity of caseworkers, now their responsibility is wider and comprises aspects of social work, too.

Counseling and placement assistance (Job Center since 2005)

The FEA offers both, financial and personal assistance to jobseekers. The FEA reimburses costs of application of up to 260 € per annum, as well as travel costs in order to enable job searchers to participate in assessment centers, interviews and the like.

Assessment of chances (profiling) and Integration agreement

Since 2003, every jobseeker who receives some unemployment benefit payments has to undergo a thorough assessment of his or her chances. Based on this profile, the caseworker and the jobseeker will elaborate a personalized placement strategy. Profiling helps match the most suitable measures to the unemployed and therefore is expected to enhance the efficiency of the measures (before 2002, unemployment duration was the key eligibility criterion for participation). The personalized placement strategy will be set out in a binding integration agreement. The agreement defines both the services provided by the local employment office (e.g. training measures) and the activities required by part of the jobseeker. For instance, the jobseeker could be expected to participate in a training measure and to make a certain number of applications in a given period.

Involvement of third parties in the placement of unemployment-assistance recipients

If the local unemployment agency was unable to place the jobseeker for a specified period, the jobseeker can claim a placement voucher from the local employment agency and employ a private placement agency for job search assistance and placement.

4.3.5 Youth programs

Support for vocational preparation training measures for young people

Young people who lack basic skills for vocational training may receive financial support for participating in preparatory training measures. Measures may last up to one year. They include basic training courses, supported courses for disabled people and combinations of ABM and preparatory vocational training (working and learning).

Intensive vocational guidance

Local employment agencies offer career counseling regarding vocational chances and prospects for young people. Measures include workshops, placement fairs as well as one-on-one interviews.

Immediate action program against youth unemployment (JUMP)

The program comprises the conventional measures of Active Labor Market Policies, mainly vocational preparation training measures, vocational training, further training and integration measures. The main difference to conventional programs is the fact that it is open to young persons under 25 years of age who do not meet all eligibility criteria set by the SGB III. The program is financed both by the FEA and by the ESF-BA program. In 2004, subsistent parts of the program became part of the SGB III.

4.3.6 Measures for the disabled

The SGB IV summarizes regulations on the integration of the disabled into the labor market. For instance, it forces employers to employ disabled people. Generally, they must fill 5% of all vacancies by disabled persons. If they fail to do so, a contribution is to be paid to the competent integration authority (Integrationsamt). The competent integration authority must approve any dismissal of a severely disabled person. Furthermore, many paragraphs of the SGB III contain measures of active labor market policy for the disabled. They comprise training measures, integration subsidies and job search assistance:

Integration subsidies for severely disabled people

In order to compensate employers for the presumably lower performance of severely disabled employees, they may receive wage subsidies amounting to up to 70% for a period of 24 months.

Measures to help integrate disabled people into working life (training)

These measures provide vocational rehabilitation measures that help physically, mentally or psychologically handicapped people and those threatened by such disabilities integrate into working life, restore, and maintain their earning capacities. Measures may take place in vocational rehabilitation institutions supported by the FEA. The participant and his or her family may receive subsistence benefit payments.

Specialized integration services for the severely disable (counseling and job-search assistance)

The FEA and the integration authority provide special integration services for disabled employees and jobseekers. They assist in adapting the workplace to the special need of the disabled worker and provide legal advice and information on financial support for both, employers and employees.

4.4   Evaluation studies

For a long time the evaluation of German ALMP suffered from the lack of suitable data. Only very recently good quality data has become available to researchers. Early studies were based on the GSOEP or, for East Germany, the Labor Market Monitor East. The main drawback of these data is that, due to rather small overall sample sizes and panel mortality, they contain only few observations on participants of active labor market measures. Researchers often had to group together heterogeneous measures and some programs could not be evaluated at all because participation was not documented in the data. Only in 1998, when the SGB III was implemented, the government acknowledged the need for a thorough evaluation of Active Labor Market

Policies, and, in the following years, considerable effort was made to derive large data sets from administrative data of local employment agencies (Bender et al. 2005). They provide many observations, cover large periods and, therefore, allow detecting short- as well as long-term effects. Furthermore, they provide enough information to better distinguish different types of treatment. Recently, these merged administrative data have become available to some researchers and seem to be able to provide robust results.

Most of the studies concentrate on training and job creation schemes, which are the most important measures in terms of expenditure and number of participants. To our knowledge, only two studies address wage subsidies and one study addresses job search assistance. We are not aware of any econometric study specifically analyzing programs for youths and the disabled. Fitzenberger/Speckesser (2000) provide a survey on early evaluation studies in Germany, most of which are based on the above-mentioned data with the corresponding limitations. For each type of measure, we will summarize early results very briefly and concentrate on the more recent results, which are based on the better data mentioned above. A summary of the preliminary results of the evaluation of the Hartz-Reforms is given in Jacobi/Kluve (2006).

Training in East Germany

Early evaluation studies on training in East Germany include Lechner (1998, 1999), Hujer/Wellner (2000)/Lechner (2000), which are based on the GSOEP. Studies based on the Labor Market Monitor East are for instance Hübler (1997), Fitzenberger/Prey (1998). Bergemann et al. (2000) use the Labor Market Monitor East of the federal state Saxony-Anhalt, as does Bergemann et al. (2004). Reinowski et al. (2003, 2004) use the Mikrozensus Saxony. Recent studies which are based on the new merged administrative data are Hujer, Thomsen/Zeiss (2004), Fitzenberger/Speckesser (2005)/Lechner et al. (2005).

Many of the early studies either find positive effects or are unable to find any significant effects of training programs in East Germany. An exception is Hübler (1997) who finds negative effects for women. This result contrasts with the finding of Bergemann et al. (2000) who find significantly positive effects of second treatments for women only. Bergemann et al. (2004) find positive effects in the early nineties and negative ones in later years. In general, studies that have been published from 2000 onwards tend to be more pessimistic. Besides Bergemann et al. (2004), also Lechner (2000) and Reinowski et al. (2003) find negative effects of training participation. By and large, the results are mixed and it is rather unclear what lesson shall be learned from these studies on the programs' effectiveness.

Recent studies based on better administrative data seem to derive more consistent results. Hujer, Thomsen/Zeiss (2004) use data from the period 1999–2002 and Fitzenberger/Speckesser (2005) cover the period 1993–1997. The most comprehensive study is the one by Lechner et al. (2004) who use data covering the period of 1993 to 2002. Due to the richness of the data, various types of training programs can be distinguished. Fitzenberger/Speckesser (2005) concentrate on "provision of specific professional skills" which is a special type of further vocational training programs. Lechner et al.

(2004) distinguish short training (up to 6 months), long training (over 6 months), retraining, and training in practice firms.

All studies based on the new data find significant evidence of locking-in effects for virtually all types of training programs. That means that the labor market performance is worse for participants compared to non-participants during and shortly after participation. The central question is whether there are positive effects in the medium and long run that are big enough to be able to compensate these negative short run effects.

The answer seems to depend on the outcome variable. For unemployment duration, Hujer/Thomsen/Zeiss (2004) do not find significant long term effects of short and medium training programs but find negative effects of long programs, which means they increase unemployment duration (here, a partici-pating person is considered unemployed). This contrasts with the other studies, Fitzenberger/Speckesser (2005)/Lechner et al. (2005), who take the employment rate as an outcome measure and find positive effects in the long run for programs that provide specific professional skills (Fitzenberger, Speckesser 2005) as well as for short training and retraining programs (Lechner et al. 2005). Lechner et al. (2005) also use monthly earnings as an outcome variable and again find positive effects in the long run.

Training in West Germany

Early studies on training in West Germany include Pannenberg (1995), Hujer et al. (1998) and Hujer/Wellner (2000). These studies use models of unem-ployment duration and are based on GSOEP data covering the second half of the 1980s and the early 1990s. Again, the results are mixed: Pannenberg (1995) and Hujer et al. (1998) do not find significant positive effects, while Hujer/Wellner (2000) find positive effects, however, for short term programs only.

Studies based on the better merged administrative data are Klose/ Bender (2000), Lechner et al. (2004) and Fitzenberger/Speckesser (2005). Klose/Bender (2000) use a preliminary version of the data. Fitzenberger/Speckesser (2005) use the final data covering the period 1993–1997, while Lechner et al. (2004) base their study on data covering the larger period of 1993 to 2002.

Klose/Bender (2000) do not find any positive effects, which might be due to the preliminary character of their data. In contrast, Lechner et al. (2004) as well as Fitzenberger/Speckesser (2005) come to quite optimistic results. Fitzenberger/Speckesser (2005) find negative locking-in effects on the em-ployment rate in the short run and significantly positive effects in the long run for training programs providing specific professional skills.

The findings of Lechner et al. (2004) suggest that short and long training have positive effects on employment rates in the short run. In the long run, short training and retraining show positive results. Furthermore, they find sig-nificantly positive effects on monthly earnings for short and long training.

Job Creation Schemes

For a long time, job creation schemes could be evaluated only for East Germany because data sources that provide information on participation in job creation schemes were limited to East Germany only. These are the Labor Market Monitor East which is used by Hübler (1997), the Labor Market Monitor of the federal state Saxony-Anhalt, which is used by Bergemann et al. (2000), Eichler/Lechner (2002) and Bergemann (2005), and the Mikrozensus Saxony used by Reinowski et al. (2003).

None of the studies finds positive effects on the employment rate, apart from Eichler/Lechner (2002) who find positive employment effects, although for men only. Reinowski et al. (2003) use the hazard rate of transition from unemployment to employment as a dependent variable, where spells of unemployment include periods of participation. They do not find positive effects of program participation. Bergemann (2005) finds that participation significantly increases the reemployment probability, but for women only. Furthermore, she reports significantly positive effects on men's and women's probability to remain employed.

Caliendo et al. (2003, 2004, 2005a, 2005b) use the recently derived administrative data for the years 2000–2002, which provides information on program effects in West Germany for the first time. Their results are pessimistic, too, revealing negative mean employment effects. Positive employment effects are limited to few socio-demographic groups, namely women over 50, long-term unemployed and hard-to-place women in West Germany as well as female long-term unemployed in East Germany (Caliendo et al. 2005a). However, since the observation period is rather short, the negative effects might represent locking-in effects like the ones that have been found for training programs.

Wage subsidies

There are only two studies on the effects of wage subsidies. Jaenichen (2002) collects administrative data from selected FEA districts throughout Germany covering the period 1999–2001. She finds that receiving integration subsidies significantly reduces the probability to be registered as unemployed. Hujer/Caliendo/Radi (2004) examine whether employing subsidized workers affects the employment development of firms. They use the IAB establishment panel data covering 1995–1999. They cannot find any significant effects.

Job search assistance

Hujer et al. (2005) is the only study on the effects of job search assistance we are aware of. It is limited to the West German federal state Hessen and studies the effects of two new measures of job search assistance ("Stellenmarkt-offensive") in 2001–2002. Firstly, the regional employment agency publishes a magazine for employers containing employment wanted advertisements among other things. The study finds positive effects of this measure, especially for women. Secondly, the employment agencies offer courses on job search activities that advise on writing application letters, CVs, participating in job interview etc. No significant effects of this measure could be found.

Macroeconomic studies

Microeconomic studies focus on the impact of labor market programs on participants, neglecting the fact that non-participants might also be affected by labor market policy measures. This is likely the case in regions, like eastern Germany, where labor market programs are implemented on a very large scale. A considerable number of studies try to grasp such indirect effects in Germany, focusing on the macro-economic impact of Active Labor Market Policies. Most recent studies include Schmid et al. (2001), Fertig et al. (2002), Hagen (2003), Blien et al. (2003), Vollkommer (2004) and Hujer et al. (2005). All studies use administrative data from regional employment agencies. Most studies focus on some indicators of matching efficiency. Exceptions are Pannenberg/Schwarze (1996) who examine wage effects, as well as Blien et al. (2003) who use regional employment growth as dependent variable.

The study by Pannenberg/Schwarze (1996) indicates a small negative impact of training measures on monthly wages in East Germany. Blien et al. (2003) provide evidence for positive effects of training and job creation programs on employment growth in East Germany. There seems to be evidence of replacement effects by job creation schemes, as Hagen (2003) suggests. Further results regarding the effect on matching efficiency and unemployment rates are very mixed and rather inconclusive.

4.5 Summary

Results of evaluation studies of German Active Labor Market Policies have been rather inconsistent for many years. Probably this was due to unsatisfactory data quality as well as the use of different, perhaps occasionally inappropriate, identification strategies. However, due to better data, advances in methodology and a higher consensus on identification strategies, recent evaluation studies seem to be able to provide more robust and consistent results. It seems to be safe to draw the following preliminary conclusions:

- Most training measures seem to show a considerable dynamic in program effects, having negative (locking-in) effects in the short-run and positive ones in the longer run. Based on such results, future cost-benefit analyses might be able to trade costs of negative short-run effects against benefits of positive long-run effects.
- There is evidence for job creation schemes performing badly on average in the short run. Whether this is true in the long run too remains an open question for future research.
- Many evaluation studies seem to prove that all programs that have been evaluated so far work differently for specific socio-economic groups. While by and large, women seem to benefit more than men, general conclusions are still difficult to draw.
- The evidence on other types of ALMP programs is very rare (wage subsidies, job search assistance), or still nonexistent (programs for the youth or the disabled, start-up subsidies).

Policy makers should also bear in mind that macro- and microeconomic evaluation studies use very specific success indicators. These might be insufficient to learn about the entire societal impact of such measures. Especially in East Germany, programs might have played an important role in alleviating the social consequences of adjusting the bad labor market conditions, even if they were unable to strongly increase individual employment probability.

5   Active Labor Market Policies in Italy

5.1   General economic situation

In the late 1990s the Italian economy reports an extremely positive employment result, with a better performance than expected on the basis of GDP growth. Figures 14 and 15 show the GDP growth rate and total unemployment rate for the period 1990–2004 respectively.

It appears that in 1998–1999 the unemployment rate starts to decrease in spite of a relative stagnation in economic growth. If we compare the period 1996–2002 with a similar, previous one, we find that in 1985–1991 GDP rose by 2,7% and employment by 1%, whereas in 1996–2002 GDP rose by 1,7% only and employment by 1,2%.

The recovery in economic growth after the slowdown in 1996 certainly furthered employment to a considerable extent. However, at the same time, Italy experienced pervasive structural improvements of the labor market mechanisms. First of all, since the Agreements 1992–1993 providing for policies of wage moderation, the social dialogue kept on improving over the years. By redefining general rules governing working conditions, company-wide contracts and wage dynamics, the social concertation succeeded in attaining a proper balance between the flexibility requirements and the security guarantees for workers.

5.2   Labor market institutions

Important reforms have affected the labor market in recent years, e.g. part-time work, temporary work, new apprenticeship schemes, tax incentives, reduction of the indirect labor costs. These interventions are slowly changing the picture of the Italian labor market, which has always been characterized by employment rates well below the EU average, high unemployment rates, especially of women, low participation, low labor market mobility and limited part-time and temporary work.

The structure of the new employment in 2000 witnesses a definite increase in female employment, in full-time and permanent employment, and a pervasive diffusion of temporary work, achieving a percentage of temporary workers over total employees equal to 10.1 percent (9.5 in 1999). Temporary workers are mainly males, less than 30 years old, employed in the industry sector and highly geographically mobile (both in 1999 and in 2000 more than one third of the workers residing in the South of Italy was working in the

North). Besides its functioning to meet the flexibility requirements in the labor market over the business cycle, temporary work seems also to play an important role in the recruitment policies. In fact, more than one fifth of the workers contacted by a firm for short collaborations are then permanently enrolled by the firm.

The positive employment growth result might also be due to the surfacing of hidden labor, as is indirectly signaled by the slower dynamics of wages with respect to labor costs. This fact, together with the higher female employment, contributes to a relatively better performance of the South of Italy, where irregular work and female unemployment have always been high historically.

Over and beyond the overall positive result in employment growth, it is worthwhile to highlight the important qualitative changes occurred over the past ten years in the composition both of the demand and in the supply of labor. The demand side reports a significant shift towards high skilled jobs, as a result of the introduction of new technologies in the production processes. The period 1995–2000 shows a decrease in the number of manual employees and workers in traditional sectors, almost entirely in permanent and full-time contracts. At the same time, the period records an increase in professional workers, mainly in the service sector and in highly specialized occupations, all in permanent and full-time contracts. However, this relocation of the labor demand is not comparable to the one observed in other countries (particularly in the US) and it was not even sufficient to meet the qualitative improvement of the labor supply.

In the period 1995–2000 the average level of education of the Italian population aged 15 and above (measured in minimal number of years necessary to achieve each qualification) increased from 9.6 to 10.3 years. This stems both from the substitution of older and less educated cohorts with younger and more educated ones and from the steep increase of the education attainment of younger cohorts. However, although the percentage of population holding a high school degree raised from 30 to 48 percent, Italy still lags behind the EU average (66 percent), with only Spain and Portugal reporting values below Italy for the percentage of high school graduates (40 and 32 percent, respectively).

The higher education level of the workforce translated in enrolling more skilled workers in the existing jobs rather than promoting the flourishing of new professional occupations with higher skill requirements. As a result, Italy experienced a decrease in wage differentials across education levels. In 1995 the average (after taxes) wage of a college graduate was 152 percent higher than the one of a worker with basic education. In 1998, this percentage dropped to 145 percent. This decrease in the education wage premium indicates a widening of the portion of the labor market where the returns to human capital are quite low.

In spite of the implementation of policies aiming at reducing the labor cost, the cost of labor per product unit keeps on raising more than in the other EU states. This slowdown in competitiveness mainly depends on the low level of labor productivity in Italy. Between 1997 and 2000 the average yearly growth rate of the value added per worker in Italy is 0.9 percent, in comparison with 1.4 percent and 1.3 percent in Germany and France, respectively. The growth

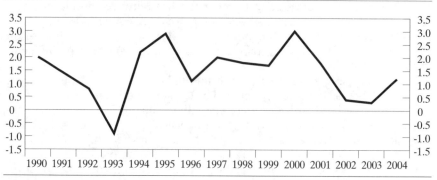

Figure 14. GDP growth rate at constant prices in Italy; 1990 to 2004; in %
Source: Eurostat.

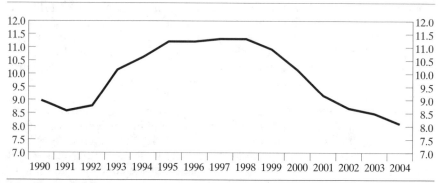

Figure 15. Total unemployment rate in Italy; 1990 to 2004; in %
Source: Eurostat, ILO unemployment definition

rate of the value added per standard employee decreased from 2.1 percent in
the period 1986–1995 to 1 percent in the period 1996-2000. This negative trend
in labor productivity seems to reflect the similar performance in total factor
productivity. The average yearly growth rate of total factor productivity
decreased from 1.2 percent in the period 1986–1990 to 0.1 percent in the
period 1996–1999.

To conclude, Italy has experienced a promising economic and employment
performance in the recent years. However, the employment rate of the
residing population between 15 and 64 years in 2000 (53.5%) remains well
below the EU average (60%) and far from the Lisbon targets (70%). The
extent of the regional differences in the Italian labor market remains substantial. For instance, in 2000 Italy realized an unemployment rate equal to
10.6 percent, the lowest level since 1994 (a year of substantial economic
growth). In the South, however, the unemployment rate remains very high, especially youth unemployment among the up-to-25-years old, being still
49.3 percent for males and 63.1 percent for females. One should note that the

unemployment rate is not an appropriate indicator of the available human resources in the South of Italy. Indeed, the requirements set in the Italian Labor Force Survey to define the group of unemployed are quite strict. In particular, the classification based on the frequency of the action actually taken in searching for jobs (e.g. a worker is unemployed if she/he has actively looked for a job in the last four weeks) is inappropriate in a context where family contacts and friends constitute the typical channel to find a job. In addition, the large use of family support, welfare benefits and irregular jobs pushes people to wait for jobs in the Public Sector, that are created with low frequency and characterized by a long time between the application for a job and its result. However, although these mechanisms and low participation rates might bias the indication obtained using the unemployment rate in the South, the magnitude of the North-South divide remains substantial.

5.3   Measures of Active Labor Market Policies

The flavor of the Italian culture in policy monitoring and evaluation is fundamental to understand both the huge delay in Italy in respect of Active Labor Market Policies (ALMP) implementation and evaluation and more generally the lack of an appropriate information system. Economic policies in Italy have always been used as instruments to please the public opinion and typically they have been designed and implemented on the basis of the "ideological principles" of the political party leading the country regardless of the real needs of the Italian economic structure. Consequently, policymakers have never been interested in monitoring and evaluating the effects of these policies. Obviously, this practice had limited relevance in a context where the leading party was changing very quickly and new policies were implemented on the basis of the new political ideas without taking into consideration what has been done by the previous government.

This general political attitude is also at the basis of the scarce importance given to the data collection process in Italy. Similarly, as borne out by the cross-country comparison of active spending (Figure 4 and Table 27 in the appendix), Italy is among the countries with relatively little ALMP expenditure, lying below the EU15 average in 2002.

However, this political culture is recently slowly changing. The essential motivation comes from the need of managing co-financed programs within the European Social Fund (ESF). In 1999, the European Commission and the Italian Ministry of Labor and Social Policies asked ISFOL's Evaluation Unit (hereafter IEU) to undertake the mid-term evaluation of the Objective 3 Community Support Fund within the new Structural Funds 2000–2006. The IEU has been created within the Italian Ministry of Labor and Social Policies in 1995 for the specific purpose of monitoring the previous ESF (1994–1999). Nevertheless, the actual evaluation research had initiated only in 2000. Indeed, this evaluation unit faces substantial difficulties.

First, consider the Italian institutional context. It is a complex and multi-actor institutional system, where a plurality of actors are involved in a specific policy. The State is no longer the single body defining the guidelines of a policy

Table 6. Labor market policies expenditure in Italy; in 1,000 €

	1996	1998	2000	2002	2004[a]
Training programs	600,383	1,407,023	594,773	611,950	1,380,042
Private sector incentive schemes	2,141,409	3,920,831	5,412,347	7,979,650	6,044,181
Public sector employment programs	426,783	671,020	712,649	481,194	184,586
Measures enhancing job search efficiency	0	0	1,346	173,458	202,317
Total active policies	3,168,575	5,998,874	6,721,115	9,246,252	7,811,126
Other measures	4,486,177	2,957,714	3,233,644	3,895,397	4,860,144
Total active and country-specific policies	7,654,752	8,956,588	9,954,759	13,141,649	12,671,270
Unemployment subsidies	6,668,857	6,334,088	6,058,631	6,765,504	7,439,864
Early retirement	2,910,689	1,886,569	1,254,155	1,244,203	1,341,218
Total passive policies	9,579,546	8,220,657	7,312,786	8,009,707	8,781,082
Total labor market policies	17,234,298	17,177,245	17,267,545	21,151,356	21,452,352

[a]Estimated values.

and the tools to use but also Regions, Provinces, Local Authorities, public and private executing agencies have a relevant role. This situation is complicated by the decentralization of the same policy into several levels (i.e., National, Regional, Local). In principle, the reorganization of the system that was implemented in the last decade was designed to enhance its efficacy and transparency, but in fact the roles of the different actors are not clearly defined and their coordination is based also on informal rules. These features of the Italian system render it quite difficult to get timely, good quality and clear information, and they leave the different bodies a large degree of discretion in the administration of the funds. In addition, the IEU faces a highly structured ESF program, proposing a large variety of types of interventions with detailed global and specific objectives and asking a detailed activity of monitoring of the different policies.

The main point is that Italy was not prepared to face this new scenario. The IEU was created within the Ministry of Labor and Social Policies by a simple reorganization of human resources that were not used to this practice. This may contribute to the delay in delivering information and/or in the scarce quality of the information being delivered. Furthermore the IEU is not an independent organization.

Nevertheless, huge steps forward have been made. Although the work of the IEU is far from a proper evaluation study, it is really important at least in the data collection stage. The figures taken from the mid-term report (2003) with respect of Labor Market Policies (LMP) are reported in Table 6.

Although the values for 2004 are still estimates, the table provides the expenditures on LMP broken down by measure for the years 1996–2004, in biannual steps. Following the common set-up adopted in the other country chapters, the policies are grouped into four (standard) types plus a fifth one (other measures) collecting country-specific programs. In Italy these measures are: a) tax-relief for workers residing in the South, b) measures supporting specific sectors (mainly agriculture), c) or specific contract schemes (in particular the ones allowing wages to be partly a function of the workers' produc-

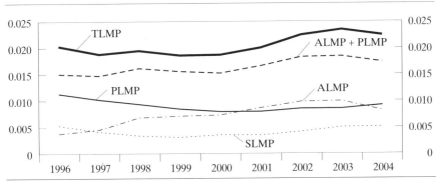

Figure 16. Labor market policy expenditure in Italy; 1996 to 2004; in % of GDP

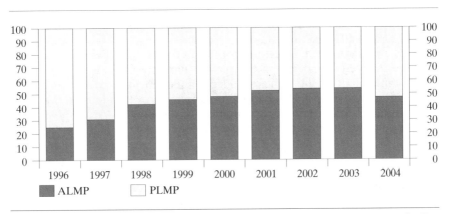

Figure 17. Active vs. passive labor market policies in Italy; 1996 to 2004; in %

tivity), d) measures to enhance higher education and professional training not targeted to specific labor market groups.

Figure 16 plots these figures as percentages of GDP. It appears evident that the year 2000 is a clear break point. In the period 1996–2000 the values for the total of labor market policies (TLMP) remain roughly unchanged. This aggregate evidence is mainly the result of a decrease in passive labor market policies (PLMP) compensated by a contemporaneous increase in Active Labor Market Policies (ALMP) over that period. The period 2000–2004, on the other hand, shows an important increase of the shares of total labor market policies in GDP, and this result is due to an increase both in active and in passive labor market policies expenditures. Also the values for the other policies, which are specific to the Italian economy (SLMP), increase over the last years.

Considering in more detail the relative importance of active and passive labor market policies, it appears that the relevance of passive policies with respect to active ones has decreased over time. Equalizing to a sum of 100%

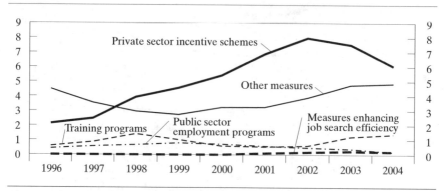

Figure 18. Expenditure on ALMPs in Italy by type; 1996 to 2004; in Mill. €

the expenditure in these two types of measures, Figure 17 shows that the active policies roughly doubled their share in the period 1996–2004 (from 25% in 1996 to almost 50% in 2004).

From a closer look at the figures for the years 2000–2004 emerges the fact that the change of tendency in total labor market policies is driven by the active component of the policies. Indeed, although passive policies expenditure rise because of the stagnation in economic growth, and new incentives to promote education and the development of specific skills are implemented over the period, the leading factor is the steep increase in active policies expenditures, starting from 2001.

Figure 18 plots the expenditures in the different types of active policies for the period 1996–2004. The apparent peak in the line for private sector incentive schemes in 2001–2003 is responsible for the steep increase in active labor market expenditures. In particular, it is due to the effects of a particular law (law 388/2000), which had a pervasive impact. This law had quite loose eligibility requirements and it was possible to cumulate the corresponding incentives with others. The design of this law has been subsequently revised, as it appears from the decrease in active policies expenditures from 2003 to 2004 already.

Private sector incentive schemes, which include mixed type contracts and other measures to promote employment growth and stability, are the most important types of ALMP in Italy, and with an increasing level of expenditures in the period 1996–2002. Observe that Figure 18 shows that the second group of measures by level of expenditures is the one collecting the policies deriving from the peculiarities of the Italian economy, whose importance seems also to be increasing in the last years.

5.4   Evaluation studies

What are the effects of these policies? As it has already been said, the period 1996–2002 corresponds to a considerable positive cycle of increase in employment in spite of a relative stagnation in economic growth. This positive cycle is certainly due to the introduction of new, more flexible forms of contracts (i.e. the so-called atypical contracts), to an increase of the employment of women and in the service sector, and to a period of wage moderation. But how much can be attributed to the implementation of LMP? Is there a substitution effect, selection effects in the eligibility criteria, are they really effective?[4] These questions are still unresolved.

The existing empirical literature on ALMP evaluation in Italy is in fact quite scarce, preliminary and fragmented. The main problem, once again, is the lack of data on program participants and on control groups. In what follows, we briefly review the main existing studies.

The available relevant studies using micro-economic data merge different administrative data sets that are available for particular regions, and thus are case-studies rather than studies with a general validity. For instance, Paggiaro et al. (2005) evaluate the Italian Mobility List, which is a policy that combines an active component, i.e. a wage subsidy to employers who hire a worker from the List, with a passive component, i.e. an income support to selected workers in the List. The aim is to investigate the effects of the Italian Mobility list on the probability of transition to a new job, dividing between workers eligible for the active component only and workers having also an income support. The analysis is made possible by the availability of detailed administrative data collected in a particular Italian region (NUTS2 area) for different purposes, which is the Veneto region, and in addition they focus their attention on two provinces (NUTS3 areas) only: Treviso and Vicenza. The time period under analysis is 1995–1999. The methodology used is propensity score matching. They find that an additional year of eligibility has a significant and positive impact on employment rates for men eligible for the active component only, whereas the effect is significant but negative for those having income support also. It is irrelevant for females.

Another existing study by Caroleo/Pastore (2001) evaluates the effects of different ALMP targeted to the youth long term unemployed. The aim is to investigate the effects of the different policies on the probability of transition to a different labor market status (unemployed, formal, informal sector, apprenticeship contract, etc.). Also in this case, the information comes from particular data, that is an ad hoc-survey within the EU Targeted-Socio-Economic-Research Program on Youth and Social Exclusion. The information is related to two regions only (Veneto, Campania). A multinomial logit model is estimated and the results show that the policy variables are never significant. Other variables seem to play the major role.

Because of this data limitation on the micro level, resorting to aggregate data might be a valuable alternative. However, to the best of our knowledge, only one paper by Altavilla/Caroleo (2004) exploits this approach. The

---

[4] The number of workers involved in each program are not reported here. Indeed, the absolute levels have a poor information content and we face data limitation problems when estimating the degree of coverage of the different policies. In fact, the only data source for the overall universe is the Italian Labor Force Survey which has very small sample sizes when selected groups are considered. As a result, quite often the coverage of one policy comes out bigger than 100%.

policies evaluated in this study are mixed-cause contracts and other employment growth and employment stability incentives. The purpose is to investigate whether ALMP effects on unemployment and employment dynamics are different across Italian regions. The analysis uses regional-level data, separated between North and South Italy for the period 1996–2002. Two methodologies are adopted: GMM panel estimation and panel vector autoregression models estimation. The study shows two main results: 1) the effects of the different ALMPs are different in the North and in the South, both on the unemployment and employment rate; 2) unemployment dynamics is differently explained in the two areas, but it is not driven by ALMP shocks.

There are also other studies on the evaluation of particular start up incentives using mainly firm level data (e.g., Battistin et al. 2002), but once again they are quite limited in number and focus on particular case-studies, having consequently a limited information content.

5.5   Summary

The message that emerges from this analysis is that while monitoring of labor market policies seems now established in Italy, little evaluation has been carried out so far. Advances in this direction are crucial to understand how the different policies relate to the marked peculiarity of the Italian labor market. In principle, an effective active labor policy implementation needs to consider the country-specific economic situation. In the Center and North of Italy, active labor policies take priority in an improvement in the rate of employment of youths, women and older workers. On the other hand, the South needs to support active policies with measures aiming at increasing the demand for labor, decreasing the labor cost as well as tackling long term unemployment and encouraging the surfacing of hidden labor and hidden enterprises. The data on LMP expenditures, showing an increase in measures deriving from the peculiarities of the Italian labor market (Figure 17), seem to indicate an effort of policy makers along these lines. However, in practice, little is known about the actual effects of these policies.

6   Active Labor Market Policies in Denmark

6.1   General economic situation

During the last decade, the Danish economy has been characterized by a long upturn actually starting in 1994 and lasting until the slowdown in the global economy in 2001. Unemployment in Denmark (Figure 19)[5] has been steadily

---

[5]   The figures on unemployment used here and in the following subsections are mostly based on national statistics from Statistics Denmark. This is the most widely used source in Denmark for research, public debate, etc. In general, these national statistics differ from standardized unemployment rates used for international comparisons (as e.g. by Eurostat). The difference is due partly to differences in concepts and definitions and partly to measurement problems. In general, the unemployment ra-

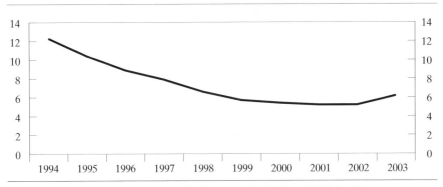

Figure 19. Unemployment rate in Denmark; 1994 to 2003; in %
Source: Statistics Denmark.

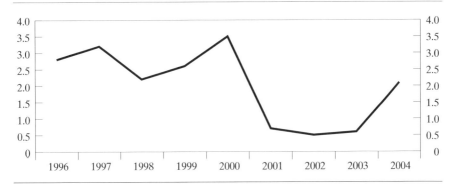

Figure 20. Real GDP growth in Denmark; 1996 to 2004; in %
Source: Eurostat.

declining from 1994 until 2002 followed by a slight increase in the most recent years, but has in 2005 started to decrease again and the unemployment rate is currently around 6 percent.

The Danish economy had a fairly strong GDP growth during the second half of the 1990s (Figure 20), but Denmark experienced an economic slow-down in 2001–2003 with GDP growing at less than 1 percent per year. This experience was in line with a low international GDP growth, but GDP growth has picked up again in 2004 and is now above 2 percent annually.

---

tes show the same development and display the same cyclical pattern, but the standardized unemployment rate is below that of the nationally defined unemployment rate, typically by about 1–2 percentage points.

6.2   Labor market institutions

Two parallel systems

In Denmark there are two parallel administrative systems for individuals ex-
periencing unemployment: one system providing active labor market policy
(related to unemployment insurance) and another system providing active
social policy (related to welfare)[6]. The distinction between the two systems is
related to the unemployment insurance system. In Denmark, membership of
an unemployment insurance fund is voluntary, and only members will receive
UI benefits if they become unemployed[7]. The active labor market policy is
designed for unemployed *insured* workers. On the other hand, non-insured
workers who become unemployed can obtain social assistance benefits, and
part of the active social policy is designed for unemployed *non-insured*
workers. In addition, the social system also covers non-workers, sick and
disabled people, and persons with other social problems. The active social
policy distinguishes between these two groups: those who have unemployment as their only problem, and those who have other social problems in
addition to unemployment. Basically, the former are unemployed workers
who receive means-tested unemployment benefits, while the latter are the
more traditional welfare recipients.

As it should be clear from this brief description, some very similar persons
(*non-insured* unemployed workers with no problems besides unemployment,
and *insured* unemployed workers) are treated quite differently in two
different systems. The systems also differ markedly with respect to benefits
and organization. The UI benefits of the labor market system are not
means-tested (apart from own labor earnings) and they are of limited duration
(up to four years), whereas the welfare benefits (social assistance) are
means-tested and they are of unlimited duration. The labor market system is
quite centralized, whereas the social system is decentralized and run by the
municipalities.

ALMP

Denmark currently has a very comprehensive, large-scale ALMP system that
originates from initiatives taken in the late 1970s. The labor market system is
responsible for the activities related to unemployed individuals insured
against unemployment and eligible for UI benefits. The public employment
service organizes various activities (e.g. job provision and ALMPs) with the
intention of alleviating the unemployment problem of the UI benefit recip-

---

[6]   This is in contrast to a number of other European countries where labor market and
social policy are organized in the same system. In Denmark, the labor market system is the responsibility of the Ministry of Employment and the social system is the
responsibility of the Ministry of Social Affairs. However, the two systems are currently being redesigned and will eventually be merged into a common system.

[7]   Around 80 per cent of the labor force is member of an unemployment insurance
fund.

ients. In the social system, the municipalities are responsible for the organization and administration of the different measures available to assist the welfare benefit recipients in becoming self-supporting. The measures that can be used to remedy the unemployment problem of UI benefit recipients and welfare benefit recipients are very similar. Since 2003, the two parallel systems have used the same types of programs, and from 2007, the two systems will be made even closer to each other, e.g. with common "jobcentres" that will be responsible for providing ALMPs to unemployed individuals regardless of their benefit status and which system they belong to.

The main guiding principle behind the active labor market and social policies can be described as a "right-and-duty" principle[8], which means that in order to receive benefits unemployed persons have to undertake an activity. The basic principle is thus that the unemployed person has a *right* to assistance in the form of an ALMP offer, but at the same time a *duty* to participate in the ALMPs and other activities when offered to retain eligibility to UI benefits or welfare benefits. Basically, the "right-and-duty" principle means that participation in ALMP is compulsory after a certain period of unemployment.

Rules for assignment

The time at which unemployed persons have to participate in ALMPs differs between the two systems and between persons at different ages. Furthermore, there have been several changes in the rules over the last decade, following a major reform of the ALMP system in 1994.

In the UI system, benefit recipients below 30 years have to receive an ALMP offer after 6 months of unemployment, whereas benefit recipients above 30 years have to receive an ALMP offer after 12 months of unemployment. The 12-months-limit has been in effect since 2000, and it is a result of a gradual decreasing of the time limit from 48 months in 1994 down to 36 months and later on to 24 months. This gradual shortening of the period until compulsory program participation has been employed in some of the evaluation studies to identify possible motivation effects (see later in this chapter). After the first 12 months on UI benefits (the "passive" period), unemployed individuals have to participate in an ALMP in return for benefits. Individuals can participate in ALMP up to three years, and until 2003 the unemployed should spend at least 75 percent of the three years in some kind of program. Individuals who refuse to participate initially lose their benefits for a limited period and eventually lose their eligibility for benefits altogether. It should be noted that program participation does not restore benefit eligibility (that possibility was abandoned in 1994). The ALMP offers are given by the public employment service and the decision to offer a specific program to an unemployed is made by a caseworker at the public employment service. There are, however, meetings between the unemployed and the caseworker, where a plan to get the person back to work is worked out.

---

[8] This is also sometimes referred to as a "mutual obligation" principle or as workfare.

The municipalities have had the possibility to assign welfare benefit recipients to ALMPs since 1977. Before 1994, when a new legislation was implemented, the ALMPs were primarily used to alleviate the unemployment problem of young welfare benefit recipients. But today, all welfare benefit recipients have to participate in an ALMP if they do not become self-supporting after a certain period.

At present, welfare benefit recipients below 30 years of age have to receive an ALMP offer not later than 3 months after the first day on welfare. If they do not succeed in becoming independent of welfare benefits after the end of an ALMP, they have to receive a new ALMP offer 3 months after the end of the previous program period at the latest. Hence, welfare benefit recipients below age 30 are subject to a more or less continuous treatment in programs while on welfare. Welfare benefit recipients above 30 years of age should participate in an ALMP after 12 months at the latest. They only have a right to receive one ALMP offer during a welfare spell. But most municipalities choose to give a new ALMP offer if the first program was not successful in bringing the welfare benefit recipients from welfare to a situation where they are self-supporting.[9] In addition, it should be noted that the time limits are minimum requirements and that many municipalities have chosen to give program offers at a much earlier stage.

The decision to assign a welfare benefit recipient into a given program is made by caseworkers in the municipality. For all welfare benefit recipients the type of the ALMP offer should depend on the background and desires of the individual welfare benefit recipient. If possible, the welfare benefit recipients should receive a selection of programs to choose from. However, apart from the desires and needs of the welfare benefit recipients, the caseworkers have to take into account the availability of different program types, the cost of the programs and the current state of the regional labor market.

The main purposes of the ALMPs are to improve the labor market prospects of the welfare benefit recipients by upgrading their skills and to increase the intensity of job search by testing job-readiness and reducing "leisure time". However, for welfare benefit recipients with problems in addition to unemployment (e.g. problems related to health, childcare or lack of self-confidence) participation in a program should primarily improve everyday life (e.g. through support for the handling of everyday activities, for the creation of a basic network, and for building of self-esteem). The hope is that the improvement in everyday life in the long run will bring this group of welfare benefit recipients closer to the labor market and towards a situation in which they are self-supporting. Ideally, the program chosen for each individual should be the program that meets these purposes in the best way.

---

[9] Before mid-1998, the current rules regarding the ALMPs for welfare benefit recipients below 30 years of age only applied to welfare benefit recipients below age 25. The rules regarding the ALMPs for welfare benefit recipients above 30 years that are effective today applied to welfare benefit recipient above 25 years. Another difference compared to the present rules is that the municipalities were not obliged to give ALMP-offers to welfare benefit recipients below 25 years of age with problems in addition to unemployment. However, a large part of the municipalities chose to offer ALMPs to this group as well, even if they were not required to do so.

Types of programs

There is a broad range of different types of programs that the caseworkers can choose from when assigning unemployed persons to active labor market measures. The programs can be categorized in four main categories:

- private sector employment programs
- public sector employment programs
- classroom training
- other programs.

The program category "private sector employment programs" consists of programs in which the participants work in a private firm. During the program period the participants receive a wage subsidy (the subsidy is actually paid to the private sector employer). The subsidy corresponds to approximately 50 percent of the minimum wage. The participants are employed on a time-limited contract typically lasting 6–9 months.

In public sector employment programs the participants either work in a public institution or in a special employment project created by the municipalities. The participants in these programs often carry out work that would otherwise not be done. This can be e.g. snow clearing for senior citizens, nature preservation and assistance of the permanent staff in municipal institutions (schools, youth hostels, theatres, sports centers, museums etc.). The jobs are temporary, typically lasting 6–12 months.

Participants in classroom training attend classes to upgrade their qualifications in different fields. This category consists of all types of classroom training including vocational training, language courses, computer courses, and in some cases even ordinary education. It typically lasts only a few months, but in some cases it may last much longer.

The residual category of programs termed "other programs" consists of programs that cannot be placed in the three other program categories. These include job-search assistance, counseling programs, self-employment grant programs (now abandoned), etc. Depending on the definition of ALMP, this category could also include rehabilitation programs. These programs are available for individuals whose working capacity is reduced (because of e.g. physical or psychological problems) to such degree that there is a very limited chance that standard ALMPs will help bring the individuals from public assistance to employment.

A more detailed description of the programs can be found in Danish Ministry of Labor (2002) and Graversen (2004).

6.3 Measures of Active Labor Market Policy

In addition to people being unemployed, there is a considerable number of persons who are participating in ALMPs in Denmark (Figure 21). Throughout the last decade, around 3.5 percent of the labor force (measured in full-time equivalents) has been participating in some kind of ALMP. More than half of the participants are welfare benefit recipients. When unemployed persons and

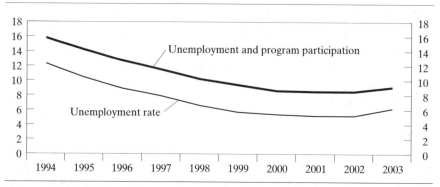

Figure 21. Unemployment and program participation in Denmark; 1994 to
2003; in %
Source: Statistics Denmark.

program participants are added together, the total rate has declined from 16
percent in 1994 to 9 percent in the early 2000s.

The declining level of unemployment in combination with the almost
constant level of program participation has resulted in an increasing relative
use of ALMP. Figure 22 shows the fraction of unemployed persons (i.e. unemployed plus program participants) participating in ALMPs during the period
1994–2003. It can be seen that the importance of ALMP participation has
increased from around 20 percent in 1994 to almost 40 percent in 1999–2002,
with a slight decrease thereafter. Since participation in ALMP is compulsory
after a certain period of unemployment, this development primarily reflects
the gradual decreasing of the time limit during the late 1990s (described in
detail in the previous subsection).

The extensive use of ALMP in Denmark is also reflected in the percentage
of GDP spent on ALMP (Figure 23). In 1997–2000 it has been between 1.6 and
1.8 percent of GDP, making Denmark one of the countries with the highest
spending on ALMPs as a proportion of GDP. All figures in this subsection
show that ALMP is a very important part of both the Danish labor market and
the Danish economy. The Danish system of ALMP extends to all unemployed
persons.

Based on the most recent published data, it is possible to calculate a distribution of participants (measured in full-time equivalents) on types of
programs in 2002:

* Training programs   44%
* Wage subsidy programs   36%
* Direct job creation schemes   14%
* Job search assistance   7%
* Youth programs   –
* Measures for disabled   –

It should, however, be noted that it is quite difficult to distinguish between the
two categories "wage subsidy programs" and "direct job creation schemes",

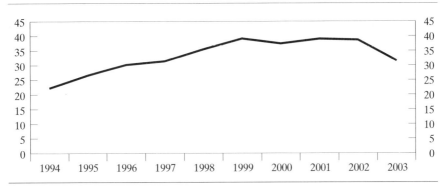

Figure 22. Fraction of unemployed persons participating in ALMPs in Denmark; 1994 to 2003; in %
Source: Statistics Denmark.

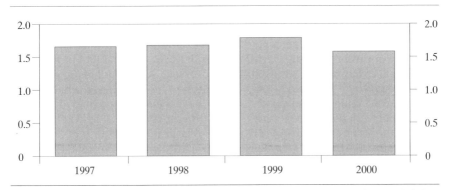

Figure 23. Expenditures for ALMP in Denmark; 1994 to 2000; in % of GDP
Source: OECD.

since e.g. some public sector employment programs may entail a wage subsidy from one public authority to another. Therefore, the distribution on these two categories is probably more equal than the figures given above. It should also be noted that the published statistics do not allow a split according to age, which is the reason that no youth programs are reported above. As mentioned earlier, the rules for assignment differ for persons below and above 30 years of age.

6.4 Evaluation studies

The extensive system of ALMP in Denmark has resulted in a number of evaluation studies that have estimated the effects of various program types for different groups of participants. In particular, the introduction of several years of compulsory participation in ALMP in Denmark inspired several Danish economists to analyze the incentive or threat effects of this policy. These studies typically analyze the UI system and the compulsory participation after 1994. Individuals could in 1994 receive UI benefits for up to four years without participating in ALMP, but the period on "passive" UI benefits was shortened during the 1990s.

A special challenge in evaluating the effects of the Danish ALMPs results from the fact that all benefit recipients have to participate in an ALMP, if they do not find employment before a certain time limit. Hence, it is not possible to create a "standard" control group for the purpose of estimating the effect of the programs. Several studies have circumvented this problem by using the variation in the timing of the programs to estimate the program effects. In this subsection, the most recent evaluation studies are discussed and their findings are summarized. Only evaluation studies done by independent researchers are included in the survey, i.e. studies by government agencies and consultancy firms are excluded. Furthermore, only quantitative/econometric studies of the employment effects are included.

Since most of the studies evaluate the universal system of ALMP in Denmark rather than single program types, this subsection first summarizes each study and its results very briefly. At the end of this subsection, the results are summarized by program type. A number of evaluation studies analyze the incentive or threat effects of ALMP (Kyhl (2001); Geerdsen (2003); Geerdsen, Holm (2004); Rosholm, Svarer (2004); Graversen (2004)) and in those studies the "threatening" program could be of any type, depending on what type of program the unemployed person would have been assigned to. The large majority of evaluation studies analyze the program effects of the whole system with all the different measures (Rosholm, Svarer (2004); Bolvig et al. (2003); Graversen (2004); Graversen, Jensen (2004); Munch, Skipper (2004); Danish Economic Council (2002); Jespersen et al. (2004)). Finally, the study by Jensen et al. (2003) analyzes the effects of a training program targeted at unemployed youth.

Kyhl (2001)

This study focuses on the incentive effect of ALMPs, i.e. the employment effect resulting from the threat of having to participate in an ALMP. The study analyzes individuals in Denmark between 25 and 60 years of age who received UI benefits in the period 1995-1998. The study is based on a 10 percent sample of the Danish population and data were drawn from administrative registers collected by the insurance funds and municipalities and handled by the Ministry of Employment. Kyhl models the transitions out of the UI system by a piecewise constant hazard model. The incentive effect of compulsory ALMP participation is not directly identified in the study. Kyhl finds increases of 20 to 70 percent in the hazard out of unemployment, when he compared hazard rates in 1996 and 1998. The increase in the hazard rate after 52 weeks of unemployment is supposed to be the result of the threat of active labor market programs. Correcting the estimates for unobserved heterogeneity reinforces the results.

Geerdsen (2003)

This study also focuses on the incentive effects of the Danish UI system in the period 1994-1998. Only individuals born between 1947 and 1969 are included. The study is based on a 10 percent sample of the Danish population. The data were collected by Statistics Denmark from various administrative bodies. Individuals' hazard rate of leaving the UI system is modeled using a discrete logistic model where the incentive effect is modeled by indicators of individuals' remaining time until compulsory program participation. The incentive effect is identified through a legislative cut in the benefit period until compulsory program participation. Geerdsen finds a significant threat effect that increased the hazard rate by up to 100 percent. The start of the program participation is set to be equivalent to the end of the period on passive UI. The threat effect is estimated using indicators for the remaining time on passive unemployment insurance benefits and without taking account of unobserved heterogeneity.

Geerdsen/Holm (2004)

This study is an extension of Geerdsen (2003). Instead of modeling individuals' time until compulsory program participation, this study models individuals' probability of participating in a program. The reason is that various aspects might reduce individuals' risk of entering a labor market program even though the law states that participation was a prerequisite for receiving benefits. If individuals knew this, they could have adjusted their labor market behavior accordingly. The empirical model as well as identification assumption resemble that of Geerdsen (2003). Geerdsen/Holm (2004) find a threat effect of more than a 100 percent increase in the hazard rate out of unemployment, which is similar to the result found by Geerdsen (2003). They use estimations of the risk of being enrolled in active labor market programs to ensure that the timing of the incentive effect was correct. They take account of unobserved heterogeneity by using a random effects model, and the results show that some of the long-term unemployed had very small probabilities of entering ALMP even though they were entitled to them.

Rosholm/Svarer (2004)

This study focuses on program effects as well as incentive effects of the Danish UI system for the period 1998–2002. The data set is a sample collected by the Danish National Labor Market Authority. Similar to Geerdsen/Holm (2004), this study models the incentive effect through individuals' risk of participating in a program. The study is based on data collected from various administrative registers. Individuals' hazard rate of leaving UI unemployment is modeled using a mixed proportional hazard model. Identification of the incentive effect is obtained through functional form assumptions on the hazard rate.

Rosholm and Svarer find a strong and significant threat effect for men prior to the start of the active labor market programs. The effect is only significant up to one year of unemployment and the magnitude is highest from the 10th to the 12th month. The average threat effect is estimated to reduce unemployment duration by nearly 3 weeks. Regarding the program effects (i.e. the "pure" effect of program participation), they find that only private sector employment programs reduce unemployment duration and that this effect is not statistically significant. Training and public sector employment programs are actually found to increase unemployment duration, primarily due to large locking-in effects. The total effect of the presence of ALMPs is to shorten unemployment duration even though actual participation in a program did not, but the threat effect is found to be large enough to make the total reduction nearly 3 weeks.

Jensen/Rosholm/Svarer (2003)

This study analyzes a Danish youth program for UI recipients under the age of 25 years initiated in 1996. According to the program, individuals without any formal education beyond secondary school who had been unemployed for 6 months within the last 9 months had to participate in a labor market program in return for benefits. Furthermore, individuals participating in a program experienced a significant cut in the level of their benefits. The ALMP had a duration of 18 months and contained various types of education. Individuals lost their right to UI benefits altogether if they refused to participate. The study is based on survey data collected from approx. 3500 individuals. Individuals are interviewed repeatedly in the period April 1996 to December 1996. The Youth Unemployment Program was gradually implemented during 1996 due to capacity constraints. Individuals, who were eligible for ALMP participation, were randomly assigned to ALMP participation during the year. However, the authors suspect that individuals were not actually selected randomly into treatment and therefore they model the selection process. Identification is based on a set of exclusion restrictions, where the excluded variables are indicators for whether the individual lives with his/her parents, an indicator for whether the individual is a homeowner, and a set of county indicators.

The authors use a competing risks duration model. They do not find a significant incentive effect of the special Youth Unemployment Program in Denmark for the treatment group. The authors suggest that the control group was not fully aware of the fact that they had not been selected for the educational program. This could have weakened the result. The increase in the baseline hazard rate for the treatment group is 150 percent, while the increase in the baseline hazard rate for the control group is 50 percent (and in both cases the hazard rate dropped again the month after to the previous levels), so the hazard rates increased for both groups, but the difference was insignificant. Participation in the program itself had an effect by significantly raising the transition rate from unemployment to schooling. A somewhat weaker effect is found on the transition rate from unemployment to employment.

Bolvig/Jensen/Rosholm (2003)

This study investigates the program effects of ALMPs for welfare benefit recipients in the period 1997–1999. The timing-of-events method is applied to estimate the effects of various types of programs. The overall effects of ALMPs are evaluated by the calculation of net effects on the expected duration of welfare spells. The results show that employment programs improve the chances of leaving welfare dependence, whereas training and other programs prolong welfare spells by decreasing the exit rate from welfare spells after participation in the programs. The optimal timing of ALMPs is also investigated and the results show that there is a case for assigning individuals to early participation in employment programs, as the net effect is larger the earlier participation begins. For all types of programs locking-in effects are found, but with the strongest effects for training programs. The study also finds differences between the effects for men and women, primarily showing that locking-in effects are stronger for women than for men.

Graversen (2004)

This study focuses on unemployed males above 25 years of age receiving social assistance (welfare benefits) in the period 1994–1998. The municipalities had an obligation to offer those who received welfare benefits participation in ALMP no later than six months after the start of the unemployment spell, but most municipalities aimed to make an offer sooner than that. The study is based on a 10 percent register sample from Statistics Denmark. Survey information is used to describe the municipalities' timing of ALMP. The incentive effect is identified by applying the differences in practice among the municipalities. The effect is modeled using a mixed proportional hazard specification.

   Graversen finds that the ALMP had an incentive effect on the hazard rate out of unemployment, but the importance of the effect was modest. The effect is estimated as the reduction of the hazard rate out of welfare benefits due to the differences in timing of implementing the ALMP to the welfare benefit recipients. The differences between the groups are largest for the first three to six months, but some of the coefficients are not significant at a five percent level. The results on the program effects show that participation in a training program or a public sector employment program would prolong the welfare spell due to a large locking-in effect and a modest treatment effect. However, participation in a private sector employment program would decrease the duration of welfare spells because of a modest locking-in effect and a large treatment effect.

Graversen/Jensen (2004)

This study also evaluates the employment effects of Danish ALMPs aimed at welfare benefit recipients. However, in this study the effect of the private sector employment programs is estimated relative to the effect of other program types. The advantage of this approach is that only participants have to be included in the empirical analyses. The disadvantage is of course that the effect of program participation relative to the effect of non-participation cannot be identified. However, given the fact that the welfare benefit recipients *had to* participate in ALMPs, the study provides essential information on which programs fulfill the purposes of the programs in the best way. The authors do not find any significant mean effects of participation in private sector employment programs compared to participation in other programs, but evidence of heterogeneity in treatment effects is found.

Munch/Skipper (2004)

This study focuses on the program effects of Danish ALMPs for UI benefit recipients. The data set used is a 10 percent random sample of entrants into unemployment in the years 1995 to 2000, but the study restricts attention to UI fund members between 19 and 66 years of age. The timing-of-events method is applied to estimate the effects of various types of programs on the unemployment duration, accounting for selection into programs based on observed and unobserved characteristics. They find that most types of programs have negative net effects on the transition rate from unemployment to employment, which is often attributed to negative locking-in effects, but sometimes also negative post-program effects. One exception are private sector employment programs, which tend to have a small positive net effect.

Danish Economic Council (2002); Jespersen, Munch, Skipper (2004)

All the evaluation studies discussed above investigate the effects of the ALMP on the job prospects of the unemployed. However, a comprehensive evaluation of the policy must take costs as well as benefits into account. Only very few studies exist that attempt to perform a cost-benefit analysis of ALMP in Denmark. Two such studies are by the Danish Economic Council (2002) and Jespersen, Munch and Skipper (2004). The latter study is actually an extension of the former. Unfortunately, the two studies do not find similar results, which basically serve to illustrate that the results are sensitive to methods. The common results are that private sector employment programs give rise to a net economic surplus, whereas training programs and public sector employment programs sometimes give rise to a surplus and sometimes to a deficit.

All the above mentioned studies can be summarized by program type as follows:

Training programs

This is the most commonly used type of program in Denmark. However, the findings of the evaluation studies about the employment effects of training programs are rather disappointing. Most evaluation studies find that training programs have negative effects by increasing unemployment duration, primarily due to large negative locking-in effects, but sometimes also due to negative post-program effects. This is the general picture found by five out of six studies (Rosholm, Svarer 2004; Bolvig et al. 2003; Graversen 2004; Munch, Skipper 2004; Danish Economic Council 2002), whereas only one study (Jespersen et al. 2004) finds some evidence that training programs give rise to a net economic surplus for some cohorts in the case in which long-term effects are analyzed. A training program targeted at unemployed youths is found to have positive effects (Jensen et al. 2003).

Private sector incentive programs

This type of program is clearly the most successful measure used in the Danish ALMP. A common result of all evaluation studies is that participation in a private sector employment program has positive effects (Rosholm, Svarer 2004; Bolvig et al. 2003; Graversen 2004; Munch, Skipper 2004; Danish Economic Council 2002; Jespersen et al. 2004), although one study does not find a statistically significant effect (Rosholm, Svarer 2004) and another study only finds a small positive net effect (Munch, Skipper 2004). One exception to the general picture is the study by Graversen/Jensen (2004). This study finds that there are no significant mean effects of participation in private sector employment programs compared to participation in other programs. However, the study finds evidence of heterogeneity in the employment effects, pointing to the need for improvements in the assignment or profiling process.

Public sector employment programs

This type of program has negative effects similar to those of training programs, i.e. participation in a public sector employment program tends to increase unemployment durations. Again, this result is primarily due to strong locking-in effects. Four out of six studies (Rosholm, Svarer 2004; Graversen 2004; Munch, Skipper 2004; Danish Economic Council 2002) find these negative effects, whereas one study (Jespersen et al. 2004) finds that public sector employment programs sometimes give rise to a net economic surplus and another study (Bolvig et al. 2003) finds positive effects, but is analyzing private and public sector employment programs together, i.e. as one type of program. Hence, the results of the latter study are not pointing directly at public sector employment programs as having positive effects.

Services and Sanctions

The studies that evaluate the universal Danish system also look at a residual category denoted "other programs", which includes job search assistance, counseling programs, etc. as well as various other programs. This residual category is very heterogeneous. In general, these evaluation studies find that participation in other programs has no effect or a negative effect. Finally, a number of evaluation studies find strong incentive or threat effects of ALMP (Kyhl 2001; Geerdsen 2003; Geerdsen, Holm 2004; Rosholm, Svarer 2004; Graversen 2004). These studies do not analyze the threat of separate program types, but of the prospect of participating in a program of any type.

6.5 Summary

Denmark has a very comprehensive, large-scale ALMP system with compulsory participation in ALMP after a certain period of unemployment. This
universal system extends to all unemployed persons and it has a broad range
of different types of programs that the caseworkers can choose from when
assigning unemployed persons to active labor market measures. ALMP is a
very important part of both the Danish labor market and the Danish economy.

In summary, the general findings that can be extracted from the recent evaluation studies are that there is strong evidence of threat effects of ALMPs in
Denmark, but more mixed results on program effects. In general, private
sector employment programs appear to have positive effects, whereas training
programs and public sector employment programs mainly have no effects, but
both positive and negative effects are found in various studies. Cost-benefit
analyses of ALMPs are very sparse in Denmark, and unfortunately the results
seem to be very sensitive to methods and the evaluated time period. Hence, no
firm evidence exists on whether ALMPs give rise to a net economic surplus or
deficit in Denmark.

7 Active Labor Market Policies in Estonia

7.1 General economic situation

Economic transition in the beginning of 1990s has led to profound changes in
the Estonian labor market. Labor force participation and employment rates
have declined remarkably and are currently well below the average of EU
countries. The average unemployment rate has risen from virtually zero in
1991 to 14% in 2000 as a result of the so called Russian crisis. Thereafter the
unemployment has been falling and was around 10% in 2004.

Recent developments in the economy and the labor market have been predominantly positive. After the initial downturn in the beginning of the 1990s
Estonia has experienced a solid GDP growth. The average GDP growth rate
during the last five years has been around 5% (Figure 24). In 1999, the
economy was hit by the Russian crisis, which was followed by a slowdown of
economic growth. From 2000 onwards the economy has been growing again,
exceeding the average growth rate of the Euro zone. However, Estonian GDP
per capita is still substantially lower than the EU average, reaching only 46%
of the average of the old EU members in PPS in 2004 (Statistical Office of
Estonia 2005).

Since 2000, the employment rates have increased and the unemployment
decreased. However, the increase in the employment rates has been modest.
Compared to 2000 the employment rate grew only by 1.5 percentage points in
2004 and reached the level of 62.6%. This is lower than the average of the old
EU members and well below the Lisbon employment target of 70% for 2010.
The reduction of unemployment has mainly happened at the cost of an
increase in the number of inactive people. Compared to 1990 the number of
inactive people in Estonia has increased by 73,500.

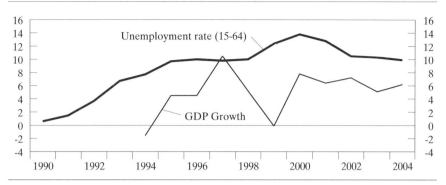

Figure 24. GDP growth and unemployment rate in Estonia; 1990 to 2004; in %
Source: Statistical Office of Estonia. Age group 1990 to 1992: 15–69.

The evaluation of a training program described below covers the period 2000–2002. During that period the business cycle was in an upturn and overall unemployment decreased. Some evaluation literature suggests that during the cyclical upturn the efficiency of active labor market policy is increased, which means that the results of the study may overestimate the true average effect (Dar et al. 1999).

7.2 Labor market institutions

There is a lot of discussion in the literature about the impact of labor market institutions on labor market performance. In Estonia, the labor market institutions have been relatively weak, and therefore it is generally believed that their impact on labor market outcomes has been small, if not nonexistent. This section focuses on institutions such as the unemployment benefit system, social assistance, early retirement, trade unions, wage bargaining and employment protection legislation; the role of active labor market policies is discussed in the following section.

The *unemployment benefit system* in Estonia consisted of a flat rate unemployment assistance benefit until 2003, which was launched in 1991 and is financed from the state budget. Since January 2003, the unemployed are also entitled to unemployment insurance benefits. The Unemployment Insurance Act came into force in January 2002 and the payments out of the Insurance Fund started in 2003. This means that currently there are two complementary unemployment compensation systems in Estonia: unemployment insurance and unemployment assistance. The last one is paid to those who fail to fulfill the insurance criteria (e.g. students) or when unemployment insurance benefits run out (Leetmaa 2004).

The unemployment insurance operates as a compulsory insurance. According to the Unemployment Insurance Act (2001) the contribution rate for the employee is 0.5–2.0% of the wages and the rate for the employer is

0.25–1% from the total wage bill paid out to all employees. The levels of the contribution rates are decided annually. Self-employed persons are not covered by the unemployment insurance scheme.

The precondition for collecting the unemployment insurance benefits is an employment record of at least 12 months during the previous 24 months. Unemployment insurance benefits are not paid to those who leave their job or service voluntarily or who lose their job because they do not perform as agreed, lost confidence of their employer or behaved in an indecent manner. These persons still receive unemployment assistance benefits.

The duration of the unemployment insurance benefit ranges from 180 days up to 360 days depending on the length of contribution payments. During the first 5 years of the system, the insurance benefits are paid up to 180 days, afterwards the entitlement period will be gradually extended up to 360 days. After expiry of the insurance benefit, the unemployed can apply for assistance benefits for the remaining 90 days and for social assistance thereafter. The replacement rate of the unemployment insurance benefit is 50% of the previous income during the first 100 days and 40% afterwards.

As with insurance benefits, in order to get the flat rate unemployment assistance, persons have to be registered as unemployed in the public employment service and been employed for 6 months during the previous year. Unemployment assistance is paid up to 270 calendar days in the amount of 400 EEK[10] (26 €) per month.

In 2003 only 17% of the newly registered unemployed were eligible to the insurance benefits and on average 49% of the registered unemployed received unemployment assistance benefits. The replacement rate of unemployment assistance benefit relative to average net wage has been very low in Estonia. In 2000–2002 the respective indicator amounted to only 6–7% (Leetmaa 2004).

After unemployment benefits are exhausted, the unemployed can apply for *social assistance*, which is called the subsistence benefit in Estonia. Subsistence benefits are means-tested and depend on the income of all family members living in the same household. Persons whose income after payment for housing expenses is below the subsistence level are entitled to these benefits. Currently, the subsistence level is 500 EEK (32 €) for the first member of the household and 400 EEK for each following one.

Taking into account the subsistence benefits and family benefits, the total benefits relative to average net wages[11] for different family types in 2000 were 33% for a single person[12], 27% for couple, 39% for a couple with two children and 48% for the single parent with 1 child. Relative to the minimum wage the respective indicators were 100% for the single parent with one child and 85% for the couple with two children. This shows that the incentive to take up a job with the minimum wage is low for these family types (Kuddo et al. 2002).

In the framework of state pension insurance system, there is a possibility to take *early retirement*, which can also be classified as a passive labor market

---

[10] 1 EUR=15.6 EEK.

[11] Relative to 66.7% of the average wage of the production worker.

[12] The ratio of the unemployment benefit relative to the 66.7% of the wage of the average production worker was 16%.

policy measure. The option of retiring 3 years before statutory retirement age has been available since 2001. If a person retires early, the pension payments will be reduced by 0.4% for each month between the actual date of retirement and statutory retirement date. In 2002 there were 2.1% of all old-age pensioners receiving early retirement pensions. Around 80% of the people who retired early were previously unemployed or inactive.

In general, there is a *decentralized collective bargaining system* in Estonia, only minimum wages are bargained centrally. Decentralized collective bargaining usually goes hand in hand with low unionization and low coverage of collective bargaining. This is also the case in Estonia, where union membership and collective agreement coverage are low compared to EU and Central and Eastern European countries and the bargaining power of the trade unions is weak. Trade union membership is small, around 14%–17% (2002) of employment, depending on the data source used[13], and declining (almost 100% in the end of the 1980s, 21% in 1996). Union membership is higher in the public sector and among non-Estonians. The low level of membership is accompanied by a low level of collective agreements coverage, for which there is no adequate estimate. The available estimates range from 18-24% depending again on the data source used (Kallaste 2003). The minimum wage in Estonia was 34% of the average wage in 2004, and around 11% of the workers are paid according to the minimum wage. The long-term agreement signed in 2001 between social partners foresees the gradual increase of the minimum wage up to 41% of average gross wages by 2008.

The *strictness of employment protection legislation* (*EPL*) is usually estimated using the EPL index, which is calculated based on the strength of the legal framework governing hiring and firing. Paas et al. (2003) calculate the respective indicators for Estonia and find that, on average, dismissals are less regulated in Estonia compared to the EU average. However, the regulations covering individual dismissals are stricter in Estonia than in the EU, while the use of fixed term contracts is less restricted. Hence, the authors conclude, that "the use of fixed-term contracts may counterbalance the negative effect of restrictions on dismissals on labor market flexibility" (Paas et al 2003).

7.3   Measures of Active Labor Market Policy

The current Employment Service Act specifies 7 types of active labor market programs in Estonia, which can be classified as follows:

- *Job Search Assistance*: information on the situation in the labor market and possibilities of employment; employment mediation; vocational guidance;
- *Labor Market Training*: general and vocational courses;
- *Wage Subsidies*: employment subsidy to start a business (business start-up grant); employment subsidy to employers to employ less competitive unemployed persons (wage subsidy);

---

[13] There is no reliable estimate on membership available. The lower estimate comes from Labor Force Surveys and the higher estimate is from unions' central organizations.

• *Direct Job Creation Schemes*: community placements (public works).

In addition there are various pilot projects for different disadvantaged groups (young people, disabled, older) financed by different sources (Phare, ESF, state budget). Unfortunately, there is no information available on the number of participants and expenditures.

The prerequisite for participating in labor market training, wage subsidies and community placement programs, or the so called "formal selection criteria", was the obligation to register as unemployed at the PES. To become registered as unemployed a person must have worked (or having had a formally equalized activity, such as being a student, being on maternity leave) at least 180 days during a previous year in 1995–2000. This was changed in October 2000, when the new Labor Market Service Act came into force. According to the Act, a previous work record was no longer required for registering as unemployed and for participating in Active Labor Market Policies. The previous employment record is now required only for applying to unemployment benefits. This means that before October 2000 most of the ALMP participants had some kind of previous work experience and there were no long-term unemployed among them.

Labor market training is the most important active labor market program both in terms of expenditures and in terms of participants (see Tables 7 and 8). Employment training may take the form of 1) vocational training or 2) more general training aimed at providing information on the labor market situation and psychological preparation for competing in the labor market. Most of the participants belong to the first group. Training is organized by the local labor offices. The duration of the courses is limited up to 6 months. In 2001 the average duration of the training course was 25 days. Participants in training receive a retraining allowance equal to 1.5 times the unemployment benefit. The number of participants in labor market training decreased between 1995 and 1999 and rose thereafter. As unemployment increased over these years the proportion of unemployed who participated in training declined and was about 10% of all annually registered as unemployed in 2002. Until 2001 there was no formal decision criteria for selecting people into training except for being registered as unemployed (see above): The decision was up to the PES officer. Since 2001, there is some kind of selection criteria established by the PES, according to which the PES officer must consider the personal characteristics and labor market situation when making the decision.

Business-start-up grant is the second largest measure in terms of expenditures. However, only a small number of unemployed (between 380 and 460 annually since 1995) participate in the program. To apply for a start-up subsidy the unemployed must be at least 18 years of age and have undergone relevant training or showing "sufficient" experience. The upper ceiling of the subsidy was 10,000 kroons in 1998–2002 and 20,000 kroons (1,280 €) since December 2002, which is about 4 times the average net wage in Estonia.

Wage subsidy to the employer for recruiting less competitive persons has been the least important active measure both in terms of expenditure and participants (only between 120 and 350 persons annually since 1995). The following persons who are registered as unemployed are considered to be less

Table 7. Number of participants in active labor market programs in Estonia; 1995 to 2002

	1995	1996	1997	1998	1999	2000	2001	2002
Participants in labor market training	9,809	9,454	8,241	7,956	7,095	8,156	10,233	10,021
Employed with subsidies to employer	121	246	216	136	265	189	332	215
Received business start-up grant	459	456	434	380	433	441	425	374
Participants in community placement	5,741	4,089	4,661	3,771	3,667	4,177	125	453
Total	16,130	14,228	13,552	12,243	11,366	12,929	11,134	10,806
in % of unemployed (LFS)	23.9	21.0	20.6	18.6	14.3	14.5	13.6	16.5

Source: Estonian Labor Market Board.

competitive in the labor market: disabled persons, pregnant women and women who are raising children under six years of age, young people aged 16–24, persons who will be retiring within 5 years and persons who have been released from prison. The level of the wage subsidy is 100% of the minimum wage during the first 6 months and 50% of the minimum wage during the next 6 months of the person's employment period.

Community placements are temporary public works organized by public employment offices. Since 2001 these are no longer financed by the state budget but local municipalities, and the number of participants has fallen remarkably as a result (Table 7).

The total public expenditures (Table 8) on labor market policies measured as a percentage of GDP have been very low in Estonia ranging from 0.2 to 0.3% of GDP. The comparable indicator in EU countries was 2.6% on average in 2000. The expenditures on Active Labor Market Policies in Estonia account for only 0.08% of GDP, which is more than ten times less than the amount spent in EU countries with comparable unemployment rates. In 2001 only 26.8% of the total spending on labor market policies was allocated to active measures in

Table 8. Expenditures on labor market policies in Estonia; 1994 to 2001

	1994	1995	1996	1997	1998	1999	2000	2001
% of GDP								
Total labor market policies	0.24	0.17	0.17	0.17	0.16	0.34	0.33	0.30
Passive policies	0.11	0.07	0.07	0.08	0.08	0.26	0.25	0.22
Active policies	0.13	0.10	0.09	0.09	0.08	0.08	0.08	0.08
% of total expenditures								
Passive policies	45.8	40.5	44.8	47.3	49.9	75.7	77.0	73.2
Active policies	54.2	59.5	55.2	52.7	50.1	24.3	23.0	26.8
Types of ALMPs, share in %								
Labor market training	62.5	55.5	57.9	59.6	55.4	59.3	58.1	63.7
Community placement	5.2	2.7	4.6	4.1	3.3	5.2	4.9	0.0
Start-up grants	4.7	9.1	7.7	7.1	6.4	6.6	6.6	5.3
Subsidy to employer	0.5	0.9	1.7	1.7	1.9	2.8	3.2	4.1
PES administration	27.2	31.9	28.2	27.5	33.0	26.1	27.1	26.9

Source: Estonian Labor Market Board, Statistical Office of Estonia.

Estonia. Furthermore, only a small fraction of the unemployed participate in Active Labor Market Policies in Estonia. In 2002, the share of participants in ALMPs amounted only to 16.5% of the unemployed according to LFS definition.

7.4   Evaluation studies

Active Labor Market Policies including various pilot projects have not been accompanied by scientific evaluations in Estonia. The main reason is lack of data as well as understanding of the rationale of these studies. The National Labor Market Board (NLMB) collects data on registered unemployed (participation in ALMPs, personal characteristics, benefit receipt). The Estonian Tax Office collects data on employment histories. However, the microdata from NLMB and Tax Office are not available, so it is not possible to carry out evaluation studies based on administrative records.

There are no macro level evaluation studies available for Estonia. The only micro level evaluation study that has been carried out so far, Leetmaa et al. (2004), follows a non-experimental research design and focuses on analyzing the individual treatment effects of labor market training participants. The study was carried out on the initiative of PRAXIS Center for Policy Studies and co-financed by the Estonian Ministry of Social Affairs.

The study is based on data gathered through a follow-up survey of registered unemployed, who had in 2000 participated either in labor market training and/or received unemployment benefits. The follow-up study was carried out in September 2002, hence, the labor market status was fixed on average 32 months after the start of training and/or unemployment benefits. The sample drawn was based on administrative records from the National Labor Market Board.

The treatment group consisted of labor market training participants and the control group of unemployment benefit recipients during the same time frame. As in 2000 both the training participants and unemployment benefit recipients were required to have a previous employment record of 180 days during the last 12 months, the pre-treatment histories of the treated and controls are similar. Furthermore, to further reduce the heterogeneity in the unemployment histories of the treated and controls, only the unemployed who registered themselves for the first time in 1999 or 2000 were considered. This means that there were no previous unemployment spells in the pre-treatment histories. Observations with inconsistent dates were dropped. In addition socio-demographic characteristics (age, sex, ethnicity, education categories, indicator for previous work experience, and region of living) were taken into account in the matching procedure.

To take into account the possible cream-skimming effects and differences in motivation between treated and controls a sensitivity analysis with different sub-samples was carried out. First, those individuals were dropped from the treatment group who in order to participate in training had to present a certificate by an employer confirming that he/she will be hired after graduating from the training course. Second, only those unemployed who made inquiries on participating in training themselves, but still ended up not participating, were taken into account for the control group. This should ensure that the control group contains only those unemployed who are as motivated as those who actually participated in training. Finally, the combination of both restrictions was used. The method used for the analyses is propensity score matching using a probit model including various socioeconomic variables.

The analysis shows a positive and statistically significant impact of labor market training on participants' employment probability, but no effect on wages, conditional on being employed. The impact of training is a 4–6% increase in employment probability after one year, and a 8–12% increase after two years from the registration as unemployed. The study also includes a preliminary cost-benefit analysis, which shows that training was cost beneficial.

Based on the study the authors conclude that as the expenditures and the number of participants in training programs in Estonia are very small, and as the programs seem to have positive treatment effects, it is likely that there is further room for the expansion of the programs. However, the expansion should go hand-in-hand with the proper monitoring and evaluation of these programs. Therefore, building up a database that could be used for evaluations, is of utmost importance (the study contains detailed recommendations for building up the database). Lack of quality data usable for evaluations is probably also a problem in most of the other new EU member countries.

7.5 Summary

Active labor market policies in Estonia have been used on a very small scale compared to the old EU member countries. Despite the economic downturn and increasing unemployment in the 1990s and in 2000, the level of expenditures on these policies remained at a low level of 0.08% of GDP. Only a small fraction of the unemployed participate in these programs.

Active labor market policies in Estonia have not been accompanied by scientific evaluations. The main reasons for that include the lack of suitable data as well as the lack of interest of policy makers for that kind of studies. The only evaluation study available follows a non-experimental approach and focuses on analyzing the individual treatment effects of labor market training in 2000–2002. The results of the study indicate that labor market training increased the employment probability of the participants and that the training was cost beneficial. This might indicate that labor market training is a suitable policy tool during the period of rapid structural changes when the skills of the workforce become obsolete quickly. However, the use of Active Labor Market Policies should be accompanied with proper evaluations based on high quality data, which is often missing in new EU member countries.

8   Active Labor Market Policies in Poland

8.1   General economic situation

The labor market in Poland is an example of a typical continental European labor market. However, on the top of this typical structure there is a number of specific features that concern, e.g., labor market outcomes such as the highest unemployment rate in the European Union, around two times higher than the EU average. The unemployment rate, although it varies with business and political cycles, has remained persistently high irrespective to a strong growth – on average – since 1990. The explanation of this situation is not straightforward and needs an analysis going beyond standard international comparisons.

Persistently high unemployment rates have characterized Poland from the beginning of transition in 1990. The unemployment rate reached a two digit level in 1991 and since that time it has been above 10 percent irrespective of various developments. The initial jump was caused by a number of reasons, of which the following ones appear to be most relevant:

• Large scale labor hoarding existed in Poland in the 1980s. Excess labor kept in enterprises was estimated to be even more than 25 percent of entire employment. Shedding the excess labor led to a large inflow into unemployment (cf. Góra, Rutkowski 1990)

• Various incentives existed (to an extent they still exist) for people from outside of the labor market to register at labor offices. In particular, easily available and rather generous unemployment benefits may have played an important role in stimulating the sharp increase of unemployment. In the early 1990s unemployment increased more than employment decreased (Góra 1997a,b).

It needs to be stressed that the two digit unemployment rate has been maintained for the entire period until now. At the same time the Polish economy has been growing very strong, reaching one of the highest average GDP growth rate among current EU-25 member countries (Figure 25).

It is a nontrivial problem how to explain developments that can be summarized as long-term coexistence of very high unemployment and very high growth. Three factors can be identified that seem to have the strongest impact on that development:

• Still a large source of inflow into unemployment exists due to unfinished reduction of labor hoarding in part of the economy, especially in public firms that usually operate within declining industries.

• The tax wedge is high in Poland. It is one of the highest in the EU and it has recently been even growing. It should be particularly stressed that the scale of the tax wedge for low income households in Poland is the highest among the EU countries.

• The Polish labor market is rather inflexible.

These factors affect the situation on the labor market in Poland. However, similar factors probably affect (to varying extent) other European labor

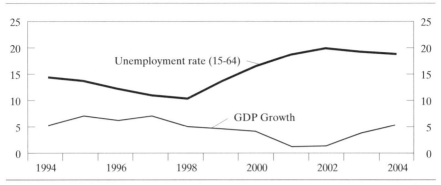

Figure 25. GDP growth and unemployment rate in Poland; 1994 to 2004; in %
Sources: Eurostat, Polish Statistical Office.

markets. The situation in Poland is different because of a large inflow into the
labor market from inactivity. This inflow is determined mostly by demography
(the largest inflow in Europe relative to the scale of the labor market). Factors
such as high tax wedge or inflexible labor market regulations create stronger
effects in the presence of pressure from outside of the labor market. Factors
that in other countries do not lead to very high unemployment, accelerate
their effect due to this pressure in Poland. The specific labor market situation
is reflected in the level of equilibrium unemployment rate that is estimated for
Poland at a very high level. The most recent estimation based on Labor Force
Survey data is 18.8 percent in 2003/2004.[14]

8.2   Labor market institutions

The institutional structure of the labor market has been changed a number of
times since 1990. Some of the changes have been substantial – such as
switching from wage related (previous) to flat rate benefits (early 1990s); decentralization the of public employment service (late 1990s). Altogether legislation defining the labor market institutional structure has been changed more
than ten times since 1990.

Two features of the institutional structure are particularly relevant for this
study. First, there are strong incentives for individuals to register as unemployed; second, there exists delegation of responsibility of labor market
policies to self-governing units at the voivodship (regional) and mostly county
level. Among the incentives, unemployment benefits do not play a major role.
What matters is a number of indirect benefits that depend on the status of the
unemployed. Examples of the incentives are: free health service for the unemployed and their families, easier access to various programs also for people
who could find a job; easier access to social assistance. On top of that

---

[14] See Bukowski, et al. (2005). Previous estimations generated similarly high level of
the equilibrium rate (see for instance Góra and Walewski 2002).

school-leavers are motivated to register just after graduation – just in case. Labor offices register without any difficulties, not even checking whether a person is really unemployed (they are not able as well as not eager to do so). At the same time deregistration procedures are weak, so many people who are not unemployed (for instance, not really seeking any job) remain in the register. That creates an impact also on Labor Force Survey (LFS) data, which we commonly perceive as independent from registration. However, answering the LFS questionnaire people often say they have been seeking a job even if they have not, since they understand that being registered means seeking a job.

The unemployment in Poland is very high, however, it is probably not as high as the statistics show. This does not mean that the statistics are wrong. In the Polish case they may be just misinterpreted. Both administrative and survey data present a similar picture of a very high unemployment rate almost reaching 20 percent. Its overestimation is caused by over-registration. There are incentives pushing people to register in many situations that are not related to the labor market. At the same time registration procedures are easy and deregistration procedures are very weak. Labor offices are focused on monitoring the unemployed eligible for benefits, while those who do not receive benefits are just registered. A large number of the registered does not seek any job and according to international definitions should not be counted as unemployed. Answering questions on whether a person has been seeking a job (standard LFS question) he or she tends to think of registering at a labor office as of seeking a job. This can be checked matching individual answers on other questions of the questionnaire.

In principle, the same may occur in other countries. In Poland, however, the scale of this situation affects the overall picture of the situation in the labor market. Table 9 presents an attempt to use Polish LFS individual data to estimate the scale of over-registration.[15]

The results presented above suggest that the rate of unemployment in Poland that can be compared with rates for other countries is somehow lower than we can see in the statistics. Similar conclusions can be drawn from other sources such as a survey conducted among local labor offices (see sections below). However, for this study another conclusion matters. Active labor market programs may have low effectiveness due to targeting some of them to participants who are not really unemployed. Targeting participants for programs is not very strict. Local labor offices' staff members do their best; however, universal procedures that can help them are non-existent or weak (cf. Bobrowicz et al. 2004).

Decentralization of the public employment service contributes to the problem discussed above. Decentralization also matters for implementation of labor market policies. Local employment offices do not have the capacity to do the job properly. There is limited co-ordination among them. On top of that subordination to local authorities creates an additional – perverse – incentive to treat labor market programs as a way to get additional financing for local-ities rather than a way of solving local labor market problems.

---

[15] A broader analysis of that phenomenon is Góra (2005).

Table 9. Estimation of the scale of over-registration in Poland; 2002

	Q1	Q2	Q3	Q4
LFS unemployed seeking a job (not only declaring that)				
U_{LFS}	3,480,000	3,432,000	3,436,000	3,375,000
Seeking a job (registration only)	493,600	524,000	529,500	502,900
$U_{LFS}*$	2,986,400	2,908,000	2,906,500	2,872,100
$U_{LFS}*/U_{LFS}$, in %	86	85	85	85
Registered unemployed (as seen via LFS) meeting criteria (checked via LFS)				
U_{adm}	3,533,000	3,502,400	3,513,600	3,547,400
Registered U not meeting criteria	943,600	961,400	1,010,100	1,020,800
$U_{adm}*$	2,589,400	2,541,000	2,503,500	2,526,600
$U_{adm}*/U_{adm}$, in %	73	73	71	71
Registered unemployed meeting criteria and really seeking a job				
U_{adm}	3,533,000	3,502,400	3,513,600	3,547,400
Registered U not meeting criteria	943,600	961,400	1,010,100	1,020,800
Seeking a job (registration only)	493,600	524,000	529,500	502,900
$U_{adm}**$	2,095,800	2,017,000	1,974,000	2,023,700
$U_{adm}**/U_{adm}$, in %	59	58	56	57

Source: Calculations based on LFS.

8.3 Measures of Active Labor Market Policy

Poland adopted a commonly accepted framework of active and passive labor market policies which have been in place since the early 1990s. However, they do not play any major role. Expenditure on the policies is limited. Would larger expenditure contribute to better situation in the labor market? Answering this question is difficult since evaluation of existing policies is rare and sophisticated methods are not always applied.

The Labor Fund was established in 1990 as a state fund dedicated to financing various expenditures related to the labor market. The Fund is in disposition of a minister responsible for labor issues (since 2002). Previously the role was played by the National Labor Office (terminated in 2002). Resources of the Fund are transferred to regional (voivodship) and local (county) self-governments that are directly involved in financing benefits and active programs. Labor Fund revenues (Table 10) come from:

- employers and self-employed contributions of 2.45 percent of social security basis of each employee or self-employed (around 63 percent of revenue in 2004);
- subsidy from the state budget (around 35 percent of revenue in 2004);
- European Union funds (not yet in 2004);
- Other minor sources.

Labor Fund expenditure (Table 11):

- Financing unemployment benefits (around 36 percent of 2004 expenditure; paid out by local labor offices);
- Financing preretirement benefits (around 47 percent of 2004 expenditure; paid out by local labor offices; expected to decrease; since 2001 new benefits are paid out by Social Security Institution out of a state budget subsidy);

Table 10. Labor Fund revenue in Poland; 2000 to 2004; in million zloty

	2000	2001	2002	2003	2004
Labor Fund revenue	6,091.7	8,316.7	9,276.0	9,812.4	8,964.0
previous year =100	–	136.5	111.5	105.8	91.4
Contribution revenue	5,105.2	5,372.2	5,355.7	5,572.4	5,640.0
previous year =100	–	105.2	99.7	104.0	101.2
Budget subsidy	838.5	2,650.0	3,634.6	3,944.0	3,144.0
previous year =100	–	316.0	137.2	108.5	79.7
Other revenue	147.9	294.6	285.7	295.9	130.0
previous year =100	–	199.2	97.0	103.6	43.9
Budget subsidy, % of total revenue	13.8	31.9	39.2	40.2	35.1

Source: Budget, 2004 estimated.

Table 11. Labor Fund expenditure in Poland; 2000 to 2004; millions zloty

	2000	2001	2002	2003	2004
Total	7,159.4	8,343.8	9,806.8	10,494.4	11,128.9
previous year = 100		116.5	117.5	107.0	106.0
PLMP	5,784.2	7,298.3	8,764.5	8,717.6	9,228.9
previous year = 100		126.2	120.1	99.5	105.9
Benefits for unemployed	3,548.0	3,914.6	4,268.8	3,741.4	4,014.9
previous year = 100		110.3	109.0	87.6	107.3
Pre-retirements allowances	1,580.0	2,189.7	2,757.5	2,596.2	2,505.0
previous year = 100		138.6	125.9	94.2	96.5
Pre-retirement benefits	655.9	1,194.0	1,738.2	2,380.0	2,709.0
previous year = 100		182.0	145.6	136.9	113.8
ALMP	1,175.4	807.1	790.6	1,406.6	1,500.0
previous year = 100		68.7	98.0	177.9	106.6
Training	84.0	43.6	57.0	109.2	175.0
previous year = 100		51.9	130.7	191.6	160.3
Wage subsidies	210.4	108.6	83.0	222.9	250.0
previous year = 100		51.6	76.4	268.6	112.2
Public works	168.8	96.5	86.1	209.8	150.0
previous year = 100		57.2	89.2	243.7	71.5
Start-up loans	125.1	64.9	68.1	196.2	-
previous year = 100		51.9	104.9	288.1	--
School-leavers	281.1	166.3	227.7	496.8	500.0
previous year = 100		59.2	136.9	218.2	100.6
Special programs	39.3	17.0	8.3	30.3	40.0
previous year = 100		43.3	48.8	365.1	132.0
Apprenticeship	349.6	338.8	292.7	225.9	350.0
previous year = 100		96.9	86.4	77.2	154.9
Other expenditure (ALMP)	42.2	36.3	35.8	24.2	35.0
previous year = 100		86.0	98.6	67.6	144.6
Other expenditure	199.8	238.4	251.7	370.3	398.8
previous year = 100		119.3	105.6	147.1	107.7

Source: Budget, 2004 estimated.

- Financing active policies excluding placement services including (since 2002) costs of the First Job program (around 13 percent of 2004 expenditure);
- Financing apprenticeship (around 3 percent of 2004 expenditure);
- Co-financing expenditure on EU programs (not yet in 2004);
- Financing other expenditure (around 3 percent of 2004 expenditure).

Local labor offices have very limited freedom of using the funds transferred from the Labor Fund. Up to 90 percent of expenditure is determined by various legal obligations. As a result labor market policies are very passive in Poland. This situation has been observed since the early 1990s. Initially it was cased by the need to pay benefits to a large number of unemployed eligible for them, while nowadays it is rather an effect of budgetary cuts affecting also the Labor Fund.

Labor Fund expenditure amounts up to around 1.2–1.3% of GDP, of which active programs (excluding active placement) constitute up to 0.2 percent of GDP. It is a rather low expenditure at international standards. On the other hand costs per participant are usually relatively low. The key question is whether the resources available are used effectively. We first present the type of programs and participation of the unemployed in the programs.

8.3.1 Passive labor market policies

Passive policies are relatively expensive. However, most of that expenditure is on pre-retirement arrangements. Unemployment benefits are nowadays much less expensive.

Unemployment benefits
Unemployed workers can receive a benefit if they have been employed or covered by social security insurance for other reasons for at least 365 days prior to registration. The benefit is granted for:

- 6 months in the regions where the unemployment rate is lower than the national average;
- 12 months in the regions where the unemployment rate is higher than the national average;
- 18 months in the regions where the unemployment rate is more than two times the national average for people who have at least 20 years of tenure or at least one child up to 15 years age, if a spouse is also unemployed and already expired his or her eligibility period.

There is a rational idea behind diversification of duration of the eligibility periods. However, as a result of that regulation some people, instead of moving to regions where unemployment is lower, tend to move to regions where unemployment is higher. Unemployment benefits are paid out very carefully. Labor offices try to reduce eligibility due to fiscal reasons. Opposite to the little care of registration itself, labor offices are focused on monitoring labor market behavior of the registered. In consequence the register is over-stated

Table 12. Registered unemployed entitled to unemployment benefits in Poland; 2000 to 2004

	Total	Entitled to benefits	Share (percentage)
2000	2,702,576	548,622	20.3
2001	3,115,056	624	20.0
2002	3,216,958	538,671	16.7
2003	3,175,674	478,105	15.1
2004	2,999,601	425,755	14.2

Source: Information service of labor offices.

while benefits are paid out to few people. The share of people registered as unemployed entitled to benefits as a share of total registration is small and constantly shrinking, reaching around 14 percent.

Pre-retirement arrangements
Pre-retirement allowances (*zasilek przedemerytalny*) were for the unemployed who worked relatively long, but had not reached an age that entitled to the old-age pension (on average the pre-retiring are 5 years "too young"). The pre-retirement allowance equaled 120% of the base amount of the unemployment benefit. Since 2002, it is not possible to apply for pre-retirement allowances anymore (those acquired in the past are paid out until regular retirement age). Pre-retirement benefits (*swiadczenie przedemerytalne*) were granted for the unemployed who had less than 5 years to be eligible for the old-age pension. Other requirements were: years of service, the employer's insolvency or difficulties that led to the employee layoff. Pre-retirement benefit is equal to 80 percent of accrued old-age pension. Since 2002, newly granted pre-retirement benefits cannot be lower than 120% of the base unemployment benefit and cannot exceed 200% of this benefit.

In principle the Labor Fund expenditure is perceived as being in line with legal guidelines. Criticism is focused on pre-retirement benefits that are extremely costly. It is due to a large number of people that are entitled. In extreme cases they are even only 41 (women) and 46 (men) years old. This policy has already led to large scale deactivation of workers from older age groups.

8.3.2 Active labor market policies

The level of expenditure on active labor market programs is very limited so the programs are unlikely to play any substantial role in labor market adjustments. However, their role cannot be fully neglected. They let local labor offices to do at least something that goes beyond just registration and paying benefits to a number of registered unemployed.

The types of programs are adjusted to the situation in Poland but do not really differ substantially from programs run in other countries. There is only one important exception. It is the exclusion of active job placement from the list of active programs. This affects statistics but much more priorities of labor

Table 13. Participants in wage subsidies in Poland; 2000 to 2004

	Total	Male	Female
2000	99,448	51,861	47,587
2001	39,315	20,603	18,712
2002	51,090	28,071	23,019
2003	114,891	64,705	50,186
2004	93,883	48,639	45,244

Source: Information service of labor offices.

offices. They tend to marginalize this activity. To an extent they have to, since this activity is heavily underfinanced in Poland. This is probably responsible for some percentage points of the unemployment rate. Additionally this malfunction contributes to lower effectiveness of other policies that are offered without clear knowledge of own labor market activity of the unemployed.

Wage subsidies
Wage subsidies aim at selected vulnerable groups to help them to integrate or re-integrate with the labor market. In practice, targeting the subsidies not necessarily works. This type of active program is broadly used, if only local labor offices can afford that. Subsidization should in principle lead to permanent employment. Program duration should not exceed 12 months. For the first 6 months the employer receives a monthly subsidy equal to the unemployment benefit plus social security contribution. If the program lasts longer the subsidy equals half of the minimum wage amount plus social security contribution per months (paid bi-monthly). If the employer keeps the person for more than 6 months after the program is completed he or she gets an additional bonus of 150 percent of the average remuneration. Wage subsidies for school-leavers are similarly designed but the subsidies are targeted at the group of registered unemployed within the 12 months period after graduation.

Program "First Job"
A new active program dedicated to school-leavers was started in 2002. The program is financed by the state via the subsidy to the Labor Fund. Employers who employ school-leavers receive refunding of disability contribution (in the part paid by the employer) and work injury contribution. The same is refunded if a school-leaver starts his or her own job. The program aims at providing the school-leavers with basic work experience and integrate them with the labor market. Participation in the program requires registration as unemployed, which contributes to stronger incentive to register even if a person could find a job without problems.

Public works
Public works aim at those unemployed whose employment prospects are the most difficult, usually these are the low skilled workers. In principle the key goal should be to shorten unemployment spells. In practice public works are often used for local infrastructure investment. Local authorities can get additional money for that purpose if only the unemployment rate in their county is

Table 14. Participants in public works in Poland; 2000 to 2004

	Total	Male	Female
2000	50,302	33,564	16,738
2001	29,025	19,172	9,853
2002	33,742	21,261	12,481
2003	100,015	65,982	34,033
2004	75,770	45,849	29,921

Source: Information service of labor offices.

sufficiently high. This perverse incentive reduces efforts to solve unemployment problems even if that could be achieved.

Labor offices initialize public works and negotiate with organizers. Previously, labor offices, being a part of special administration independent from local authorities, could have played the role. Since 2002 it has been much more difficult, since labor offices are subordinated to local authorities who organize the works or are involved in negotiated projects. For a period of up to 6 months public works organizers receive an amount of up to 75 percent of average remuneration plus social security contribution per unemployed enrolled on the program. After the 6-month period is expired, the organizers receive a bi-monthly subsidy up to the average remuneration plus social security contribution. In counties belonging to the regions recognized as being severely hit by unemployment, public works organizers can additionally receive a partial reimbursement of non-labor costs of the program (up to 25 percent of the subsidy to cover the labor cost).

Training courses
Training courses are meant to improve or change skills of the unemployed. The courses should increase employability of program participants. Additionally, this type of activities should be in line with restructuring of local industries. The courses are in the educational domain. Labor offices initialize the courses and finance participation of the unemployed but the offices are not involved in running the courses. There is a large number of specialized training institutions that offer their services in the market. Training courses typically last no longer than 6 months. In this period participants receive a training allowance amounting up to 120 percent of the unemployment benefit. The allowance is to be paid back if a participant fails to complete the course for reasons other than starting a job. Out of the resources available for active

Table 15. Participants in training in Poland; 2000 to 2004

	Total	Male	Female
2000	98,651	48,283	50,368
2001	47,587	24,600	22,987
2002	68,564	35,592	32,972
2003	132,230	68,877	63,353
2004	127,785	66,890	60,895

Source: Information service of labor offices.

Table 16. Participants in start-up loans in Poland; 2000 to 2004

	Total	Male	Female
2000	5,251	2,677	2,574
2001	2,679	1,340	1,339
2002	2,763	1,472	1,291
2003	5,255	2,846	2,409
2004	4,272	2,279	1,993

Source: Information service of labor offices.

programs relatively little share is spent on training. According to a survey in 2004 only 8.8 percent of offices spent more than 20 percent of resources available for active programs on training (Bobrowicz et al. 2004).

Start-up loans
The unemployed can apply for a start-up loan. Similar opportunities exist for firms intending to create a new job for an unemployed. In both cases the loan equals up to 20 average monthly remunerations. If the newly started workplace still exists after 24 months, the amount of the loan is reduced 50 percent.

The start-up loans are not common. A special selection process meeting strict criteria is used. The fact that the criteria exist is good. However, they are not necessarily focused on expected ability of an unemployed to become self-employed but they are focused rather on social characteristics of the unemployed. For instance those with unemployment spells over 12 months or lonely parents should be accepted for the program in the first order (Bobrowicz et al. 2004). This appears strange given the challenges of being self-employed.

8.4 Evaluation studies

Academic attempts to evaluate effectiveness of the policies have been seldom and produce ambiguous results. The latter stems – among others – from poor data sources. Active programs are narrowly used, so the number of participants dropping into the sample of the Polish Labor Force Survey (PLFS) is limited. At the same time administrative data does not allow for controlling selection of participants of programs. Nevertheless, evaluation of effectiveness of Active Labor Market Policies in Poland is possible and really needed. Otherwise discussions on whether to extend or not the scope of active programs will be based on pure beliefs that can be wrong and lead to wasting resources.

As mentioned above relatively few studies exist that are focused on the evaluation of active programs' effectiveness in Poland. Prior to 2002 a specialized labor market administration coordinated activities of regional and local offices. Since 2002 labor offices are subordinated to local self-government. Apart from the already mentioned perverse interest of local authorities, this situation means that local labor offices are responsible for implemen-

Table 17. Role of various active programs in Poland as seen by local labor offices

Type of active program	Average range
Subsidized employment	6.69
Start-up loans	5.65
Professional advice	6.82
Training courses	7.37
On the job training	4.79
Apprenticeship	8.29
Special programs	1.96

Source: Bobrowicz et al. 2004. Based on a survey; 0: no role to 10: crucial role.

Table 18. Average number of people on various active programs per local labor office in Poland

Type of program	Number of participants	
	entire sample	per labor office
Subsidized employment	44,527	215
Start-up loans	1,840	9
Professional advice	108,942	526
Training courses	54,135	262
On the job training	5,359	26
Apprenticeship	46,705	226
Special programs	657	3

Source: Bobrowicz et al. 2004. Based on a survey.

tation of active programs, being virtually left without institutional support. This affects the methods of program evaluation. Typically local labor offices calculate and announce the share of program participants to the number of participants who started a job afterwards. So there is little to comment on from the point of view of more sophisticated evaluation of program effectiveness.

Labor offices staff members do, however, their best trying to use the resources in a rational way. A recently conducted survey presents methods applied and opinions on what should and could be done in the area of active program (Bobrowicz et al. 2004). Tables 17 and 18 present a small part of results of the survey. The rationale for the approach applied in the labor offices surveyed is mostly their own experience.

The survey briefly presented here gives additional light on the problem of over-registration leading to over-estimation of the scale of unemployment in Poland. Local labor offices staff members who directly work with the unemployed and know the most on their labor market behavior strongly support the view based on LFS individual data analysis mentioned above (Table 19).

There is a limited number of academic studies on Active Labor Market Policies. They are usually based on individual data from the Polish Labor Force Survey. The data set is occasionally extended by adding questions (supplements to the regular questionnaire) focused on particular issues. One of such supplements (conducted in 1996 and covering the period from 1992 to 1996) was focused on Active Labor Market Policies. It brought additional in-

Table 19. Average estimated shares of registered unemployed representing attitudes towards labor market involvement in Poland

Type of attitude	% of registered unemployed
Persons not interested in starting any job	20.2
Very passive, not believing in finding a job and usually not taking one if there is a chance to do so	17.8
Passive, seeking a job means noting more but registration, usually taking a job if offered by a labor office	28.6
Active, wishing to take a job, ready to take offers such as training	21.1
Very active, use available opportunities, actively seeking a job	12.4

Source: Bobrowicz et al. (2004). Based on a survey: observed by local labor offices staff members

formation on labor market behavior of active programs participants. Individual data from that supplement were used by various economists for the evaluation of effectiveness of active policies during the early stages of transition.

Typically the studies lead to the conclusion that active programs analyzed were ineffective. This particularly applies to public works (Góra et al. 1995; Kluve et al. 1999). Wage subsidies programs have been analyzed much more, and results suggest the same. The programs do not create the desired effects. Virtually all studies present a similar picture: Subsidization is ineffective (Góra et al. 1995; Puhani 2003) or may even create some negative effects on employment probability (Kluve et al. 2005). The only type of active programs that these studies find to be effective is training. The studies lead to a conclusion suggesting concentration of available resources on training courses. This is a conclusion that is in line with the needs that are natural in an economy such as the Polish one that is quickly modernized and restructured.

8.5 Summary

The very high level of unemployment in Poland needs urgent political attention. Well designed active labor market programs can contribute to a reduction of unemployment in the future. However, before more resources are allocated to active programs clear procedures on the way of evaluating their effectiveness need to be developed and delivered to those who are to implement the programs. Without easy-to-use procedures spending more money may lead to wasting resources rather than to a reduction of unemployment.

New research on active programs' effectiveness needs repetition of the data collection on individual labor market behavior, similar to the one used in the PLFS in 1996. This would bring new data for research and possible policy advice. Additionally, a comparison of the situation after 10 years would create an interesting and possibly fruitful research topic.

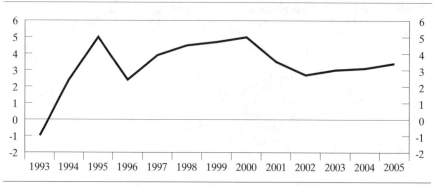

Figure 26. GDP growth in Spain; 1993 to 2005; in %
                Source: Eurostat.

9   Active Labor Market Policies in Spain

9.1   General economic situation

Since the 1990s, the Spanish economy has been characterized by high GDP growth, caused by increasing domestic demand, and relatively low inflation. Between 1995 and 2003, the average GDP growth rate was 3.25% (Figure 26), which is well above the EU average. The dynamic growth performance came hand in hand with a process of outstanding job creation resulting in an average increase in employment rates of 3.5%, which is among the highest within the EU. At the same time, the unemployment rate has steadily fallen from a peak of around 20% at the beginning of the 1990s to slightly above 11% in 2003 (Figure 27).

Despite these positive trends, the unemployment rate as well as long-term unemployment are still among the highest within the European Union, and in fact the highest within the Euro area. Spanish labor market outcomes vary

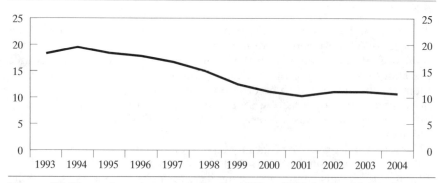

Figure 27. Unemployment rate in Spain; 1993 to 2004; in % of labor force
                Source: Eurostat.

substantially by gender and age. While the 80% participation rate of men is rather high by EU standards, the participation rate of women was only around 55% in 2003. The unemployment rates of women are persistently twice as high as unemployed rates of men. The Spanish labor market also shows large regional disparities. In the southern regions Extremadura and Andalucía the unemployment rates were around 18% in 2003, while the unemployment rates in the regions of Navarra and La Rioja are only around 6%. This high disparity across regions points to a rather low geographical mobility of the labor force.

9.2   Labor market institutions

One of the most frequently discussed features of the institutional framework of the Spanish labor market seems to be the coexistence of permanent contracts with high employment protection on one side and temporary contracts available for regular activities on the other side. Temporary contracts were introduced in 1984 with the intention to reduce (long-term) unemployment by raising flexibility in the labor market. In fact, unemployment rates decreased sharply over the following decades. At the same time, however, the labor market became increasingly segmented with highly paid permanent employees protected by high dismissal costs on one side and lowly paid employees who are continuously working on fixed term contracts and who are exposed to a high degree of precariousness on the other side. Today, temporary contracts account for nearly one third of total employment, which is more than twice the EU average. The high share of temporary contracts kept wages on a low level and is considered detrimental in terms of labor productivity (Dolado et al. 1999). Since 1997, several reforms tried to limit the excessive use of temporary contracts by easing employment protection legislation for permanent workers and providing financial incentives for the creation of permanent contracts. However, these measures did not result in a significant reduction of the share of temporary workers (Dolado et al. 2002).

It appears that successive Spanish governments put much effort in first increasing and later decreasing flexibility of the labor market. At the same time, activating unemployed people directly by means of classic active labor market measures has played a rather marginal role for many years. It is widely acknowledged in this context that the launch of the European Employment Strategy played a crucial role in the further development of Active Labor Market Policies in Spain (Ballester 2005; Consejo Económico y Social 2005; Alonso-Borrego et al. 2004).

It is worth noting, however, that even in the field of active labor market policy the problem of excessive use of temporary contracts plays a central role: the highest share of active labor market expenditures in Spain, almost 40%, is spent on measures for the promotion of permanent contracts. These are subsidies paid to employers who create a permanent employment contract for unemployed workers or who convert a temporary contract in a permanent one. In the context of this study, it is clearly worth discussing whether such incentives should be regarded as active labor market policy in the sense of a cross-country analysis of ALMP effectiveness.

The Spanish unemployment benefit varies between 75% and 170% of the national inter-professional minimum wage (100% to 220% if the unemployed has dependent children) and lasts for 120 to 720 days, depending on previous contributions to the unemployment insurance system. After that period, the unemployed person is entitled to unemployment assistance, which amounts to 75% of the national inter-professional minimum wage. After a maximum period of 18 months, eligibility for unemployment assistance expires, and social assistance applies. A so-called active integration wage (75% of the national minimum wage), is available for up to 10 months to persons who are not entitled to unemployment benefit or subsidies but who agree to undertake a profiling and to sign a binding integration agreement. These people will get priority access to active labor market measures. In general, receiving unemployment assistance is not a necessary condition for participating in active labor market measures; however, recipients usually get priority access.

9.3   Measures of Active Labor Market Policy

At the beginning of the 1990s, Spanish spending on ALMP measures was among the lowest in the European Union. Since 1998, Spain has increased its spending on ALMP at a higher rate than any other European country. Finally, in 2002, the expenditure level as a share of GDP reached the average of the EU-15 member states. However, given the relatively high unemployment rate, this indicator remains rather low. Furthermore, as discussed above, if the promotion of permanent contracts is not considered an active labor market policy in the sense of this study, Spanish expenditure levels are even smaller relative to other countries.

The Spanish spending profile shows a high share spent on the promotion of permanent contracts, as well as on start-up incentives. This share is higher than in any other EU-15 country. Furthermore, the share spent on training measures is relatively low, amounting to less than half the EU-15 average. In terms of participants, schemes for the promotion of permanent contracts are the most important ones, followed by training and direct job creation schemes.

The National Employment Institute (INEM), an autonomous administrative body attached to the ministry of labor and social affairs, manages active and passive measures of labor market policy. In recent years, the INEM transferred more and more competencies to the realm of the autonomous regions. Today, the division of functions between the national level and the level of the autonomous regions is quite complex, including parallel structures in some cases. The autonomous regions and the municipalities may set up their own employment promotion bodies to complement INEMs measures. They may implement placement services and job search assistance, vocational training of the unemployed and most have agreed on their own regional employment pact with the social partners. Furthermore, the INEM gave up its monopoly on placement services when the government legalized non-profit agencies and temporary work agencies in 1994. Today both private and public regional or national entities may offer placement services. The following paragraphs describe Spanish active labor market measures in more detail.

Training

Training targets the young, the low skilled and the long-term unemployed, women, disabled and migrants. Training schemes include vocational training measures for unemployed workers and workshop schools for the youth and for adults, respectively. These measures combine training with practice, sometimes via internships in private or public firms. For instance, the INEM set up an experimental program on training and employment integration in the area of information and communication technologies. It is financed partly (35%) by the participating company. The social partners organize further vocational training for employed workers. Since many different bodies both on the national level and on the level of the autonomous regions provide training for different target groups, the National Vocational Training Plan 1998–2002 established a National System of Qualifications and Vocational Training that provide unified and coherent training plans and certifications.

(Financial) Incentive Schemes: The most important financial incentive scheme in terms of expenditure and participants is the promotion of open-ended contracts. Target groups are unemployed workers, older workers and workers who hold an apprenticeship, training, replacement or substitution contract. The second incentive scheme is the promotion of start-up activities. For instance, unemployed workers may receive an advance payment of their full unemployment benefit to start up their own business, as well as subsidies for costs of feasibility studies, auditing and counseling. Measures for the promotion of start-up incentives also include the promotion of employment in local employment initiatives and co-operatives. A further incentive scheme is the support of domestic migration, which aims at the promotion of workers' geographical mobility.

Direct Job Creation Schemes

The INEM, in cooperation with other public or private non-profit organizations, contracts long-term unemployed people and employs them for so-called socially useful activities in these organizations. Furthermore, the autonomous regions Andalucía, Extremadura and some under-developed rural areas run job creation schemes for agricultural employment. Employment workshops, which are already mentioned above in the training category, might also be considered a form of job creation measure.

Services and Sanctions: Public employment services play a rather small role in job placement, especially for high-risk groups (Ballester 2005; Bertelsmann Stiftung 2004). A reform in 2002 aimed at improving the monitoring and placement of job searchers via an enforcement of the so-called principle of rights and duties. Beside a substantial reduction of benefit entitlements, the reform intended that unemployment benefits were to be paid only to those who make a written commitment to accept all proposals, which would help them find work. It re-defined a suitable job that has to be accepted as one that resembles any job previously held by the applicant for a period of 6 to 12 months at any time in his or her working life. The public opinion criticized these measures as being far too restrictive. A general strike finally forced the government to abandon most elements of the reform. The integration agreement is now voluntary and the definition of suitable jobs is less restrictive than initially intended and left at the discretion of the employment service. It is often criticized that the public employment services fail to provide effective job search assistance to the unemployed (Bertelsmann Stiftung 2004; Arellano 2005a). In recent years, redundant workers increasingly employed private outplacement services as an alternative to the public employment services (Arellano 2005a).

9.4 Evaluation studies

Rigorous evaluation studies of active labor market policy in Spain are scarce. One reason seems to be the unavailability of appropriate data. Only recently, process data has become available to researchers. Moreover, other issues than active labor market policy, such as the evaluation of successive reforms of the regulation of fixed-term contracts, as well as the introduction of a minimum wage, absorbed a great deal of attention from the scientific community. Rigorous evaluation studies in this context are the studies by Kugler et al. (2003) and Arellano (2005c) on the effect of reforms of fixed-term contracts, and the study by Dolado/Felgueroso (1997) on the effects of the introduction of a minimum wage.

Evaluation studies of classic active labor market measures are Mato (2002) and Arellano (2005a) on training measures, as well as the study by Cueto (2003) on hiring subsidies and self-employment programs. Moreover, Arellano (2005b) evaluates job search assistance by comparing the effect of private outplacement services compared to public employment services. Furthermore, the study by Davia et al. (2001) evaluates active labor market programs on a macro-economic level.

Training

Mato (2002) evaluates training programs for unemployed and employed workers in Asturias. As a control group, he uses data of individuals who applied for training courses but could not participate because the number of places was limited. The results suggest that training slightly increases the employability of unemployed and employed workers but has no effect on earnings. Arellano (2005a) assesses the effect of four types of training courses (general training, professional training, retraining, and further training) on the duration of unemployment. The control group is composed of registered unemployed workers who do not participate in any training measure. All training programs apart from general training exhibit significant positive effects. Training participation increases the probability of women to leave unemployment by 50% and the one of men by 40%.

Employment incentives

Cueto (2003) compares two types of employment incentives in the region Asturias: start-up subsidies and hiring subsidies for employing an unemployed worker on a permanent contract. The results indicate that start-up subsidies perform better than hiring subsidies in terms of job stability and occupation rates.

Services and sanctions

The study by Arellano (2005b) on the effect of private job search assistance by outplacement services uses two data sources: individual data generated by Creade, a private outplacement service firm, for the treatment group, and individual process data from INEM in the region Madrid for the control group. The study employs several matching methods, which lead to similar results. The results indicate that outplacement services compared to public services have significantly positive effects on the duration of unemployment, except for men.

Macro-economic evaluation

The study by Davia et al. (2001) studies the impact of active labor market programs on a macro-economic level. The results suggest that training programs and employment incentives significantly reduce the overall unemployment rate, the long-term unemployment rate as well as the overall exit rate from unemployment. The exit rate from long-term unemployment is reduced by employment incentive programs only.

9.5   Summary

Although the launch of the European Employment Strategy entailed a considerable increase in spending on Active Labor Market Policies in Spain, Active Labor Market Policies still play a rather small role both in public policy and in the scientific community. The most concerning issue for policy makers seems to be the promotion of permanent contracts, which accounts for the largest shares in spending on active labor market measures. Only few studies carry out a rigorous evaluation of labor market policies. Two studies suggest positive but small effects of training measures. Another two studies do not compare treatment to non-treatment but rather compare the effects of two treatments to one another. These studies suggest that start-up subsidies perform better than hiring subsidies and that private placement services work better compared to public ones.

10   Active Labor Market Policies in France

10.1   General economic situation

It was at the very beginning of the 1970s when unemployment started to increase in France. Especially the youth unemployment rate has been rising rapidly and became one of the highest in the European Union. At 13% already in 1979, youth unemployment increased to a maximum of about 29%

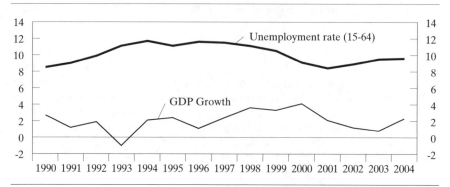

Figure 28. GDP growth and unemployment rate in France; 1990 to 2004; in %
            Source: Eurostat.

in 1995. More recently, the youth unemployment rate was 21.8% in 2004, while
the total unemployment rate was 9.6%. As can be seen in Figure 28 the annual
GDP growth of the last 15 years has averaged around 2%, with a slight peak at
the end of the 1990s, and rather small increments over the last years.

10.2 Labor Market Institutions

Active labor market schemes were introduced in France in the beginning of
the 1970s. The high unemployment rates, and especially the high youth unemployment rates, led to many reforms in the labor market policy in the 1980s
and 1990s. One of the most notable changes in these two decades was the
Emergency Plan for Youth Employment (*Plan d'Urgence pour l'Emploi des
Jeunes*) introduced in 1986 with strong incentives for private firms to offer
training places. Alternating work schemes (*formations en alternance*) with alternating spells of training and work were supported. The lower bound on the
entry age for these contracts has been lowered to 16 years, and the upper
bound has been raised from 20 to 25 years.

The PAP program (*Programme d'action personnalisé*), a more generous
benefit system (for eligible unemployed persons) with intensified counseling
of the unemployed, was introduced as part of the policy reform in 2001 called
"Plan d'aide au retour à l'emploi" (PARE). It is a combination of benefits and
placement. As part of it, the maximum duration of drawing unemployment
benefits was lowered. While a more extensive reform was intended, these
main points of the reform were realized. A meeting with an unemployment
agency caseworker is now compulsory for all newly registered unemployed individuals and recurs at least every 6 months. Before the reform measures were
open only to long-term unemployed workers.

10.3 Measures of Active Labor Market Policy

Since 1974 more than 50 measures were introduced in total, but only ten still exist. Because of the high youth unemployment rate most measures are designed for youth. About 800,000 youths between 15 and 25 years old take part in one of these measures each year.

Training

The institutional setting of the apprenticeship system in France is similar to the German one: Part-time work in a private firm is combined with part-time education in a public training centre. Young People between 15 and 25 years of age without any diploma or formal education can reach a national diploma after completion of the contract and passing a test. Therefore there are differences of involved persons due to the differences in the education systems. The number of participants is much smaller in France than in Germany. The length of such an *apprenticeship contract* varies between one and three years with a usual length of two years. The wage of the apprentice is a fraction of the level of the minimum-wage. The individual level depends on the age and seniority of the apprentice. At the end of the temporary contract the employee may be hired under a fixed term labor contract.

The *Qualification Contract (Contrat de Qualification, CQ)* is very similar to the apprenticeship contract and is a fixed-term contract for about 6 to 24 months, where at least one fourth of the period must be training with the objective that participants prepare for a diploma, similar to an apprenticeship. This program is addressed to unskilled or long-term unemployed young adults and is approved by collective agreement. The participant is paid by the employer. The wage is a fractional amount of the minimum wage. The fraction again depends on age and job tenure. Employers are private firms who are exempt from paying social security contributions and apprenticeship tax.

The *Adaptation Contract (Contrat d'Adaption)* can be a fixed-term contract for about 6 to 12 months (since 1987 at least 200 hours) or a perpetual contract. Target group are skilled youths having problems finding an employment. Employing firms work in handcraft, trade and industry, and provide some job-specific training. The amount of training depends on the contract, the occupation and the skill level. The wage is at least the legal minimum wage, and is paid by the employer. The employers do not have to pay the apprenticeship tax but the Social Security contributions.

Apprenticeship Contracts, Qualification Contracts and Adaptation Contracts are generally addressed to young workers with low labor market experience. Thus applicants are mainly young people who leave school or college.

Special *training courses* for 16 to 25 years old are offered by state training centers. These courses are aimed to facilitate social and professional integration of young people leaving the educational system without any diploma or qualification and have a length of 6 to 9 months. Trainees receive a lump-sum from the state.

The *programs for insertion and training (Action d'insertion et de formation, AIF)* were introduced in 1990. Participants take part in training courses of 40 to 200 hours and receive a lump-sum from the state. This program is now the main program addressed to long-term unemployed.

The *courses for preparation to the working life* (*stages d'initation à la vie professionelle, SIVP*) were non-renewable temporary contracts and are no longer in use. This measure was targeted at youths without any professional experience and long-term unemployed youths. Participants received an education or training in a firm or a public education centre with a lump-sum from the state and complementary allowance from the firm. This measure was completely replaced in 1991 by the "*Contrats de Retour à l'Emploi*", which is targeted at long-term unemployed, benefit recipients and old-age employees. The contract could be either a long-term or a fixed-term contract. The firms are exempt from paying Social Security contributions.

The retraining program "*Convention de conversion*" was set up in 1987 to improve labor market prospects of displaced workers. For a period of six months retraining and job search assistance are proposed to displaced workers. The target group consists of workers up to the age of 57 who have at least two years of seniority in their former firm. The main purpose of this measure is to increase the employment probability of displaced workers and to avoid long-term unemployment spells for employees who were laid off for economic reasons. During the first two months of the program, the worker receives a specific allowance representing 83% of her former wage. During the following four months this reduces to 70%.

Private sector incentive schemes

French ALMP measures targeting private sector incentives regard mostly firms taking part in the apprenticeship system. Firms without any apprenticeship contracts have to pay an apprenticeship tax. As described above, for several measures employers are sometimes exempt from Social Security contributions if they employ participants of these measures.

Since the mid-90s there are two big strands of labor market policy: distribution of labor because of a reduction in working time and a decrease in welfare contributions for low income jobs.

The *35-hours-law* is the result of different attempts to reduce working hours. Firms were forced to reduce the working hours to 35 hours per week or less until January 2000 (January 2001 for small firms). They received compensations dependent on the date of carrying out the change.

Also introduced was the *bonus for employment (prime pour emploi)* which is some kind of income tax or combined wage for individuals in the low wage sector. The bonus is subtracted from the income tax, or directly paid if no income tax has to be paid. Because the bonus was not attractive enough to start working for all recipients of social benefits it has been increased in 2006.

Public sector employment

The program of *community jobs* (*Travaux d'Utilité Collective, TUC*) was set up in 1984 and discontinued in 1990, being replaced by the *Contrat Emploi Solidarité*. Low-skilled youths aged 16 to 21 years and long-term unemployed

22 to 25 years of age are recruited by public institutions, local administrations or non-profit associations to do work for public utility. It is a non-renewable temporary and part-time employment with the legal minimum wage as salary paid by the State. The employer is exempt from Social Security contributions except of Unemployment Insurance contributions.

The *Employment-Solidarity Contracts (Contrats Emploi Solidarité, CES)* are part-time (20hrs a week) and fixed-term (from 3 to 12 months) employment contracts. They can be renewed two and even three times for recipients with poor employment prospects and are similar to TUC. The target group is extended to adults with bad perspectives on the labor market. Participants receive the legal hourly minimum wage, entirely paid by the state. Employers are exempt from Social Security contributions except of Unemployment Insurance. This measure is still in use.

In 1997 the socialist government introduced *Employment for youths (Emplois Jeunes)*. The aim of this program was the creation of 700,000 new jobs for young adults (aged 26 or younger) in the public and also in the private sector. To avoid displacement in the public sector new job profiles were created. This program was very cost-intensive and was entirely discontinued after the change of government in 2002.

Services and sanctions

The basic *Skill Assessment* lasts typically one day. The provider helps the individual assess his professional skills. It was introduced as part of the reform in 2001. The *Project Assessment (Bilan de competences approfondi)* is another skill assessment with an average duration of 20 hours. It is aimed at individuals with professional experience who have difficulties finding a job corresponding to their skills. Individuals who wish or have to change profession and need time or help can take part in the *Project Support*. It lasts three months, during which participants have frequent contacts to a personal advisor. A similar program targeted at individuals with higher skills is *Job-search support*. It lasts up to 3 months, during which a personal advisor assists and teaches (sometimes group-based) the unemployed person.

10.4 Evaluation of the schemes

As described above, the problem of high unemployment rates in France is mostly a problem of very high youth unemployment rates. Thus, measures are mostly targeted at youths and most of the evaluation literature confines itself to programs for youth and young adults. The set of studies evaluating ALMPs in France remains limited.

Training programs

Three studies evaluating training programs are presented in the following section. Bonnal/Fougère/Sérandon (1997) focus on programs of the late 1980s, Cavaco/Fougère/Pouget (2005) discuss programs of the late 1990s, and

Brodaty/ Crepon/Fougère (2002) compare these two periods with the datasets used in the first two studies.

Bonnal et al. (1997) use the dataset *"Suivi des chômeurs"*, an extraction of the Unemployed Follow-Up-Survey collected by INSEE between 1986 and 1988 covering all individuals who were unemployed in August 1986, to estimate the effects of different training measures. The sample is randomly drawn from the files of the public employment services (*Agence Nationale Pour l'Emploi, ANPE*). 7450 individuals were interviewed four times between Nov 1986 and May 1988. The data contain monthly retrospective records for this time period.

Cavaco et al. (2005) use the survey *"Trajectoires des demandeurs d'emploi et marché local du travail"*, which was collected by the French Ministry of Employment and Social Policy (DARES) between 1995 and 1998. The sample has been drawn randomly among workers entering unemployment between April 1995 and June 1995 in three French administrative regions. The surveys are not representative of all regions in France. The data record retrospectively every month between the second quarter of 1995 and the first quarter of 1998. 8125 individuals were interviewed three times. The dataset was complemented by a second survey conducted in the same local areas as the first one, but focusing only on displaced workers who joined the retraining program *convention de conversion*. The studies are cast into a continuous time framework with one or two-factor individual random-effects. Only Cavaco et al. (2005) observe adults in their study, while the other two studies use only data on young workers and young male workers, respectively (Bonnal et al. 1997).

Cavaco et al. (2005) examine the effects of the retraining program *convention de conversion* for displaced workers on the probability to find a long-term contract after participating. Their estimation of a duration model suggests that the probability to obtain a permanent job increases by 8 points for participants, while non-participants would have had an increased probability of 28 points if they had participated. The authors conjecture that the program might have been offered more frequently to those individuals with a low re-employment probability.

Bonnal et al. (1997) find that SIVP have positive effects on the transition intensities of young men from unemployment to employment. Measures like apprenticeship contracts and adaptation contracts have only positive effects for young men without any diploma. A positive effect of the other training courses can only be identified for young men without any diploma. Using a propensity score matching approach to assess the effectiveness of training, Brodaty et al. (2002) distinguish between long-term and short-term unemployment. Although the two sub periods considered (1986–1988 and 1995–1998) are similar from a macroeconomic point of view, programs are generally found to be less effective in the second period. While participants, both short-term as well as long-term unemployed, experience a higher transition rate to employment in the first sub period, in the second sub period the short-term unemployed experience lower transition rates, and the effect for long-term unemployed is insignificant.

Overall, training measures have positive effects on employment. The positive effects were higher in the 1980s than ten years later. Brodaty et al.

(2002) suppose that reasons might be that more unemployed workers became eligible to these programs in the late nineties or young eligible workers were more heterogeneous in the 1990s as ten years before.

Public incentive schemes

Two of the studies on training measures described above also estimate effects of public incentive schemes using the same datasets. Contrary to the results for training measures, Bonnal et al. (1997) observe negative effects of participating in public employment measures on the transition rates to employment for young men with a technical school certificate. No effects can be found for young men without any diploma. While no significant effects are found for the first sub period (the late 1980s) in the study by Brodaty et al. (2002), participation in such a measure has a negative effect on the transition rates to employment in the late 1990s.

On the basis of this limited set of studies, Public Employment Programs in France seem to have zero or negative effects on the individual employment probability after participation.

Services and sanctions

Crépon/Dejemeppe/Gurgand (2005) evaluate the effects of intensive counseling schemes by using duration models. Their dataset is a longitudinal administrative dataset containing about 400,000 individual unemployment spells from ANPE records. It is a 1/12 nationally representative sample of all unemployed persons. They analyze individual transitions from unemployment to employment and time spent out of employment and detect a positive and significant impact on the transition rate from unemployment to employment (increase by 1 percentage point) and on the unemployment recurrence (decrease by more than 6 percentage points). The schemes without skill assessment have some impact on both unemployment and employment duration. The job-search support program has the strongest effect, while project assessment and project support display some lock-in effect.

Fougère/Pradel/Roger (2005) use the survey "*Suivi des Chômeurs*", covering the years 1986 to 1988, to examine the disincentive effects of the public employment service on the search effort of unemployed workers and on their exit rate from unemployment. They find an increased exit rate from unemployment through a higher job contact arrival rate by the public employment service, especially for low-educated and low-skilled workers.

10.5 Summary

The French labor market has been characterized by a very high youth unemployment rate for several decades. Therefore most active labor market measures are targeted at youths, and the evaluation literature mostly focuses on these programs. In fact, few empirical studies analyzing French ALMP exist. Training schemes in terms of apprenticeships and similar contracts, as well as the program for displaced (older) workers, have positive effects on the transition to employment for participants. The measures enhancing job search activity introduced with the labor policy reform in 2001 also seem to be effective.

Among the programs discussed above only the public employment schemes show zero effects in the 1980s and negative effects in the 1990s for young workers. However, these are measures designed for adults, and not for young workers specifically.

11   Active Labor Market Policies in the UK

11.1   General economic situation

For more than a decade now, the British labor market has been performing excellently compared to most European countries. The British economy has continuously kept on growing at a growth rate between 2 and 4 percent per year while maintaining inflation at a low level. The unemployment rate and long-term unemployment rate have fallen steadily and are now on a level not seen since the 1970s. In addition, the employment rate of 71.6% in 2004 is at historic highs, with a level well above the Lisbon and Stockholm employment targets. However, not all groups benefit equally from the favorable conditions. The increase of the employment rate has been driven mainly by rising female employment, while male employment has decreased since the 1970s. Furthermore, there is concern on inactivity of certain groups, especially older persons, younger persons and lone parents. For example, the UK has the highest proportion of 18-year-old men who are neither in school nor in the labor force. For 22-year-old men the UK is second after Italy in this category (Van Reenen 2003).

We also observe an overall increase in wage inequality since 1979. Inequality has been increasing between younger and older age groups, and even

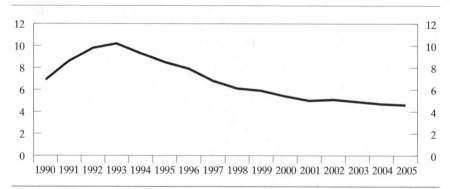

Figure 29. Unemployment rate in the United Kingdom; 1990 to 2005; in % Source: Eurostat.

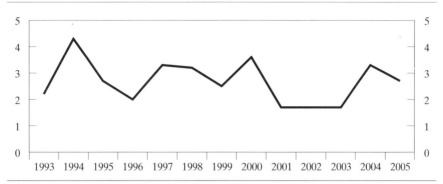

Figure 30. GDP growth in the United Kingdom; 1993 to 2005; in %
         Source: Eurostat.

within gender and skill class. This is not only caused by diverging wages but
also by the substantial cutback of benefits and pensions.

11.2 Labor market institutions

Compared to most European countries, British labor market institutions
appear relatively market orientated. Employment protection is low, limiting
the minimum period of dismissal notice to only 1 to 12 weeks, depending on
the duration of employment (although in practice many employment
contracts will specify a longer period than the minimum legal requirement).
Regulation on temporary contracts is therefore obsolete. During the 1980s,
trade unions and employer associations lost most of their influence and roles
as coordinators of wage negotiations. Over the past 40 years, the structure of
wage determination has been progressively decentralized to the point that it is
now very fragmented and more decentralized than elsewhere in Europe. This
trend has been accompanied by the development of flexible payment systems
that are responsive to performance and local labor market conditions. The
coverage of collective bargaining has fallen from around 75% in 1980 to under
40% at present.

Spending on active labor market measures in UK is lower than in any other
EU-15 country. Against this background, it seems that the British labor
market policy achieves excellent performance with a minimum input in terms
of expenditure on active labor market policy. However, it is important to bear
in mind that the UK employment strategy has been accompanied by steady
employment growth, a tight benefit system and an extensive fiscal policies that
are designed to "make work pay". The Active Labor Market Policies have to
be viewed in this context.

Since the 1980s, several reforms cut back benefit levels and introduced
threats of sanctions for benefit recipients to enforce their attachment to the
labor market. The introduction of Restart in 1986 made compulsory inter-

views with the Employment Service a condition of benefit receipt for all those whose unemployment claims had reached a duration of six months or more. The program combines counseling and encouragement with tighter enforcement of the conditions necessary to qualify for unemployment benefits. Since 1997, the labor government introduced several New Deal programs involving compulsory participation for long-term unemployed. Today the British system can be viewed as an employment assistance regime geared to remind the unemployed of their job-seeking obligations and, through regular contact, to encourage them to seek and take up available unsubsidized jobs.

An equally important feature of the British employment policy mix is the UK tax system, which provides high incentives to take up work. Fiscal policies that "make work pay" include the national minimum wage, the exemption of social security payments for low wage earners, an income tax system favoring low wage earners, child-care subsidies, and various forms of tax exemptions for households of low wage earners. These measures cannot be regarded as Active Labor Market Policies, though they may work via the same mechanism as for example targeted subsidized employment in the private sector does (Blundell and Meghir 2001).

Also the unemployment benefit regime, the so-called Jobseeker's Allowance (JSA), which was introduced in 1996, is strictly committed to the rights and responsibility agenda. There are two types of Jobseeker's Allowance: the contribution-based Jobseeker's Allowance, which is paid for up to 6 months, and the non-contributory Jobseeker's Allowance, which is means tested and available for people who are not entitled to contribution-based Jobseeker's Allowance or whose needs are not met by the contribution-based allowance. The non-contributory Jobseeker's Allowance automatically entitles recipients to other types of benefits, e.g. housing benefits. Both benefit types require certain labor market conditions: Recipients have to be under 60, be available for work, seek work actively and are not allowed to claim income support. They have to sign a Jobseekers' Agreement, which sets out what they will do to look for work within any agreed restriction. The Jobseekers Agreement will be signed jointly by the jobseeker and a caseworker, and is reviewed regularly for the duration of their claim. If individuals do not take-up a job offer satisfying the agreed restrictions they may be denied further JSA payments. People who are out of the labor market may receive other benefits, like a means-tested Income Support or disability benefits. However, working-age benefit recipients who are inactive as well as partners of benefit recipients may also be asked to attend compulsory work-focused interviews. It is the aim of the employment service to reduce welfare dependency by assisting any benefit recipient with job search and increasing help as duration of benefit receipt increases.

Until 2001, the welfare and benefits system was administered through different delivery organizations, while Jobcentres dealt solely with Jobseekers. Since then, there has been gradual closure of Jobcentres and Social Security offices and the creation of an integrated service known as "Jobcentre Plus", offering both employment and benefit services under one roof. The re-organization intends to implement the principle of rights and responsibilities, which links benefit receipt to certain obligations, in a more efficient way.

11.3   Measures of Active Labor Market Policy

As already mentioned, the UK employment strategy relies heavily on services and sanctions while training, employment incentive programs and direct job creation schemes only play a minor role. Such active labor market measures are mainly part of New Deal programs. Therefore, in this chapter we will not describe them separately, but rather within the context of the New Deal programs.

The New Deal programs are universal measures for the long-term unemployed. They are packages of treatments, tailor made for certain target groups. Joining one of the New Deal programs is compulsory for most unemployed after claiming Job Seekers Allowance for a given period. Unemployed people with severe disadvantages may be eligible for early entry to the programs. Everyone on a New Deal program gets a personal adviser who will be his or her point of contact throughout the program. The program consists of several stages. The first stage is a series of individually tailored advisory interviews, which may be followed, if necessary, by measures like confidence building courses, help with job applications, grants to meet the costs of starting work, or even help with issues like drug or alcohol misuse. The second stage involves compulsory active labor market measures if the long-term unemployed person fails to integrate in the regular labor market within the first stage. There are special New Deal programs for age groups 18–24, 25+, and 50+, as well as New Deal for Lone Parents, New Deal for Disabled People, and New Deal for Partners of Unemployed People.

For example, the New Deal 18–24, which is the largest program, is compulsory for benefit recipients aged 18-24 after six months of unemployment. First, participants go through a period of intensive job-search, known as Gateway, which lasts for up to 4 months. Second, if the participant is still unemployed, she must enter one out of four options, which encompass temporary work experience and training. These are a) full-time education and training option, aimed at those lacking basic qualifications, b) employment option, with wage subsidies paid to employers, c) voluntary sector, and d) environment task force. The work options b) to d) also include education and training of one day a week. The employment option (b) usually takes place in the private sector and may be viewed as an employment incentive program. The options c) and d) could be labeled direct job creation schemes. These options last up to six months, with the exception of full time education and training which can last up to one year. Alternatively, participants may receive promotion to set up their own business (Youth Enterprise Initiative). Depending on the chosen activity, participants continue to receive Jobseeker's Allowance or an equivalent allowance or wages. Finally, those who could not be placed during the program enter the follow-through stage which is essentially the same as the Gateway period with intensified help and guidance. Participants can only leave the program by entering employment or ceasing to claim Jobseeker's Allowance for more than 13 weeks.

The design of other New Deals is similar. Unemployed people aged 25 and older have to join the New Deal 25+ after 18 months of unemployment. The options of the second stage are either full time subsidized employment or full-time education or training for up to 6 months. Those aged 50 and older can participate in a New Deal 50+ on a voluntary base. In the second stage, they may receive an Employment Credit and in-work training and support. Furthermore, there is a New Deal for Lone Parents, a New Deal for Disabled People and a New Deal for Partners of Unemployed People. These programs are on a voluntary basis, too, and may include training programs. The New Deal for Partners of Unemployed People illustrates the serious intention of the UK employment strategy to reduce welfare dependency. If an unemployed person claims Jobseeker's Allowance for himself and a partner for six months or more, not only the jobseeker himself but also the partner can get involved in New Deal.

11.4   Evaluation studies

Since active labor market programs only play a minor role in the United Kingdom, it is not surprising that there are only few evaluation studies. Several macro-econometric evaluations exist; however, in these studies the policy being evaluated is essentially indicated by a set of time dummies. It is therefore difficult to assess whether the observable effects are due to the introduction of a labor market program, or due to other macro-economic events occurring simultaneously. For example, using a time series model the Employment Service suggests that a rule changes in Jobseeker's Allowance reduced claimant unemployment by about 15,000 to 20,000 (Sweeney, MacMahon 1998). Large positive effects of Restart were found by Dicks/Hatch (1989)/Disney et al. (1991). More recently, Riley and Young (2001a, 2001b) found moderate effects of the New Deal 18-24 when they used a macro-economic approach (about 28,000 extra jobs).

The micro-econometric evaluation is difficult, since many programs are compulsory, which makes it difficult to find an appropriate control group. Fortunately, however, there was an experiment in 1989 that provides useful insights for the effect of the Restart program from a micro-econometric perspective. A sample of just fewer than 9000 individuals approaching their sixth month of unemployment were identified. Of this set a random control group of 582 persons were selected who were not asked to participate in a Restart interview at the usual point in time but six months later. Both groups were followed up in successive individual surveys. This information was matched to administrative records using the unique social insurance numbers. Dolton/O'Neill (1995, 1996) analyze this data and find that the group who were randomized out of Restart had median unemployment duration one month longer than those who did receive Restart. Using a competing risks model, they also find that the strongest effects of Restart came from exits into jobs rather than to training and non-participation. The effect appeared to work both through increasing the arrival rate of job offers and by making the treated group more likely to accept a job if they received an offer. A further study examines the long run effects of the random delay in Restart interviews (Dolton, O'Neill 2002). They find that members of the treatment group had unemployment rates that were six percentage points lower than the control group five years after the initial interview. The authors also examine the channels through which Restart operates and find that the threat component of Restart is important in generating the short-run positive effects, while the services provided at the interview played an important role in generating the positive long-run effects.

Furthermore, researchers can exploit the fact that many programs are piloted in certain areas before they are rolled out nationwide. For example, Van Reenen (2003) evaluates the first stage Gateway period of the New Deal 18–24, comparing pilot areas to other areas in 1998. Additionally, he constructs a control group of unemployed people aged 25–30 who are ineligible for the New Deal 18–24 because of age restrictions. The study focuses on men because three quarters of all New Deal participants are male. According to the estimation results, young unemployed men are about 20% more likely to find jobs each month because of the New Deal. An increase in steady state youth employment of over 17,000 is estimated. Though the effect is rather small, van Reenen estimates that the economic benefits of the program still exceed the economic costs. Also Blundell et al. (2004) find an increase in the probability of young men finding a job in the next four months after participation started.

Dorsett (2004) uses matching methods to assess the relative effectiveness of the four options in the second stage of the New Deal 18–24 program. He uses administrative data for males entering New Deal at the end of 1998. The results suggest that a period of subsidized employment is the most effective means of exiting unemployment and securing unsubsidized employment compared to other options. Also, remaining on an extended Gateway stage is more effective than the other options of education, voluntary sector or environmental work. The differences between these last three options are more subtle; however, environmental workers are likely to remain unemployed longest. The relative good performance of an extended Gateway stage suggests that participants of the second stage search for jobs less intensively and therefore are less likely to exit unemployment.

11.5 Summary

The British employment strategy strongly emphasizes universal but tailor made services and sanctions, while other categories of active labor market policy only play a minor role. Not only the low levels of unemployment but also the evidence of rigorous evaluation studies suggests that the strategy is successful in bringing the unemployed into unsubsidized employment. However, it is important to bear in mind the wider institutional and economic context. Continuous economic growth and the consistently implemented "make-work pay" policy may have contributed considerably to the UK success story.

Chapter 5: The effectiveness of European ALMPs

1 Findings from previous research

Accompanying the increased interest by European policy makers in the evaluation of comprehensively utilized active labor market measures, especially in the context of the EES, recent years have also seen a growing academic interest in the evaluation of ALMPs. This has resulted in an increasing number of evaluation studies, entailing both a huge step forward in the amount of empirical evidence available, and remarkable advances in analytical techniques for program evaluation (cf. also chapter 3). The report at hand focuses mainly on what could be called "third-generation" evaluation studies, i.e. studies that were conducted at some point in time since the late 1990s, predominantly already in the 2000s, and that are characterized by applying a set of relatively mature and standard (by now) methods from the econometric toolbox. At the same time, these studies discuss recent programs that were implemented in the 1990s and the 2000s. Before turning to these third-generation studies in detail, this section provides a concise overview about evaluation studies that have been conducted and whose results have been summarized beforehand.

Previous econometric research has been analyzed in overview studies by Heckman et al. (1999) on European program evaluations before 1994 and by Kluve/Schmidt (2002) for subsequent evaluation studies on programs until 1999. The former could be called "first-generation" evaluation studies, since they entail, in general, evaluations of rather new policies at the time, applying rather new econometric techniques on the basis of often still rudimental data. The latter constitute the second generation of European evaluation studies and are mostly characterized by both more mature and a more extensive set of policies, by a deepened and rapidly developing methodological know-how, and frequently much improved data. Both overview studies also juxtapose the respective US and European "evaluation cultures". Additional surveys of ALMP experience are given in Martin (2000) and Martin/Grubb (2001), who give a descriptive account of OECD countries' experience with active labor market measures.

Heckman et al. (1999) give a thorough overview about microeconomic studies for the US and for Europe, in which they emphasize several differences between the two. Whereas US researchers began conducting evaluation studies already in the mid-1970s, European efforts in this field began later, much in line with the later beginning of comprehensive use of such policies.

Another difference is that many European evaluations focus on unemployed youths, whereas the US studies focus on more disadvantaged unemployed of all ages. Overall, they stress that no clear pattern emerges about the performance of different active measures. For the US, the evidence suggests that government employment and training programs (a) can improve the economic prosperity of low-skilled persons, and (b) have markedly varying impacts on different demographic and skill groups. In particular, the evidence for youths is not encouraging. The general conclusion regarding ALMP effectiveness in the US is that if there are any positive treatment effects at all, then these will be small. Frequently, individual gains from programs are not sufficiently large to lift many participants out of poverty, as is the principal goal in many US programs.

Kluve/Schmidt (2002) investigate European evaluation studies covering programs conducted during the time period 1983–1999, but mostly during the 1990s. They conclude that studies on ALMP show a large heterogeneity regarding their effects. One of their main results emphasizes that training programs seem likely to improve the labor market prospects of unemployed workers. Furthermore, direct job creation in the public sector has been of little success, whereas subsidies in the private sector might show at least some positive effects. One consistent result for both Europe and the US are positive effects for job search assistance programs, which are in general the least expensive measures. By contrast, youth programs usually show negative effects also in Europe.

Moreover, Kluve and Schmidt conduct a quantitative analysis with a small set of 53 observations based on the evaluation studies reviewed in their article and those European evaluation studies reviewed by Heckman et al. (1999, Table 25), i.e. in this empirical analysis each program evaluation represents one data point. They investigate the correlation of the binary dependent variable "study finds a positive treatment effect yes/no (1/0)" with several indicators representing (a) the type of ALMP program, (b) the research design and timing of the program, and (c) several variables capturing the economic environment and the institutional context for the respective country and the point in time when the study was conducted. Overall, the results from this quantitative analysis strengthen the findings that result from merely surveying all the studies: Studies on training programs and job search assistance appear more likely to report positive treatment effects than "subsidy-type" programs. Regarding the time period, they report negative correlations for the 1990s relative to the base category, the 1970s, which could e.g. be due to a better economic climate in the 1970s, but also to improved evaluation techniques in the 1990s.

Moreover, the positive and significant coefficient for the unemployment rate indicates that positive results were usually found in times of high unemployment. The authors conclude that training programs and subsidies appear to have the potential to combat unemployment if they are well implemented and targeted. Nevertheless, effects of training for program participants are rather modest in size. However, Kluve/Schmidt (2002) emphasize that the results from this quantitative analysis are tentative findings that have to be taken with caution. Limitations of the study regard the relatively small sample size, a constrained set of covariates, and the fact that private and public sector employment schemes are pooled.

Adding to these reviews on academic evaluation work, in 2002 the European Commission and the member states conducted the "Impact Evaluation of the European Employment Strategy" to assess its impact following the first five years after the launch at the Luxembourg Jobs Summit in November 1997. The member states held the responsibility of completing national policy impact evaluation studies, which comprised eight thematic chapters. The Commission analyzed these national reports and added a macroeconomic analysis and an assessment of the EU-wide labor market performance. The results on "Unemployment Prevention and Active Labor Market Policies" are based on the results from national evaluations which were conducted by the member states. The national reports display some variation in terms of methodological rigor: While some countries apply quasi-experimental approaches to evaluate the impact of active measures, other countries rely on purely descriptive methods or literature surveys.

Overall the results are very similar to the findings presented by Kluve/Schmidt (2002). They highlight the general success of job search assistance and the better performance of subsidies in the private sector compared to job creation in the public sector. Additional results indicate that training programs are more likely to have positive results for specific target groups. Positive rewards are found mainly among women reentering the labor market as well as educated immigrants, whereas low-educated individuals usually have lower benefits. In addition, positive impacts were found for self-employment grants, although these measures only have a limited scope. It is also emphasized that programs implemented on a large scale are less convincing, indicating that large programs might suffer from inadequate targeting and tailoring.

It is stressed that there is little evidence about macroeconomic effects of ALMPs. However, some studies report a long-term increase of labor supply. Further, some studies from Sweden indicate that active measures prevented a large drop-out out of the labor force during the economic downturn in the early 1990s and therefore maintained labor force participation. Some evaluations report an increase of human capital and a reduced wage pressure or increasing national incomes. Nevertheless, numerous studies emphasize negative displacement and substitution effects associated with ALMPs. Overall, it is mentioned that the results are comparable to the results from evaluation studies in OECD countries.

The impact of active measures in OECD countries has been summarized by Martin (2000) and Martin/Grubb (2001), whose results are mostly in line with the aforementioned literature. Direct job creation in the public sector often seems to fail, whereas subsidies in the private sector and training programs may prove to have some positive effects on some target groups. Job search assistance may be a promising tool if it is combined with measures that enhance the pressure on participants to accept jobs.

2   Summary of the results from recent European evaluation research

As borne out by our reports from selected EU member states in chapter 4, the use of ALMPs and their respective evaluations are remarkably heterogeneous across countries in many dimensions. Some countries (e.g. Sweden) have a fairly long tradition of ALMP practice accompanied by a relatively exhaustive evaluation literature. In contrast, there are hardly any impact evaluation studies available for the new member states (with a few exceptions for Estonia, Hungary, Poland and the Slovak Republic). In some countries (e.g. Spain) ALMPs play a minor role, and therefore few evaluation studies exist. Other countries such as Germany have used ALMPs heavily for more than a decade, yet evaluation research has emerged only recently, even though the output has been remarkable over a short period of time.

The existence of good empirical practice and of reliable evaluation results in a given country is intimately related to the data that are collected, and their availability: The Swedish evaluation culture, for instance, is characterized by its availability of extremely informative and large data sets. German evaluation research only began to soar once access to administrative data was facilitated, which has proved to be a rather sluggish process that still has not resulted in entirely open and transparent data access procedures. Nonetheless, the development in Germany has been remarkable. In the new member states, appropriate data sets had to be set up from scratch. Only very few countries have had policies evaluated using social experiments, but those who have done so (the Netherlands, in particular) appear to have come up with strong, reliable evidence on the effectiveness of the programs evaluated in this way.

Most of the recent empirical evidence still comes from the microeconomic field, investigating average treatment effects for the treated individuals and neglecting aggregate-level impacts, in particular potential displacement and substitution effects. Relative to this increasingly large set of micro studies, the existing literature on the macroeconomic effects of ALMPs has remained small. This chapter therefore focuses mainly on a summary of the third generation of microeconomic studies that have been conducted since 2002, adding to the overview of the previous two generations of evaluation studies in Heckman et al. (1999) and Kluve/Schmidt (2002).[1]

2.1   Results from microeconomic studies

Recent microeconomic studies differ substantially in various aspects. There is a large variety of programs with different design and focus on different target groups. Furthermore, across countries it is clear that programs take place in differing economic environments against a backdrop of specific institutional settings.

---

[1]   The analysis also includes a few evaluation studies conducted before 2002 which have not been reviewed in Kluve and Schmidt (2002).

Table 28 in the Appendix depicts key features – specifically program type, target group, study design, observation period, outcome variables and identification strategy – and results of 77 microeconomic evaluation studies of European ALMPs. Most of these studies are discussed in detail in the corresponding country chapters. In addition, Table 28 includes evaluation studies from the remaining EU member states, as well as from Norway and Switzerland.

Looking at the features of the studies in Table 28, we observe that the studies show some disparity of evaluation design and estimation techniques. The vast majority of studies is based on non-experimental data. Regarding identification strategies in this regard, the "third generation" of program evaluation generally uses either matching estimators or duration models, with few exceptions. It is still common to focus solely on short-run impacts, though some more recent studies try to assess long-term effects if suitable data are available (e.g. Lechner et al. 2004; 2005). While few studies take into account the effects on the participants' income, most studies estimate the impact of participation on unemployment and employment as the main outcome variables, which is in line with the general objective of such policies in Europe to combat unemployment, rather than alleviate poverty (as is often the case in the US). Unfortunately, it remains uncommon to conduct rigorous cost-benefit analyses about the efficiency of labor market programs, and only few of the studies mentioned includes such an effort.

The remaining part of this section discusses the main findings from the country reports and the studies surveyed in Table 28 by program type.

(Labor market) Training

Given the fact that labor market training amounts to the largest share of spending on active measures across the EU with almost 40% in 2003, it is not surprising that numerous studies investigate the impact of training programs. Overall, more than half of the studies in Table 28 investigate a measure with training content.

Given the established tradition of running and evaluating ALMPs in Sweden, numerous studies exist that estimate the impact of Swedish training programs. The largest Swedish program, the Adult Education Initiative (AEI) also known as Knowledge Lift, was implemented in 1997 and aims at raising the skill level of low-skilled workers. Stenberg (2005) investigates the impact of AEI on unemployment incidence and duration relative to the vocational part of labor market training. He reports a decreasing incidence of unemployment, but an increase of the unemployment duration compared to participation in labor market training. Albrecht et al. (2005) examine the impact on income and the employment rate. They report positive employment effects for young men, but no significant impact on their average income. The results for women are insignificant for both outcomes; there is at best a slight increase in income for young women, but a slight decrease for older women. Finally, the authors stress that the participants among young men are on average more disadvantaged than the non-participants.

The study by Richardson/van den Berg (2001) investigates the impact of Swedish labor market training, AMU. The authors report a substantial and significant effect on the transition rate from unemployment to employment for vocational training after participation, which diminishes with time. Nevertheless, taking the time from the beginning of the program into account, the resulting net impact is about zero, which indicates the presence of locking-in effects during participation.

Andrén/Andrén (2002) distinguish between Swedish-born and Foreign-born participants in AMU in the years 1993–1997, a time with a continuous high unemployment rate after the peak in summer 1993. The study generally finds small positive employment rewards for Swedish-born participants. The rewards for Foreign-born are negative in the first year, but positive for following years. In contrast to these findings is the study by Fredriksson/Johansson (2003), who, for the same time period, investigate whether job creation programs and training programs increase employment probability and mobility in the longer run. They estimate an outflow to employment for participants of training programs that is reduced by around 40 percent. Moreover, participation is associated with locking-in effects reducing regional mobility.

In conclusion, the most frequently used and most expensive measure in Sweden, the labor market training AMU, does not seem to be a very effective program. Whereas studies on the 1980s frequently established positive income or employment effects, estimates for the 1990s tend to be insignificant or negative (cf. also Calmfors et al. 2002). Among other possible explanations, this could be due, for instance, to either differentially effective programs depending on the respective economic situation (having been much better in Sweden in the 1980s than in the 1990s), or to the fact that more sophisticated econometric methods were available to evaluate the measures in the 1990s.

An early study also for the 1980s focuses on public training programs in Austria (Zweimüller, Winter-Ebmer 1996), indicating positive treatment effects on employment stability. A more recent, specific training scheme in Austria is evaluated in Winter-Ebmer (2001). The program was offered to workers affected by large-scale downsizing during privatization and restructuring of the national steel firms in the late 1980s. One special feature that these "Steel Foundations" were financed jointly by the unemployment insurance funds and the steel firms themselves. The other feature is that the long-term program was composed of orientation, re-training and placement assistance elements. The program resulted in considerable wage gains and improved employment prospects for the participants.

In Germany a set of various training measures exist, such as e.g. short (up to 6 months) and long training (over 6 months), retraining, and practical training in firms. Early studies on training measures in both East and West Germany do not come to consistent conclusions: Some studies find positive effects, whereas many studies do not detect any effect of training measures at all. The more recent literature, based on much more informative administrative data, seems to point to slightly more positive results (cf. Lechner et al. 2004, 2005; Fitzenberger, Speckesser 2005): In general, training measures seem to show a considerable dynamic in program effects, having negative (locking-in) effects in the short-run and positive ones in the longer run. Based on such results, future cost-benefit analyses might be able to trade the costs of negative short-run effects against the benefits of positive long-run effects.

Similar to Germany and Sweden (cf. also Table 26), training is the most commonly used type of program in Denmark. However, the findings of the Danish evaluation studies about the employment effects of training programs are rather disappointing. Most analyses find that training programs have negative effects by increasing unemployment duration, primarily due to large negative locking-in effects, but sometimes also due to negative post-program effects. This is the general picture found by a majority of recent studies (Rosholm, Svarer 2004; Bolvig et al. 2003; Graversen 2004; Munch, Skipper 2004; Danish Economic Council 2002). Only one recent Danish study (Jespersen et al. 2004) finds some evidence that training programs give rise to a net economic surplus for some cohorts in the case where long-term effects are analyzed, a finding similar to recent results from German studies.

For a set of EU countries, in particular the new member states and countries with a limited ALMP practice such as e.g. Italy and Spain, only few evaluations of training exist. Mato (2002), for instance, evaluates training programs for unemployed and employed workers in the Spanish region *Asturias*. The results suggest that training slightly increases the employability of unemployed and employed workers, but has no effect on earnings. Arellano (2005a) assesses the effect of four types of training courses in Spain (general training, professional training, retraining, and further training) on the duration of unemployment. All training programs apart from general training exhibit significant positive effects. Training participation increases the probabilities of women and men to leave unemployment by 50% and 40%, respectively.

One evaluation study for Estonia (Leetmaa, Vork 2003) analyzes individual treatment effects of labor market training. The results indicate that labor market training increases the employment probability of the participants and that the training is cost beneficial. This might imply that labor market training is a suitable policy tool during the period of rapid structural changes when the skills of the workforce become obsolete quickly. Similarly positive experiences appear to have been made with Polish training measures in the early years of transition (Kluve et al. 1999). More recent evidence, unfortunately, does not exist.

An evaluation study about the impact of vocational training has been conducted by Cockx (2003) for Belgium. The analysis reports a decreased transition rate from unemployment during participation, indicating locking-in effects. The transition rate after participation, however, exceeds the previous decrease and the results of a simulation exercise suggest a reduction of duration of unemployment by 4 to 6 months.

Cavaco et al. (2005) analyze the impact of retraining for displaced workers in France and report an increased employment probability for participants. They emphasize that the program was not targeted towards individuals who would benefit the most and assert that the employment probability for non-participants would have been higher had they participated. Moreover, participants were slightly older than non-participants and facing very low re-employment probabilities. This underlines that training programs might have higher rewards for individuals with better labor market prospects.

The Finnish study by Hämäläinen (2002) considers the impact of LMT for three different cohorts, facing a dramatically deteriorating economic situation. The study reports positive treatment effects that decline considerably, corresponding to the macroeconomic development. In addition, LMT is most effective for unemployed with poor employment probabilities during periods of high unemployment; this is reversed during the periods with low unemployment, in which individuals with good labor market prospects profit the most. Moreover, Hämäläinen (2002) concludes that in this case "the effectiveness of training programs is negatively related to overall unemployment". This differs from the results presented by Cavaco et al. (2005), which indicate that training had no positive effects for individuals with low re-employment probabilities during high and persistent unemployment.

Zhang (2003), on the other hand, reports a pro-cyclical pattern for training measures in Norway, implying that stronger impacts are felt the better the labor market prospects are. The study also estimates a positive overall impact on the transition rate from unemployment to employment, with higher benefits for women. Another Norwegian study by Raaum et al. (2002) investigates the long-run impact for LMT on earnings. This is the largest program in Norway and mainly comprises vocational training and to a lower extent basic courses. The authors find increased earnings for participants with recent labor market experience over the post-treatment period of 5 years, whereas labor market entrants have lower and insignificant effects. The cost-benefit analysis indicates positive gains for experienced participants, whereas the direct costs exceed the benefits for labor market entrants. In addition, the program is cost-beneficial for experienced women, whereas the benefits for experienced men are limited by their costs.

Private sector incentive programs

The two prevailing ALMP measures that target incentives regarding private sector employment are wage subsidies and start-up grants for self-employment. The former receive much more attention in the evaluation literature. For Germany, Jaenichen (2002) collects administrative data from selected Federal Employment Agency districts throughout Germany covering the period 1999–2001. She finds that receiving integration subsidies significantly reduces the probability to be registered as unemployed. Hujer et al. (2004) examine whether employing subsidized workers affects the employment development of firms, but do not find any significant effects.

The evaluation of the Italian Mobility List by Paggiaro et al. (2005) concerns a policy that combines an active component, i.e. a wage subsidy to employers who hire a worker from the List, with a passive component, i.e. an income support to selected workers on the List. The aim is to assess the effects of the Italian Mobility list, for the time period 1995–1999, on the probability of transition to a new job, dividing between workers eligible for the active component only and workers having also an income support. The authors find that an additional year of eligibility has a significant and positive impact on employment rates for men eligible for the active component only, whereas the effect is significant but negative for those having income support also. For women no effect is found.

The country report from Denmark (cf. section 6 of chapter 4) finds that this type of program is clearly the most successful measure used in the Danish ALMP. A common result of virtually all evaluation studies is that participation in a private sector employment program has positive employment effects (Rosholm, Svarer 2004; Bolvig et al. 2003; Graversen 2004; Munch, Skipper 2004; Danish Economic Council 2002; Jespersen et al. 2004). One study does not find a statistically significant effect (Rosholm, Svarer 2004) and another study only finds a small positive net effect (Munch, Skipper 2004). One further exception to the general picture is the study by Graversen/Jensen (2004), which finds that there are no significant mean effects of participation in private sector employment programs compared to participation in other programs.

By contrast to the positive effect of Polish training measures in the 1990s mentioned above, private sector wage subsidies displayed negative treatment effects at the time (Kluve et al. 2005). This finding, however, seems to be mostly the result of unemployment benefit regulations that restore eligibility after program participation. Again, more recent evidence does not exist. For Spain, Cueto (2003) compares two types of employment incentives in the region *Asturias*: start-up subsidies and hiring subsidies for employing an unemployed worker on a permanent contract. The results indicate that start-up subsidies perform better than hiring subsidies in terms of job stability and occupation rates.

Forslund et al. (2004) evaluate the impact of Swedish employment programs in the private sector targeted at the long-term unemployed. The subsidies cover 50% of wages for a maximum period of 6 months. They report positive treatment effects on unemployment duration, which decreased by an average of 8 months, following a locking-in period due to participation. Although they do not examine the macroeconomic impact, the authors stress that there is evidence for large deadweight and substitution effects, which might offset the overall positive results.

Zhang (2003) examines the impact of numerous active measures for Norway. Regarding wage subsidies, Zhang (2003) reports significant positive effects on the employment probability for participants. Whereas the transition rate to employment is negative at the beginning of the treatment, it turns positive with elapsed treatment duration. Benefits for women are higher than for men. However, participants in the scheme are mainly qualified and ready-to-work individuals. Moreover, Zhang (2003) reports a pro-cyclical pattern, implying that wage subsidies have higher pay-offs in times of better labor market conditions.

Direct employment in the public sector

Direct job creation in the public sector is an important active labor market program in many countries (Tables 26 and 27). In Germany, for instance, public employment schemes have been used on a large scale since the early

1990s, in particular in the Eastern part shortly after reunification. For quite some time these measures could be evaluated only for East Germany, because corresponding data sources were limited to East Germany only. A set of evaluation studies exists, most of which do not find positive effects on the employment rate. Eichler/Lechner (2002) find positive effects for men only, Bergemann (2005) for women only.

Caliendo et al. (2003, 2004, 2005a, 2005b) use the recently derived administrative data for the years 2000-2002, which provides information on program effects in West Germany for the first time. Their results, too, reveal negative mean employment effects. Positive employment effects are limited to few socio-demographic groups, namely women over 50, long-term unemployed and hard-to-place women in West Germany as well as female long-term unemployed in East Germany.

The Danish experiences with public sector employment programs are equally disappointing. Overall, the evidence for Denmark suggests negative effects similar to those of training programs (cf. above), i.e. participation in a public sector employment program tends to increase unemployment durations. Again, however, this result is primarily due to strong locking-in effects. Four out of six recent studies (Rosholm, Svarer 2004; Graversen 2004; Munch, Skipper 2004; Danish Economic Council 2002) find these negative effects, whereas one study (Jespersen et al. 2004) finds that public sector employment programs sometimes give rise to a net economic surplus. Another study (Bolvig et al. 2003) finds positive effects, but is analyzing private and public sector employment programs together, i.e. as one type of program. Hence, the results of the latter study are not pointing directly at public sector employment programs as having positive effects.

A Public Works scheme in Poland in the 1990s displayed negative treatment effects (Kluve et al. 2005), and more recent evidence has not been produced. France has some direct employment schemes for youths that also show zero or negative effects on employment probabilities (cf. also below). The review by Zhang (2003) for Norway also investigates the impact of employment programs in the public sector. These programs are mainly targeted towards long-term unemployed and participants with low qualifications. Overall, the programs have no positive effects on the transition rate to employment, but at least some positive effects for youths. A different target group, social assistance recipients, was the subject of the Norwegian study by Lorentzen/Dahl (2005). The overall results indicate a negative and insignificant effect for employment programs.

These negative overall results are in accordance with the Swedish findings by Fredriksson/Johansson (2003), who report a reduced outflow to employment of around 40% for job creation in the public sector, with even more negative long-run effects. Further, participation is strongly associated with locking-in effects. These effects do not only reduce the overall outflow rate, but even more strongly the outflow to jobs outside the home region.

Also for Sweden, Korpi (1994) finds significant positive effects of relief work on the duration of employment of youth in the first half of the 1980s. Recent Swedish studies evaluate relief work only in comparison to other measures. For instance, Sianesi (2002) finds that recruitment subsidies and trainee replacement schemes generate significantly better results as relief work. Carling/Richardson (2001) compare, among other things, relief work and the workplace introduction, API. The reduction in unemployment duration is significantly lower for API as for relief work participants.

Services and sanctions

As detailed in chapter 2, this category comprises all measures that aim at increasing job search and job match efficiency. This includes different types of services, e.g. job search assistance, interviews at the PES offices, job clubs, counseling, and the monitoring of the participants' job search behavior. In addition, this category comprises "stick-type" measures like benefit sanctions that are imposed if individuals do not comply with required search behavior or refuse acceptable job offers.

Across countries, there exists a relatively large economic literature that focuses on counseling and monitoring. This is the one measure for which several studies have used social experiments to access its effectiveness. In a first experiment in the Netherlands, Gorter/Kalb (1996) analyze the effects of *extended* counseling and monitoring on the duration of unemployment. Gorter/Kalb (1996) find that the effect of counseling and monitoring on the job finding hazard is modest and insignificant for individuals who previously had a permanent contract and significantly negative for individuals who previously had a temporary contract. They explain this big difference by stating that the aim of counseling and monitoring is to provide unemployed workers with a permanent contract, which might be difficult to obtain for individuals who were previously in temporary employment. Furthermore, they find that counseling and monitoring significantly increases the job application rate.

Similarly/van den Berg/van der Klaauw (2006) investigate the effect of the *regular* counseling and monitoring in the Netherlands on unemployment duration, on the basis of a randomized experiment, for the less disadvantaged workers. The empirical results show a very small and insignificant positive effect of counseling and monitoring on the probability of finding work. Since counseling and monitoring is a relatively inexpensive policy, the benefits in terms of unpaid unemployment insurance benefits are – 6 months after inflow into unemployment – approximately the same as the costs of providing counseling and monitoring.

In another experiment in the UK, Dolton/O'Neill (2002) examine the impact of the Restart program, which combines monitoring and job search assistance. Overall, the Restart program has a significant positive effect in qualitative terms of a 6 percentage points lower unemployment rate for men even after 5 years, but no substantial long-run impact for women. A cost-benefit analysis indicates that these programs are a cost-effective means to reduce long-term unemployment. In addition, the authors elaborate that the threat component might be responsible for the short-run effects, whereas job search assistance may account for the long-run impact of the programs.

Finally, in an experiment conducted in Hungary, Micklewright/Nagy (2005) find that stricter monitoring only increases the re-employment of women above 30 years old. This is a group of individuals that typically does not devote much effort to job search. A feature of the monitoring in Hungary is that the case worker also acts as a matching agent that offers suitable vacancies to unemployed workers.

The non-experimental research on Job Search Assistance seems to arrive at mostly positive conclusions across countries. In Denmark, these measures are usually captured in the residual category "other programs", against which training, wage subsidies, etc., are being evaluated. While this residual is clearly a rather heterogeneous category, the fact that the other programs mostly display zero or negative effects does shed some positive light on job search assistance.

For France, Crépon et al. (2005) find a significantly positive impact in qualitative terms on the transition rate from unemployment to employment (higher) and on unemployment recurrence (lower) for individuals with higher risks of unemployment. Centeno et al. (2005) examine the Portuguese Inserjovem and Reage programs, which are targeted towards youth and long-term unemployed. They report at most a small and insignificant impact on the unemployment duration (a reduction less than 1 month). In addition, they find a negative but insignificant effect on wages; this effect is greatest for men, whereas women do not see benefits from the program at all.

The studies by Hofer/Weber (2004a) and Hofer/Weber (2004b) investigate the impact of Austrian programs. The former one reports an increased employment probability by 15% within the first four months, and the latter one reports a decrease of the unemployment duration by 20–30% in the first year. Nevertheless, these positive results occur only in the short-run, and diminish over time. They also conclude that the more disadvantaged individuals and long-term unemployed require different programs, because they face substantial problems that cannot be solved by job search assistance only.

Regarding the effects of sanctions, Abbring/Van den Berg/Van Ours (2005) focus on unemployment insurance recipients and Van den Berg/Van der Klaauw and Van Ours (2004) study welfare recipients in the Netherlands. In the empirical analyses the unanticipated nature of imposing sanctions is exploited. The empirical results of the former study indicate that the sanction probability increases during the first 16 weeks of collecting unemployment insurance and remains constant afterwards. The effects of imposing a sanction on the transition rate from unemployment to employment are substantial and significant. Imposing a sanction increases the re-employment probabilities of the sanctioned worker. Sanctions seem to have a somewhat larger effect on the re-employment probabilities of females than of males.

Van den Berg/Van der Klaauw/Van Ours (2004) find that the sanction rate is highest between the 6th and 12th month of collecting welfare benefits, which coincides with the time period in which the first thorough investigation of files occurs. The effect of imposing a sanction on the transition rate from welfare to work is both substantial and significant. A sanction raises the exit rate to work with about 140%.

Despite these two evaluation studies on sanctions in the Netherlands, and despite the fact that Grubb (1999) notes in his survey that sanctions exist in many countries, the empirical literature on the effects of sanctions remains limited. Lalive/Van Ours/Zweimüller (2005) find for Switzerland a smaller effect of actually imposing sanctions than the ones found in both Dutch studies. There are two important differences between the Swiss and the Dutch policy regime on sanctions. First, in Switzerland there exists a system of warning unemployed workers prior to imposing a sanction. Roughly one third of the warnings is followed by a sanction. Lalive/Van Ours/Zweimüller (2005) show that the effect of a warning is as large as the effect of actually imposing a sanction. Second, Switzerland has a much stricter sanction regime than the Netherlands (e.g. Grubb, 1999). Whereas in the Netherlands, the annual sanction rate during an spell of unemployment is below 5%, in Switzerland, this can be as high as 12%. In the Netherlands, re-employment rates of sanctioned individuals are often very low and there is much room for increases. In Switzerland, also individuals who already have higher re-employment rates get punished and therefore there is less room for increases in re-employment rates for sanctioned workers.

Youth programs

This category encompasses a substantial variety of programs, including training programs, wage subsidies or job search assistance, specifically targeted towards youth. Their main objectives often are not only to enhance employment prospects but also to foster the education of young unemployed. Tackling youth unemployment plays a very important role due to potential negative long-term effects like discouragement or stigmatization. As mentioned earlier, the results from previous research about the impacts of youth programs are rather disappointing.

Since the French labor market has been plagued by high youth unemployment for several decades, ALMPs targeted at youths play a particularly important role in this country. Brodaty et al. (2002) analyze the impact of workplace training programs in the private sector, workfare programs in the public sector and other programs (e.g. training) for the two cohorts 1986-1988 and 1995–1998. Despite a similar macroeconomic environment they report differing results for both periods. Whereas all programs show positive effects between 1986 and 1988, the results turn negative for the second cohort. One possible explanation might be the labor market situation with higher overall and youth unemployment rates in the second cohort. Finally, they stress that private subsidies yield better results for the short-term unemployed, whereas other programs including training work better for the long-term unemployed youths. In general, from the available evaluations on youth programs in France (cf. also Bonnal et al. 1997; Cavaco et al. 2005) it follows that training schemes in terms of apprenticeships and similar contracts have positive effects on the transition to employment for participants. The measures enhancing job search activity introduced with the labor policy reform in 2001 also seem to be effective (Crepon et al. 2005; Fougère et al. 2005).

Cockx/Göbel (2004) evaluate the impact of subsidized employment for the young unemployed in Belgium and find rather mixed results. They report positive effects for women on the transition rate from unemployment. The transition rate is positive for men only in the first year, and afterwards turns negative. The Finnish study by Hämäläinen/ Ollikainen (2004) finds positive effects of increased employment and earnings for employment programs in the private and public sector even after four years. They report similar results for labor market training with the difference of vanishing positive effects in the fourth year. Nevertheless, they find a slightly negative impact for youth practical training, which is the least expensive but also the largest Finnish program for youth unemployed.

Similar to other EU countries, also in Sweden special attention is paid to the problem of youth unemployment, and special active measures for youths exist. Larsson (2002) examines the impact of youth practice and AMU on employment and earnings for youths aged 20–24. The study finds that participation in youth practice or labor market training has negative short-term effects on employment and earnings, which become insignificant regarding the long-term effects after two years of the program start. In summary, the author concludes that youth practice is "less harmful" than AMU.

The "New Deal for Young People" was implemented in the U.K. in 1998. It is a rather extensive program combining mandatory job search assistance with an additional option of training, subsidized employment, voluntary work or work with the environmental task force for young individuals within their first six month of unemployment. Blundell et al. (2003) restrict their evaluation to the assessment of job search assistance and the employment subsidy option. They report positive and significant effects for men within the first four months, which diminish over the subsequent two periods. The effects for women are also positive, but they are smaller and less precise. Furthermore, van Reenen (2003) extends this evaluation with an additional cost-benefit analysis. He finally concludes that the social benefits exceed the social costs. Moreover, he finds that job search assistance is the most cost-effective method. An additional evaluation of the New Deal has been conducted by Lissenburgh (2004) who compares the impact of all four options. He reports that the employment option was the most effective, followed by extended job search assistance, whereas work in the environmental task force was the least effective. However, participants in the employment schemes were usually more advantaged and therefore it is questionable if an extension of this option might yield equally favorable results.

Several studies remain that report no or even negative effects for youth programs. The study by Centeno et al. (2005) investigates the impact on wages for job search assistance and small basic skills courses for Portugal. They show that the Inserjovem program targeted specifically towards youth had a negative but insignificant impact on wages. Hardoy (2001) investigates the impact of employment, vocational, training and combination courses in Norway and reports a rather dismal performance. Moreover, she finds no positive effect for any program, and negative effects for vocational and training programs. Nevertheless, there were at least some small positive effects for female participants in employment and combination programs, and for the 16–20 year old participants in employment programs. Finally, the Italian study by Caroleo/Pastore (2001) concludes that training and ALMPs in general are unlikely to be effective for youth unemployed.

Measures for the disabled

It is obvious that disabled persons are often disadvantaged on the labor market, facing lower employment probabilities and longer durations of unemployment compared to the non-disabled. Despite the fact that some countries spend a relatively large amount on active measures for disabled individuals (Netherlands, Norway and Sweden with spending of around 0.5% of GDP, and Denmark and Germany with spending of around 0.3% of GDP in 2000) very little empirical evidence exists on measures targeted at disabled individuals.

One exception is the study by Aakvik (2002) who investigates the long-term impact of vocational rehabilitation programs in Norway. These programs offer general education, which can be either the integration of disabled individuals into the ordinary public school system or specific classroom training for these unemployed. He reports that participants have an eight percentage points higher employment rate than non-participants. However, there are some indications for cream-skimming participants who are more likely to be employed, although this is contradicted by an increased participation probability for unemployed living in areas with higher local unemployment rates. Adjusting for observed differences between treatment and control group yields an employment rate for participants which is only three percentage points higher compared to the control group. Overall, he concludes that the program has no significant impact on the employment rate of participants.

Another study for Norway has been conducted by Aakvik/Dahl (2004). They investigate the impact of labor market enterprises, which are a combination of training and work experience schemes available for a maximum period of two years. If these measures are unsuccessful for the individuals' transition to ordinary employment they can enter an additional sheltered work option. Unfortunately, the authors cannot answer the counterfactual question due to a lack of suitable data. Instead, they merely provide a comparison of exit rates into ordinary employment over time which increased from 28 percent to 39 percent during the period 1995-1999. Under the assumption of constant effects for non-participants over this period, they indicate a treatment effect of 11 percentage points. At best, this is a tentative finding providing an upper boundary for the true impact of the program.

The study by Høglund/Holm (2002) examines the impact of vocational rehabilitation programs for long-term sick-listed workers in Denmark. The study distinguishes between employment with an old employer and a new employer as the outcome measures of interest. Estimation results indicate that educational measures only have a positive but insignificant impact on the transition rate to a new employer, whereas they have no direct effect on the transition rate to an old employer. Due to negative locking-in effects that offset the small positive effect of the program the authors conclude that the net effect on the transition rate to new employers is zero.

2.2   Results from macroeconomic studies

Numerous evaluation studies emphasize the importance to further investigate net effects on aggregate employment and unemployment for a "more accurate assessment of the impacts of the programs" (Heckman et al. 1999). However, the assessment of general-equilibrium effects requires extensive data and a theoretical framework that explains the relevant labor market variables. As already pointed out several times above, the number of macroeconomic studies on European ALMP has remained relatively small; Table 29 in the Appendix displays 12 recent macroeconomic studies.

The Spanish study by Davia et al. (2002) examines the effects of various active measures at the aggregate level. The authors find a significant reduction of the unemployment rate for training programs and measures promoting employment contracts without economic incentives. Nevertheless, only the latter ones yield positive and significant effects on the outflow rate from unemployment to employment, whereas training programs fail to enhance employment. In a study for the Netherlands, Jongen et al. (2003) examine the macroeconomic impact of subsidized employment in the private sector, relief jobs and training programs in the public sector. The results of their simulation indicate a positive net employment effect for relief jobs. Nevertheless, the effects on the aggregate level are reversed, because a higher participation in relief jobs crowds out regular employment. These results are in accordance with the results for training programs, which increase the employment rates for participants, but also exert crowding out effects resulting in a decreased output. In contrast, subsidies in the private sector only have a rather modest employment effect, whereas they raise the overall output and hence are more effective than training programs on an aggregate level.

Albrecht et al. (2005) investigate the impact of the Swedish Knowledge Lift on the individual level (cf. above), but they also utilize an equilibrium search model to examine the impacts on labor market equilibrium. They report positive effects for the treated and a shift in the job composition across the two skill categories. The upgrading of skills from low-skilled to medium-skilled workers increases the number of vacancies and the wage levels for medium-skilled, whereas the remaining low-skilled face decreasing wages and more difficulties to find a job. Finally, they conclude that the general equilibrium effects are 1.5 to 2 points larger than the positive effects on the individual level. Johansson (2001) examines the impact of Swedish labor market programs on labor force participation and indicates substantial positive effects, although these positive effects are only temporary. Nevertheless, she concludes that labor market programs might reduce business-cycle variation; they may prevent that individuals drop out of the labor force during an economic downturn.

Hujer/Zeiss (2003) examine the macroeconomic impacts of training and direct job creation measures in West Germany. The authors report a negative and significant impact for job creation schemes, which tend to reduce the search efforts among participants. Moreover, they emphasize that the negative impact mainly arises because of the institutional setup of this program. The created jobs are only additionally generated jobs failing to enhance the employment probability for a regular job. In addition, the study finds no effects for vocational training programs. The economic situation was characterized by a shortage of labor demand, leading the authors to conclude that a program that intends to affect the supply side might not have positive effects during a period with problems arising from the demand side.

Another study by Hujer et al. (2002) analyzes job creation schemes and vocational training to point out differential effects between East and West Germany. Regarding West Germany, they conclude that job creation schemes show positive effects only in the short-run, but they fail to reduce the job seeker rate in the long-run. Furthermore, vocational training has a positive impact on the labor market situation not only in the short-run but also in the long-run. In contrast, the results for East Germany are less precise. Whereas job creation schemes have no significant effect on the job seeker rate, the results for vocational training vary considerably with the choice of estimator, which does not allow a profound statement about their impact.

Fertig et al. (2002) investigate the impact of several ALMPs on a (semi-) aggregate level. Their results for Germany indicate that training programs for unemployed with no formal job qualification and for employed individuals at risk of becoming unemployed have a positive effect on the net-outflow from unemployment. Moreover, positive effects are also reported for wage subsidies, whereas public employment programs in East Germany have a significantly negative impact on the net-outflow from unemployment.

The only study that evaluates the macroeconomic impact of youth programs has been conducted by Filges/Larsen (2001) for Denmark. The YUP program provides vocational training and involves an incentive and a sanction component. The incentive entails the participation in a specially designed program for 18 months, whereas the sanction entails a cut of unemployment benefits by 50 percent during treatment. The analysis concludes that these programs do not crowd out ordinary employment if the participation spell is sufficiently long. Even if crowding out may occur this may be offset by an increase of skilled workers, which finally results in a reduction of unemployment. The authors emphasize the importance of the incentive for the success of the program. If the incentive is not successful and only the sanction is effective, this induces more workers to acquire ordinary education.

The Finnish study by Kangasharju/Venetoklis (2003) uses a different outcome measure and investigates the impact of wage subsidies on the employment in firms. They report an increased employment effect, which is nevertheless not large enough to avoid a substitution effect. Moreover, the subsidies are mainly a substitute for private employment expenditures by firms. Finally, there are no indications for a displacement effect; subsidized firms do not harm non-subsidized firms in the same industry and geographical region.

Van der Linden (2005) utilizes an equilibrium matching model to estimate the impact of counseling programs in Belgium. He reports that increased entry into the programs exerts positive direct effects on the employment rate, but also detrimental indirect effects through wage shifts and a changing search behavior among non-participants. Boone/van Ours (2004) investigate the impact of training, job search assistance through PES and subsidized jobs for the OECD 20. They report positive effects for labor market training and PES, with stronger effects on the reduction of the unemployment rate for LMT. In contrast, subsidized jobs have no positive effect on the unemployment rate. Boone et al. (2002) apply a search equilibrium framework to assess the design of optimal unemployment insurance combined with monitoring and sanctions. They conclude that introduction of monitoring and sanctions is associated with a welfare improvement.

This contrasts the results in the French study by Tanguy (2004), which reports negative effects for monitoring and sanctions on the search intensity. The results of a simulation analysis indicate that the effects on the search intensity increase the unemployment rate and finally reduce welfare. The author argues that these effects are the result of a shift in job search behavior from informal channels like personal job search to formal channels through PES.

2.3   Overall assessment

The preceding overview has summarized the main findings from current European evaluation studies, and illustrated the substantial heterogeneity that exists across countries, regarding types and details of measures, rationales for their implementation, and, in particular, estimates of program effectiveness.

Training programs are the most widely used active labor market measure in Europe. The assessment of the effectiveness shows rather mixed results; treatment effect estimates are negative in a few case, and often insignificant or modestly positive. Still, there are several indications that training programs do increase participants' post-treatment employment probability, in particular for participants with better labor market prospects and for women. However, this pattern does not hold for all studies. Locking-in effects of training are frequently reported, though it remains unclear to what extent these are really entirely undesirable, and not rather a necessary element of this type of program.

The more recent literature on the evaluation of training emphasizes the need to consider long-run impacts. Such an assessment has become increasingly possible due to extended data. There are indeed indications from these studies that positive treatment effects of training exist in the long-run. Moreover, if negative locking-in effects were to matter, these would be outweighed by the long-run benefits of program participation. The existence and direction of a relation between the business cycle and the effectiveness of training programs is not clear from the evidence: Some studies report a pro-cyclical pattern, while others report the opposite.

Private sector incentive programs entail wage subsidies and start-up loans. Whereas the latter have rarely been evaluated in European countries, several evaluations of wage subsidy schemes exist. The findings are generally positive. Virtually all studies that evaluate private sector wage subsidy programs – such as several studies from Denmark, but also evidence from Sweden, Norway, Italy, etc – assert beneficial impacts on individual employment probability.

These encouraging findings, however, have to be qualified to some extent, since the studies usually disregard potential displacement and substitution effects or deadweight loss that may be associated with wage subsidy schemes.

In contrast to the positive results for private sector incentive programs, direct employment in the public sector rarely shows positive effects. The evidence across countries suggests that treatment effects of public sector job creation on individual employment probabilities are often insignificant, and frequently negative. Some studies identify positive effects for certain socio-demographic groups, but no clear general pattern emerges from these findings. Potentially negative general-equilibrium are usually not taken into account. Though these measures may therefore not be justified for efficiency reasons, they may be justified for equity reasons, possibly exerting positive social impacts by avoiding discouragement and social exclusion among participants. Corresponding outcome measures, however, are difficult to assess empirically, such that the literature has focused on treatment impacts on actual employment.

A general assessment of Services and Sanctions across countries indicates that these measures can be an effective means to reduce unemployment. The results appear even more promising given that these measures are generally the least expensive type of ALMP. Moreover, several experimental studies exist for this program type, producing particularly robust evaluation results. There are some indications that services such as job search assistance or counseling and monitoring mainly work for individuals with sufficient skills and better labor market prospects, but less so for the more disadvantaged individuals. This pattern, however, is not entirely clear, since some studies conclude that the opposite is the case.

Whereas in many countries some type of sanction for non-compliance with job search requirements exists, only few sanction regimes have been evaluated. The studies generally find a positive effect on re-employment rates, both for actually imposing sanctions and for having a benefit system including sanctions. A particularly well-balanced system of job search services and sanctions, combined with a set of other active measures such as training and employment subsidies, appears to be the "New Deal" in the UK. This points to the conjecture that the interplay between the services provided by the PES, the requirements demanded from the unemployed individual, and the portfolio of active measures plays an important role regarding ALMP effectiveness. The comprehensive activation approach implemented in Denmark, for instance, also appears promising, even though it clearly requires substantial effort.

For youth programs, no clear pattern arises from the cross-country summary of studies. There are some indications that wage subsidies work for young unemployed individuals, especially the ones with a more advantaged background. However, some studies do not find this effect, and again potential general-equilibrium effects are disregarded. Youth training programs sometimes display positive treatment effects on employment probability, but negative results are also reported. Whereas the extensive "New Deal" in the UK illustrates the potential effectiveness of Services and Sanctions for youths, this result is not found in evaluations from other countries (e.g. Portugal).

Regarding programs for the disabled, due to a lack of evaluation studies no conclusive evidence exists. The results of the limited empirical evidence available are rather disappointing. Vocational rehabilitation programs seem to have no positive and significant impact on the employment rates of disabled unemployed.

The limited set of available macroeconomic evaluation studies also does not point to a consistent pattern. There are some indications for positive effects on net employment for training programs in general and also for youth, while other results indicate that these programs only reduce unemployment but do not enhance employment, or have no net employment impact due to crowding out effects. Several macro studies, however, underline the dismal performance of direct job creation schemes in the public sector. Rather mixed results are reported for wage subsidies in the private sector. Some studies reveal an overall positive net employment effect, but substitution effects may outweigh a positive employment effect. Finally, job search assistance and counseling exert positive direct effects on the employment rate, but may have negative effects through shifts in wages and job search behavior as well. Monitoring and sanctions have the potential to improve welfare. These results underline the importance of collecting further empirical evidence on an aggregate level, since some macroeconomic results confirm corresponding microeconomic evidence, whereas other results indicate reinforced or even reversed effects. The number of macro studies is quite small relative to the set of microeconomic program evaluations in Europe.

In summary, looking at the overall assessment of the available evidence, it is difficult to detect consistent patterns, even though some tentative findings emerge. The following quantitative analysis builds on these tentative findings and constitutes an attempt to identify such consistent patterns.

3   Quantitative Analysis

The previous chapters – in particular the country reports – have summarized a large number of studies and a substantial body of evidence on the effectiveness of ALMPs across Europe. Several preliminary hypotheses are suggested by this collection of evidence. First, sanctions and job search services appear to be relatively effective in raising employment outcomes. Second, training programs seem to have relatively small effects at best, and often have a significant employment impact only in the longer run. Third, programs based on direct employment in the public sector typically have no significant effect, or even a negative effect, on participants' post-program employment outcomes. Given the substantial heterogeneity across the programs reviewed in the earlier chapters, however, and the difficulties in comparing programs across countries, it is difficult to draw any firm conclusions on the fundamental questions of "Which programs work? For whom? And under what conditions?"

The goal of this chapter is to try to systematically synthesize the evidence reviewed in the earlier chapters, and to assess whether the available data support a set of stronger conclusions than can be derived from any single study. The framework is that of *meta-analysis:* a technique for analyzing and summarizing the results of different studies, each of which is focused on the same question (in our case, the size and direction of the impact of a particular ALMP on post-program employment probabilities). This idea was first implemented by Kluve/Schmidt (2002), who summarized a total of 53 European active labor market programs. In this chapter we describe the meta analysis approach in more detail, and attempt to summarize all European evaluation studies that are available to date.

The basic idea of a meta-analysis is to construct and analyze a data set in which each observation represents a particular program evaluation. For each observation in the data set the outcome of interest is an indicator for whether the program was found to have a positive, zero, or negative effect. The goal of the meta-analysis is to relate this outcome to quantitative information on the nature of the underlying program – including the type of program and the institutional and economic environment in which it was offered – and on the evaluation methodology used to derive the estimated impact. Using standard multiple regression techniques, it is possible to obtain a *quantitative* assessment of the factors associated with relative success or failure of various types of ALMPs, in different European countries and in different economic and institutional contexts. Meta-analysis techniques are widely used in the medical sciences, and have also been used with great success in other areas of social sciences. They are particularly appropriate in the ALMP context because of the wide variety of different programs and evaluation methods that have been used in the literature, and because of the clear importance of being able to draw palpable and credible findings from this diverse literature to inform future policy choices. A meta-analysis has significant advantages over simple descriptive reviews of existing programs and studies (such as Martin 2000; Martin, Grubb 2001) because the analysis helps to identify systematic differences across the different types of ALMPs, while controlling for other factors, like economic conditions during the period of the evaluation or the particular methodology used to derive the estimated impact. Given the rapid growth in the number of ALMP evaluations in the past few years, it is also an opportune time to incorporate the newest studies into our summary.

3.1 Structure of the data

The meta analysis is based on a data set that is constructed from available microeconometric evaluation studies across European countries. A similar exercise would clearly be desirable for macroeconomic studies as well; unfortunately, however, the small number of macro studies precludes such an analysis. The micro studies listed in Table 28 constitute the basis of the data. The sample includes a large number of recent studies, as well as many studies from the 1980s and early 1990s that are analyzed in Kluve/Schmidt (2002) and Heckman et al. (1999).

Each observation in the data corresponds to the evaluation of a particular program. That is, it is possible that a given evaluation *study* yields two or more data points, if e.g. if the study evaluates both a training program and a wage subsidy program in a given country. In sum, we have N=137 observations in the data, a substantially larger number than Kluve/Schmidt (2002) were able to use for their meta-analysis (N=53). These 137 observations originate from 95 different evaluation studies[2].

For each observation, the outcome variable of interest is given by the treatment effect that is found for the program being evaluated. The quantitative analysis (below) first considers a binomial outcome, i.e. whether the study finds a positive treatment effect or not. This is the procedure used in Kluve/Schmidt (2002). Given the much larger number of studies, it is also possible in a second step to refine this analysis using a trinomial outcome, and take into account whether the effect is positive, zero, or negative. We present results for both approaches. In the overall sample, 75 studies (i.e. 54.7%) find a positive effect, whereas 62 (i.e. 45.3%) do not. Further distinguishing between zero and negative treatment effect estimates, 29 studies (21.2%) find a negative impact, whereas 33 studies (i.e. 24.1%) attribute an effect of zero to the program.

In the meta-analysis the program effect from each study is related to four broad "categories" of independent variables, capturing (a) the type of program, (b) the study design, and (c) the institutional context and (d) the economic background in the country at the time the specific program was run. This analysis is conducted using either a probit framework (in the case where outcomes are classified as positive or not) or a multinomial probit (in the case where the evaluation outcome is classified into three categories). The types of ALMP programs considered are exactly those outlined above and discussed in the country reports, i.e. training programs, private sector incentive schemes, direct employment programs in the public sector, and Services and Sanctions. Slightly more than half of the observations (70) investigate the impact of training programs. 23 studies analyze private sector incentive schemes; whereas 26 studies investigate public sector employment programs and 21 studies focus on Services and Sanctions.[3] We also include a dummy variable for programs specifically targeting the young among the unemployed, which is frequently the case (25.6% of the available evaluations) [4].

A key feature of our analysis is that we control for the methodology or "study design" used to derive the estimated impact. The gold standard of scientific evaluation is a randomized design. Hence, we include an indicator for whether the evaluation was based on a randomized experiment, which is the case for N=9 observations. Also, we include dummies for the decade in which

---

[2]   Not all studies in Table 28 could be included in the quantitative analysis. For some this is not feasible, if e.g. the study merely pools several programs together and only reports overall effects, or if treatment effects are reported relative to results from other programs, rather than non-participation.

[3]   These numbers sum up to 140 rather than 137, since three observations consider incentive schemes mixing private and public sector and therefore cannot be differentiated in this regard.

[4]   The indicator for disabled has been excluded, because only three observations were available.

the program was run. Most programs for which evaluations exist were implemented in the 1990s (81 observations), whereas only 4 observations are from the 1970s. 16 observations come from the 2000s, and 36 from programs run in the 1980s. Moreover, in one specification we distinguish whether the size of the sample that the study uses is small (N<1000), medium (1000=N=10000), or large (N>10000)[5]. 43% of the studies are small, 40% are medium-sized, and 17% are based on large samples.

Four indicators are used to capture the institutional labor market context, particularly the regulations that may influence the willingness of employers to hire ALMP participants, and the willingness of participants to take jobs. In the former category, we include an index for dismissal protection, and two indicators regarding fixed term and temporary employment. The dismissal protection index takes on values between 0.8 (for the UK in the early 1980s) to 4.3 (for Portugal in the late 1990s). The indicator of regulation over fixed-term contracts takes on values from 0 (for several countries including the UK) to 5.3 (for Belgium in the early 1990s). The index of control over temporary-work agencies takes on values from 0.5 (for several countries including Denmark) to 5.5 (for Sweden, during the period from the 1970s to the early 1990s). All three indicators are taken from the 2004 OECD Employment Outlook. The variable representing the willingness of participants to take jobs is the gross replacement rate, taken from OECD 2004 "Benefits and Wages: OECD Indicators". This takes on values between 17.5% (for UK in the late 1990s) and 63.7% (for Denmark in 1996).

Finally, the economic background against which we would like to interpret program effectiveness is captured by three variables: the unemployment rate; the annual growth rate of GDP; and the current rate of expenditures on ALMP as a percentage of GDP. These variables are measured at the time when the particular program was actually running. If the period of program operation spans several years, the respective averages are considered. In the data, the unemployment rate ranges from 1.9% (for Sweden in the late 1970s) to 16.5% (for Ireland in the late 1980s). GDP growth varies between –0.7 (for Finland during the time period 1990–1995) and +7.1 (for Estonia during 2000–2002). The ALMP spending index ranges from 0.03% of GDP (Slovak Republic 1993–1998) to 2.68% of GDP (Sweden in the early 1990s). The country studies above provide further details on the economic context and development for each specific country.

3.2 Empirical results

As outlined above, the implementation of the quantitative analysis first considers a binomial outcome, i.e. whether the evaluation of a program finds a positive treatment effect or not. Table 20 reports the marginal effects of the basic specification of a corresponding probit regression.

---

[5] Besides these thresholds on total sample size it is required that both treated and comparison samples are sufficiently large (about half the corresponding threshold) to enter a higher category. That is, for instance, a study using a sample of 100 program participants and 900 comparison individuals would still be a „small" study.

Table 20. Effectiveness of European ALMP: Quantitative Analysis, Specification 1

	Marginal Effect	t-ratio
(a) Type of program and target group:		
Direct employment program	**−0.314**	−2.32
Private sector incentive scheme	**0.283**	2.26
Services and Sanctions	**0.377**	2.11
Young workers	***−0.357***	−2.99
(b) Study design and time period:		
Experimental design	−0.351	−1.43
Program implemented in the		
1970s	0.353	1.52
1980s	0.224	1.55
2000s	0.077	0.59
(c) Institutional context on the labor market:		
Index for dismissal protection regulation	**−0.151**	−2.11
Index for fixed-term contracts regulation	0.042	0.85
Index for temporary work regulation	0.005	0.13
Gross replacement rate	−0.006	−1.53
(d) Macroeconomic background:		
Unemployment rate	***0.051***	2.81
ALMP expenditure (% of GDP)	−0.077	−0.84
GDP growth	−0.036	−0.89

Number of observations = 137. – Pseudo R^2 = 0.204. – Notes: The dependent variable is an indicator (1/0) variable, reflecting a positive estimate of the program effect. Table entries document the marginal effect (evaluated at the sample mean) in the corresponding probit regression, i.e. the difference in the predicted probability for achieving a positive treatment effect which arises from a marginal change in a continuous explanatory factor (such as the GDP growth rate) or which arises from changing an indicator among the explanatory factors (such as the indicator for an experimental study design) from 0 to 1. T-ratios of the marginal effects are reported in the third column. Marginal effects printed in *italics* indicate marginal significance (10%-level), marginal effects printed in **boldface** indicate statistical significance (5%-level), and marginal effects printed in ***boldface and italics*** indicate high significance (1%-level). The underlying standard errors adjust for clustering by study.

Looking first at the set of variables summarizing the program type (in panel (a)), we adopt as a base category the "classic" ALMP training programs aimed at human capital enhancement. Relative to this baseline, the estimates show that both private sector incentive schemes and Services and Sanctions are associated with a higher probability of yielding a positive treatment effect. For Services and Sanctions, the increased likelihood of a positive impact is 37.7 percentage points (evaluated at the sample mean) – a very large effect. At the same time, direct employment programs in the public sector are associated with a significantly lower probability of showing positive treatment effects. A highly significant negative relation also exists between programs targeted at young workers and the probability to display positive treatment effects; that probability is almost 36 percentage points lower if young people are the target group of the program.

The variables summarizing the study design and time of implementation of the program (panel (b)) do not show significant relations with the outcome variable. With respect to the time period, the 1990s are used as a base category. Most studies in the sample originate in the 1990s, and since that time it can be assumed that the main methodological challenges of program evaluation along with a set of feasible solutions are widely recognized.

The institutional background controls (panel (c)) show a statistically significant negative correlation between the degree of strictness of dismissal protection regulation and the probability of estimating positive treatment effects on employment probability. This result is consistent with the notion that regulatory barriers to job dismissal generate a barrier to new hiring, making firms reluctant to hire new workers if these cannot be dismissed again. Such behavior would then affect unemployed workers, decreasing their employment chances even after participation in ALMP. The other institutional features do not significantly affect the likelihood of finding a positive program impact.

Finally, the covariates on the macroeconomic context (panel (d)) seem to indicate that a higher unemployment rate is highly significantly associated with a higher probability of estimating positive treatment effects, although the size of the marginal effect is small (indicating a 5 percentage points higher probability). One possible explanation of this phenomenon is that in times of high unemployment the share of better qualified individuals in the unemployment pool will be higher, so that the estimate might result from "cream skimming" of the potentially more successful program participants. The remaining economic variables on ALMP expenditure and GDP growth do not play a significant role. It is interesting to note that spending more money on active measures at the aggregate level does not necessarily seem to relate to increasing individual participants' employment probability.

Table 21 reports empirical results for a second specification, which includes country dummies. Again, the outcome variable is a binomial indicator of positive treatment effects or not. The advantage of this specification is that it controls for any permanent features of different countries that may influence the relative success of ALMPs. We use Sweden as the omitted country in the base category, i.e. the country effects are judged relative to Sweden. Sweden is the European country with the longest tradition of ALMP. It also has a tradition of extensive data collection and thorough evaluation of the active labor market programs. A total of 23 observations in the data originate in Swedish evaluation studies, 9 of which find a positive impact. Note that the last country dummy in Table 21 is labeled "Small country". This category collects those countries from which only one or two program evaluations exist in the data, leading to perfectly predicted outcomes in the estimation. Also, regarding the time period, all decades other than the 1990s are used as a base category.

The results presented in Table 21 are generally consistent with the findings from our first specification. Direct employment programs in the public sector are associated with a significantly lower probability of displaying positive treatment effects (−33.8 percentage points), relative to training, while the opposite is the case for private sector incentive schemes (+30.9 percentage points). Services and sanctions also show a positive and marginally significant effect. As in Table 1, programs for young workers are particularly unlikely to

Table 21. Effectiveness of European ALMP: Quantitative Analysis, Specification 2

	Marginal Effect	t-ratio
(a) Type of program and target group:		
Direct employment program	**-0.338**	-2.33
Private sector incentive scheme	**0.309**	2.34
Services and Sanctions	*0.346*	1.70
Young workers	***-0.519***	-3.90
(b) Study design and time period:		
Experimental design	*-0.462*	-1.93
Program implemented in the 1990s	-0.211	-1.46
(c) Institutional context on the labor market:		
Index for dismissal protection regulation	-0.326	-1.64
Index for fixed-term contracts regulation	-0.166	-1.40
Index for temporary work regulation	0.085	1.43
Gross replacement rate	0.004	0.34
(d) Macroeconomic background:		
Unemployment rate	0.013	0.38
ALMP expenditure (% of GDP)	0.036	0.15
GDP growth	-0.030	-0.60
(e) Country dummies:		
Austria	0.299	0.69
Denmark	-0.308	-0.59
France	0.481	1.57
Germany	0.226	0.84
Ireland	0.367	1.04
Netherland	-0.087	-0.18
Norway	0.257	0.72
United Kingdom	-0.062	-0.09
Switzerland	-0.422	-0.79
Finland	*0.469*	1.71
Small country	0.256	0.57

Number of observations = 137. – Pseudo R^2 = 0.246. – Notes: The dependent variable is an indicator (1/0) variable, reflecting a positive estimate of the program effect. Table entries document the marginal effect (evaluated at the sample mean) in the corresponding probit regression, i.e. the difference in the predicted probability for achieving a positive treatment effect which arises from a marginal change in a continuous explanatory factor (such as the GDP growth rate) or which arises from changing an indicator among the explanatory factors (such as the indicator for an experimental study design) from 0 to 1. T-ratios of the marginal effects are reported in the third column. Marginal effects printed in *italics* indicate marginal significance (10%-level), marginal effects printed in **boldface** indicate statistical significance (5%-level), and marginal effects printed in ***boldface and italics*** indicate high significance (1%-level). The underlying standard errors adjust for clustering by study.

yield positive employment impacts. It is worth emphasizing that these relative program effects are identified by comparing the relative impacts of different types of programs in the same country, and are therefore unaffected by unobserved country-specific factors that are correlated with the relative use of different types of ALMPs. For this reason, the findings on program type are particularly credible.

There is some indication from the model in Table 21 that experimental evaluations are less likely to produce positive treatment effect estimates. Regarding both the institutional and the economic context, no significant correlations are found. Interestingly, the marginal effect of the unemployment rate is insignificant, and almost zero in size. This implies that the significant positive coefficient found in specification 1 is largely driven by cross-country differences in unemployment rates that happen to be correlated with the relative impact of ALMPs, rather than by temporal variation in unemployment and the estimated program impacts. Looking at the country dummies themselves, only studies from Finland seem to have a slightly higher probability of finding positive effects.

In a final specification using the binary outcome, we restrict the sample to evaluations of programs that were implemented in 1990 or later. One reason for considering the later programs is that more recent evaluations presumably use more sophisticated evaluation methods, and may be more reliable. This restriction slightly reduces the sample to 109 observations. We continue to include indicators for the size of the sample used in the evaluation study (for the classification cf. section 3.1 above). The estimates are reported in Table 22.

The results regarding program type and target group are even more pronounced in this specification. The marginal effects on both private sector incentive programs and Services and Sanctions are highly significant and fairly large, amounting to 43.9 percentage points and 55.7 percentage points, respectively, relative to the base category. Public sector employment programs again show a statistically significant negative correlation with the probability of positive treatment effects. Programs targeted at young workers also are markedly less likely to display positive effects, with a probability 62.6 percentage points lower than that of adult workers.

The covariates in Panel (b) do not show any relation between the sample size of a study and the corresponding treatment effect estimate. Experimental study design, however, is significantly negatively associated with the likelihood of finding a positive effect. This finding is potentially worrisome, since the vast majority of evaluations are non-experimental, and the negative coefficient in Panel (b) suggests that there may be a tendency toward "overly optimistic" results in the non-experimental evaluations. Another possible interpretation is that experimental designs have been used selectively to evaluate programs that are somewhat less successful than average.

Panel (c) shows a significant negative correlation between the strictness of dismissal protection legislation and program effectiveness among evaluations in the 1990s. This parallels the finding in specification 1. It is also worth noting that even in the broader sample used in Table 21, the impact of dismissal legislation is marginally significant ($t = 1.64$). Taken as a whole, the series of specifications therefore provide relatively consistent evidence on the impact of this form of labor market regulation on the measured effectiveness of ALMPs. By comparison, in all three specifications none of the other institutional factors are found to affect the measured impact of the programs. The country dummies display weak associations only for Denmark and Switzerland, whose program evaluations appear to be less likely to estimate positive treatment effects, relative to Sweden.

Table 22. Effectiveness of European ALMP: Quantitative Analysis,
            Specification 3

	Marginal Effect	t-ratio
(a) Type of program and target group:		
Direct employment program	**-0.336**	-2.20
Private sector incentive scheme	*0.439*	2.68
Services and Sanctions	*0.557*	3.70
Young workers	***-0.626***	-3.31
(b) Study design, timing, and sample size:		
Experimental design	***-0.632***	-3.23
Program implemented in the 1990s	-0.229	-1.20
Small	-0.115	-0.65
Large	0.033	0.15
(c) Institutional context on the labor market:		
Index for dismissal protection regulation	**-0.485**	-2.04
Index for fixed-term contracts regulation	-0.093	-0.74
Index for temporary work regulation	*0.122*	1.74
Gross replacement rate	0.019	1.18
(d) Macroeconomic background:		
Unemployment rate	0.066	1.33
ALMP expenditure (% of GDP)	-0.315	-1.08
GDP growth	-0.000	-0.00
(e) Country dummies:		
Austria	-0.373	-0.65
Denmark	*-0.713*	-1.85
France	-0.205	-0.34
Germany	-0.267	-0.77
Ireland	-0.087	-0.14
Netherland	-0.580	-1.53
Norway	-0.487	-1.05
United Kingdom	-0.538	-0.82
Switzerland	*-0.622*	-1.87
Finland	0.121	0.26
Small country	-0.638	-1.42

Number of observations = 109. – Pseudo R^2 = 0.339. – Notes: The dependent variable is an indicator (1/0) variable, reflecting a positive estimate of the program effect. Table entries document the marginal effect (evaluated at the sample mean) in the corresponding probit regression, i.e. the difference in the predicted probability for achieving a positive treatment effect which arises from a marginal change in a continuous explanatory factor (such as the GDP growth rate) or which arises from changing an indicator among the explanatory factors (such as the indicator for an experimental study design) from 0 to 1. T-ratios of the marginal effects are reported in the third column. Marginal effects printed in *italics* indicate marginal significance (10%-level), marginal effects printed in **boldface** indicate statistical significance (5%-level), and marginal effects printed in ***boldface and italics*** indicate high significance (1%-level). The underlying standard errors adjust for clustering by study.

As we noted earlier (section 3.1) we have access to a much larger set of evaluation studies than was used in Kluve/Schmidt (2002). The larger sample size has an important payoff, allowing us to fit more richly specified models (including the models in Tables 21 and 22 that include country dummies), and better identify some of the key patterns in the data. In the second main step of our analysis, we extend the specification to distinguish not only between positive and non-positive outcomes, but also between evaluation studies that report negative versus zero impacts. That is, we complement the previous analysis by considering a trinomial dependent variable taking on the values -1 for a negative treatment effect estimate, 0 for an estimate of zero, and $+1$ for a positive estimate. The following tables 23 through 6.6 present the results for the corresponding ordered probit regressions. In these regressions the same three specifications for the set of covariates as in the binomial case are used.

Table 23 presents estimates of the marginal effects for obtaining a negative (column 2) and positive outcome (column 4), respectively, for the entire sample without the country dummies. In interpreting these estimates it is useful to compare the sign and magnitude of the coefficients for each independent variable on two margins: the margin between a negative versus a zero effect (coefficients reported in column 1); and the margin between a positive versus a zero effect (coefficients reported in column 3). Note that one would generally expect these coefficients to be opposite in sign: a covariate that is associated with a higher likelihood of a positive versus a zero effect will tend to be associated with a lower likelihood of a negative versus a zero effect.

The results in Table 23 tend to reinforce our findings from Table 20. In particular, we find that ALMPs based on private sector incentive schemes and Services and Sanctions are significantly more likely to yield a *higher* probability of positive treatment effects and a *lower* probability of negative treatment effects, relative to ALMPs based on conventional training programs. On the other hand, direct public sector employment programs are associated with a significantly higher probability of negative treatment effects and a significantly lower probability of positive treatment effects. For youths, the same pattern holds, though the effects are a little less pronounced. There is also some indication that experimental studies have a lower probability of yielding positive effects, that strict dismissal protection is associated with both a higher probability of negative impacts and a lower probability of positive impacts, and that higher unemployment lowers the probability of a negative estimated program impact while raising (slightly) the likelihood of a positive impact. Other factors, including the variables representing the time period and the institutional and economic background do not seem to play a role.

The model in Table 24 parallels the specification in Table 21, and includes the same variables as in Table 23, along with country dummies. As we found using a binary outcome variable, the addition of the country dummies has little impact on the size or significance of the coefficients representing the different program types, but does lead to a reduction in the estimated effect of unemployment. Indeed, a striking result in Table 24 is that – with the sole exception of the variable indicating whether the evaluation used an experimental design – not a single variable describing the time period (Panel b), the institutional setting (c), the macroeconomic background (d), or the country (e) displays an even marginally significant correlation with either a negative or positive treatment effect estimate. Looking at the program types in Panel (a), on the other hand, a clear and statistically significant picture emerges once again: Relative to the base category of training programs, private sector incentive schemes and Services and Sanctions have lower probabilities of negative

Table 23. Effectiveness of European ALMP: Quantitative Analysis, Specification 4

	Negative treatment effect		Positive treatment effect	
	Marginal Effect	t-ratio	Marginal Effect	t-ratio
(a) Type of program and target group:				
Direct employment program	**0.165**	2.06	**–0.227**	–2.30
Private sector incentive scheme	***–0.141***	–3.39	***0.270***	2.76
Services and Sanctions	***–0.203***	–3.82	***0.427***	4.45
Young workers	*0.135*	1.78	*–0.195*	–1.92
(b) Study design and time period:				
Experimental design	0.263	1.25	*–0.312*	–1.67
Program implemented in the				
1970s	–0.120	–1.40	0.248	1.05
1980s	–0.116	–1.59	0.205	1.61
2000s	0.036	0.41	–0.056	–0.43
(c) Institutional context on the labor market:				
Index for dismissal protection regulation	*0.072*	1.83	*–0.115*	–1.84
Index for fixed-term contracts regulation	–0.023	–0.79	0.037	0.80
Index for temporary work regulation	–0.001	–0.04	0.001	0.04
Gross replacement rate	0.003	1.52	–0.006	–1.55
(d) Macroeconomic background:				
Unemployment rate	**–0.022**	–2.07	*0.035*	1.86
ALMP expenditure (% of GDP)	0.059	1.07	–0.094	–1.08
GDP growth	0.010	0.37	0.016	–0.37

Number of observations = 137. – Pseudo R^2 = 0.133. – Notes: The dependent variable is a categorical variable indicating whether the estimate of the program effect is negative (–1), zero (0), or positive (+1). Table entries document the marginal effects (evaluated at the sample mean) from the corresponding ordered probit regression for the negative and positive outcomes, respectively. I.e. the difference in the predicted probability for achieving a negative (positive) treatment effect which arises from a marginal change in a continuous explanatory factor (such as the GDP growth rate) or which arises from changing an indicator among the explanatory factors (such as the indicator for an experimental study design) from 0 to 1. T-ratios of the marginal effects are reported in the third and fifth column, respectively. Marginal effects printed in *italics* indicate marginal significance (10%-level), marginal effects printed in **boldface** indicate statistical significance (5%-level), and marginal effects printed in ***boldface and italics*** indicate high significance (1%-level). The underlying standard errors adjust for clustering by study.

treatment effects, and higher probability of positive treatment effects. The opposite is the case for direct employment in the public sector. The opposite is also the case for programs targeting young workers.

The results from our final specification are presented in Table 25. This model is fit to the subset of evaluations for programs conducted in the 1990s, and includes controls for the sample size used in the evaluation. In general, the results are very similar to the findings in Table 24. In the 1990s subsample the country dummies for Denmark, Switzerland, and for the group of small countries all show a more pronounced negative effect on the likelihood of a positive program impact, relative to the baseline country (Sweden). In this subsample there is also a stronger tendency for experimental studies to yield more negative impact estimates. But apart from these small differences, the

Table 24. Effectiveness of European ALMP: Quantitative Analysis, Specification 5

	Negative treatment effect		Positive treatment effect	
	Marginal Effect	t-ratio	Marginal Effect	t-ratio
(a) Type of program and target group:				
Direct employment program	**0.181**	2.06	**−0.250**	−2.32
Private sector incentive scheme	*−0.145*	−3.75	*0.291*	3.13
Services and Sanctions	*−0.194*	−3.56	*0.422*	3.92
Young workers	**0.165**	2.20	**−0.239**	−2.45
(b) Study design and time period:				
Experimental design	0.358	1.53	**−0.395**	−2.23
Program implemented in the 1990s	0.090	1.02	−0.152	−1.04
(c) Institutional context on the labor market:				
Index for dismissal protection regulation	0.106	1.11	−0.175	−1.08
Index for fixed-term contracts regulation	0.028	0.41	−0.046	−0.41
Index for temporary work regulation	−0.023	−0.70	0.039	0.69
Gross replacement rate	−0.002	−0.26	0.003	0.26
(d) Macroeconomic background:				
Unemployment rate	−0.014	−0.78	0.024	0.77
ALMP expenditure (% of GDP)	−0.057	0.46	−0.095	−0.46
GDP growth	0.014	0.55	−0.024	−0.55
(e) Country dummies:				
Austria	−0.035	−0.13	0.061	0.12
Denmark	0.205	0,48	−0.268	−0.59
France	−0.064	−0.34	0.118	0.30
Germany	−0.045	−0.34	0.080	0.32
Ireland	−0.136	−1.58	0.308	1.25
Netherland	0.116	0.34	−0.165	−0.40
Norway	−0.085	−0.63	0.162	0.55
United Kingdom	0.012	0.03	−0.020	−0.03
Switzerland	0.350	0.65	−0.382	−0.96
Finland	−0.122	−1.15	0.259	0.89
Small country	0.018	0.07	−0.287	−0.07

Number of observations = 137. – Pseudo R^2 = 0.149. – Notes: The dependent variable is a categorical variable indicating whether the estimate of the program effect is negative (−1), zero (0), or positive (+1). Table entries document the marginal effects (evaluated at the sample mean) from the corresponding ordered probit regression for the negative and positive outcomes, respectively. I.e. the difference in the predicted probability for achieving a negative (positive) treatment effect which arises from a marginal change in a continuous explanatory factor (such as the GDP growth rate) or which arises from changing an indicator among the explanatory factors (such as the indicator for an experimental study design) from 0 to 1. T-ratios of the marginal effects are reported in the third and fifth column, respectively. Marginal effects printed in *italics* indicate marginal significance (10%-level), marginal effects printed in **boldface** indicate statistical significance (5%-level), and marginal effects printed in ***boldface and italics*** indicate high significance (1%-level). The underlying standard errors adjust for clustering by study.

results confirm our earlier conclusions from the model in Table 24. In particular, none of the variables representing the timing, institutional setting or economic situation appears to have an important effect on program effectiveness. Rather, the likelihood of a positive program impact seems to be

Table 25. Effectiveness of European ALMP: Quantitative Analysis, Specification 6

	Negative treatment effect		Positive treatment effect	
	Marginal Effect	t-ratio	Marginal Effect	t-ratio
(a) Type of program and target group:				
Direct employment program	**0.195**	2.11	**-0.275**	-2.36
Private sector incentive scheme	***-0.181***	-4.18	***0.391***	3.60
Services and Sanctions	***-0.230***	-3.98	***0.535***	9.06
Young workers	*0.166*	1.93	**-0.244**	-2.15
(b) Study design, timing, and sample size:				
Experimental design	***0.736***	5.17	***-0.586***	-9.16
Program implemented in the 1990s	0.079	0.79	-0.142	-0.77
Small	0.079	0.85	-0.131	-0.90
Large	0.119	0.83	-0.176	-0.95
(c) Institutional context on the labor market:				
Index for dismissal protection regulation	0.116	1.08	-0.198	-1.08
Index for fixed-term contracts regulation	-0.012	-0.17	0.020	0.17
Index for temporary work regulation	-0.045	-1.33	0.076	1.32
Gross replacement rate	-0.006	-0.89	0.011	0.88
(d) Macroeconomic environment:				
Unemployment rate	-0.032	-1.40	0.055	1.34
ALMP expenditure (% of GDP)	0.195	1.24	-0.331	-1.34
GDP growth	0.005	0.15	-0.008	-0.15
(e) Country dummies:				
Austria	0.472	0.76	-0.457	-1.38
Denmark	0.630	1.40	**-0.584**	-2.51
France	0.488	1.07	*-0.496*	-1.83
Germany	0.185	0.68	-0.255	-0.87
Ireland	-0.062	-0.30	0.118	0.27
Netherland	0.294	0.63	-0.341	-0.91
Norway	0.207	0.52	-0.273	-0.67
United Kingdom	0.414	0.51	-0.427	-0.84
Switzerland	*0.718*	1.71	***-0.574***	-3.99
Finland	0.071	0.25	-0.109	-0.28
Small country	0.606	1.58	***-0.577***	-2.86

Number of observations = 109. – Pseudo R^2 = 0.202. – Notes: The dependent variable is a categorical variable indicating whether the estimate of the program effect is negative (–1), zero (0), or positive (+1). Table entries document the marginal effects (evaluated at the sample mean) from the corresponding ordered probit regression for the negative and positive outcomes, respectively. I.e. the difference in the predicted probability for achieving a negative (positive) treatment effect which arises from a marginal change in a continuous explanatory factor (such as the GDP growth rate) or which arises from changing an indicator among the explanatory factors (such as the indicator for an experimental study design) from 0 to 1. T-ratios of the marginal effects are reported in the third and fifth column, respectively. Marginal effects printed in *italics* indicate marginal significance (10%-level), marginal effects printed in **boldface** indicate statistical significance (5%-level), and marginal effects printed in ***boldface and italics*** indicate high significance (1%-level). The underlying standard errors adjust for clustering by study.

largely determined by the type of ALMP program. The base category, training, has a reasonably large share of positive effects. For the 70 evaluations of training programs, 38 yield a positive impact, 14 are zero, and 18 are negative. Relative to this baseline, Private Sector incentive schemes and Services and

Sanctions perform significantly better, while public sector employment programs and programs targeted at young workers perform significantly worse.

3.3   Summary of findings

This chapter has used a meta-analytical approach to assess the effectiveness of Active Labor Market Policy across European countries. The objective of the analysis is to draw systematic lessons from the more than 100 evaluations that have been conducted on ALMPs in Europe, and to complement the more descriptive analyses and country-level summaries in the preceding parts of the study. Most of the evaluation studies included in our meta-analysis have been conducted on programs that were in operation in the period after 1990. The past 15 years have seen an increasing use of ALMPs in a variety of European countries, and some improvement in the methodologies used to evaluate these programs. Thus, we believe that lessons drawn from our meta-analysis are highly relevant to the current policy discussions throughout Europe on the appropriate design of ALMPs.

The picture that emerges from our quantitative analysis is surprisingly clear-cut. Once the *type* of the program is taken into account, our analysis shows that there is little systematic relationship between program effectiveness and a host of other contextual factors, including the country or time period when it was implemented, the macroeconomic environment, and a variety of indicators for institutional features of the labor market. The only institutional factor that appears to have an important systematic effect on program effectiveness is the presence of more restrictive firing regulations. But even this effect is small relative to the effect of the program type. Traditional training programs are found to have a modest likelihood of recording a positive impact on post-program employment rates. Relative to these programs, private sector incentive programs and Sanctions and Services show a significantly better performance. Indeed, we find that evaluations of these types of programs are 40–50 percent more *likely* to report a positive impact than traditional training programs. By comparison, evaluations of ALMPs that are based on direct employment in the public sector are 30–60 percent less *likely* to show a positive impact on post-program employment outcomes.

Chapter 6: Conclusions and policy recommendations

The importance of ALMPs has been underlined by the launch of the European Employment Strategy (EES). The EES highlights employment as a key objective receiving the same attention as the other EU economy objectives. Moreover, the EES encouraged member states to shift their policies from a preventive towards a more active approach and to improve the effectiveness of active measures. Nevertheless, there are still substantial differences among EU Member States, both in terms of unemployment rates and expenditures for AMLPs. Some countries have relatively high spending, whereas numerous countries continue to spend relatively small GDP shares on ALMPs.

In line with the large heterogeneity across countries regarding spending on ALMPs and types of programs, the evaluation practice also differs substantially. Some countries have a tradition of evaluating active policies and collecting the corresponding data (Sweden being the outstanding example), while other countries show relatively little interest in assessing the effectiveness of their policies. For the new member states, this has to be seen mainly in the context of rather recent implementation of ALMPs, of having to construct appropriate data sets from scratch, and of necessitating some time to develop an "evaluation culture". In general, the "European evaluation culture" has made substantial advances, and the sobering picture about that culture at the turn of the millennium drawn in Kluve/Schmidt (2002) does not continue to be true. Most of these advances are likely directly related to the evaluation endeavors as part of the EES. Room for improvement, however, remains: for instance, the distribution of available evaluation studies is strongly skewed across countries, and the concept of conducting experimental studies that provide the most reliable evidence on policy effectiveness has become anything but popular.

Moreover, the vast majority of evaluation studies continues to focus on effectiveness at the microeconomic level. Clearly, such evaluations can be very informative, yet as pointed out above – and as also recognized by most policy makers – a more complete assessment of ALMP effectiveness requires an investigation of general-equilibrium effects. Such analyses have remained the exception. Also, it is still not common to conduct thorough (or even back-of-the-envelope) cost-benefit analyses, although they would be highly desirable for a more complete assessment of ALMP usefulness, in particular for drawing policy conclusions on continuing, extending, changing, or abolishing specific policies. Perhaps unsurprisingly, thus, most evaluation studies are noticeably reluctant to develop any such recommendations.

The assessment of recent studies aims at elaborating a more precise pattern about ALMP impacts in Europe. The main part of the analysis is set against the backdrop of three frames. First, we have discussed the role of the European Employment Strategy in shaping member states' labor market policies, and have described the current situation on European labor markets regarding core indicators such as the unemployment rate and GDP growth. The second frame has been given by a discussion and definition of active labor market program types, and program expenditure by country and type of measure. The most important ALMP categories across European countries are (i) training programs, which essentially comprise all human capital enhancing measures, (ii) private sector incentive schemes, such as wage subsidies to private firms and start-up grants, (iii) direct employment programs, taking place in the public sector, and (iv) Services and Sanctions, a category comprising all measures aimed at increasing job search efficiency, such as counseling and monitoring, job search assistance, and corresponding sanctions in case of noncompliance. It is important to note that many active labor market programs in European countries specifically target the young workers (25 years of age and younger) among the unemployed. Whereas several countries also have specific active labor market programs for the disabled, very few evaluations of these measures exist.

The third frame regards the methodology of program evaluation. Since the cross-European analysis of ALMP effectiveness must necessarily rely on credible evaluation studies from all countries involved, appropriate outcome variables and cost measures, as well as feasible identification strategies that can help solve the so-called "evaluation problem" (i.e. the inherent unobservability of the counterfactual no-program situation) must be discussed and properly specified.

Logically building on these three frames as a backdrop, the subsequent analysis of ALMP effectiveness has concentrated on two focal points. The first focus regards a set of country studies from selected EU member states. Specifically, we discuss Austria, Denmark, Estonia, France, Germany, Italy, The Netherlands, Poland, Spain, Sweden, and the UK. While taking into account idiosyncrasies of each country, for purposes of comparability the studies follow a homogeneous structure to the extent possible, discussing (a) the economic context, (b) labor market institutions, (c) ALMP practice, and (d) evaluations. Unsurprisingly, both the economic background and the institutional set-up vary substantially across countries, from currently well-performing (e.g. Denmark, Estonia) to rather sluggish economies (e.g. Germany), and from fairly flexible (e.g. the UK) to rather heavily regulated labor markets (e.g. France, Germany). Substantial differences exist with respect to ALMP practice, too. Some countries spend a substantial share of GDP on active measures (e.g. The Netherlands, Denmark, Sweden) and run a comprehensive set of various types of ALMP (e.g. Germany), while other countries spend considerably less (UK, Italy) and run a relatively narrow set of programs (e.g. Estonia, Spain). Denmark certainly has the most comprehensive ALMP strategy with substantial effort to activate all unemployed persons.

Similar to differences in the implementation of ALMP, also the evaluation practice varies across countries. Sweden is well-known to have a long tradition of running and thoroughly evaluating ALMP, possible also because of a correspondingly comprehensive collection of data. The Netherlands and the UK, along with the one existing study from Hungary – stand out as countries implementing some evaluations based on randomized experiments. These experimental studies analyze the effects of job search assistance programs. On the other hand, in Spain and Italy, for instance, an "evaluation culture" hardly exists, which is probably in line with a limited ALMP practice that is only just emerging. Germany is an example of a country in which – despite a fairly long tradition of running ALMPs – program evaluations were almost nonexistent until few years ago, and in which a practice of evaluating labor market policies has developed very rapidly. It is true for all countries that almost every evaluation study exclusively discusses microeconomic treatment effects, and that only very few macroeconomic studies exist.

Succeeding the country studies, the second focus regards the appropriate summarizing of the available evidence. After first reviewing the experiences from the country reports and several studies from the remaining member states (as well as Norway and Switzerland) in a descriptive manner, the study then concentrates on a meta-analysis of the available evidence. While the review produces some tentative findings – Services and Sanctions may be a promising measure, direct job creation in the public sector often seems to produce negative employment effects, training measures show mixed and modestly positive effects –, no palpable pattern emerges from the descriptive cross-country assessment.

The objective of the meta analysis is thus to draw systematic lessons from the more than 100 evaluations that have been conducted on ALMPs in Europe, and to complement the more descriptive analyses and country-level summaries in the preceding parts of the study. Most of the evaluation studies considered have been conducted on programs that were in operation in the period after 1990. This reflects the fact that the past 15 years have seen an increasing use of ALMPs in EU member states, and some improvement in the methodologies used to evaluate these programs. Thus, we believe that lessons drawn from our meta-analysis are highly relevant to the current policy discussions throughout Europe on the appropriate design of ALMPs.

The picture that emerges from the quantitative analysis is surprisingly clear-cut. Once the type of the program is taken into account, the analysis shows that there is little systematic relationship between program effectiveness and a host of other contextual factors, including the country or time period when it was implemented, the macroeconomic environment, and a variety of indicators for institutional features of the labor market. The only institutional factor that appears to have an important systematic effect on program effectiveness is the presence of more restrictive dismissal regulations. But even this effect is small relative to the effect of the program type.

Traditional training programs are found to have a modest likelihood of recording a positive impact on post-program employment rates. Relative to these programs, private sector incentive programs and Services and Sanctions show a significantly better performance. Indeed, we find that evaluations of these types of programs are 40-50 percent more likely to report a positive impact than traditional training programs. By comparison, evaluations of

ALMPs that are based on direct employment in the public sector are 30–40 percent less likely to show a positive impact on post-program employment outcomes. Also the target group seems to matter, as programs aimed specifically at young workers fare significantly worse than programs targeted at adults, displaying a 40–60 percentage points lower probability of reporting a positive effect.

The general policy implications that follow from these findings are rather straightforward. Decision makers should clearly focus on the type of program in developing their ALMP portfolio, and the European Commission should spell out similar recommendations to member states within the European Employment Strategy: Training programs should be continued, and private sector incentive schemes should be fostered. Particular attention should be paid to Services and Sanctions, which turns out to be a particularly promising and, due to its rather inexpensive nature, cost-effective type of measure. A well-balanced design of basic services such as job search assistance and counseling and monitoring, along with appropriate sanctions for non-compliance, seems to be able to go a long way in enhancing job search effectiveness. If further combined with other active measures such as training and employment subsidies, this effectiveness could be increased, even for youths, as promising results from the UK's "New Deal" show.

Direct employment programs in the public sector, on the other hand, are rarely effective and frequently detrimental regarding participants' employment prospects. On this account they should be discontinued, unless other justifications such as equity reasons can be found. Some countries have already resorted to redefining the objective of direct employment programs such that they should increase "employability" rather than actual employment, an outcome that is notoriously difficult to assess empirically.

Young people appear to be particularly hard to assist. It is not clear if it follows from this disappointing result that youth programs should be abolished, or rather that such programs should be re-designed and given particular attention. It might also be the case that Active Labor Market Policies are not at all the appropriate policy for this group, and public policy should therefore focus on measures that prevent the very young from becoming disadvantaged on the labor market in the first place.

The development of an "evaluation culture" has been positive in basically all member states, though different countries clearly find themselves at different stages of that development. One evident conclusion of this study is that evaluation efforts should be continued and extended. An ever-refined meta-analysis of an ever-extended set of European evaluation studies would continue to produce important insight into the effectiveness of ALMPs, in particular as data quality and methodology will likely continue to improve. The substantial advances in non-experimental program evaluation notwithstanding, more member states' governments interested in the effectiveness of their policies should consider implementing randomized experiments, in light of the strength of the evidence they produce.

Appendix

Table 26. ALMP expenditures by category; 2000 to 2002; share in %

	(2) Training	(3) Job rotation and job sharing	(4) Employ-ment incentives	(5) Integra-tion of the disabled	(6) Direct job creation	(7) Start-up incen-tives	(2–7) Total
2000							
Belgium	15.6	11.7	14.9	12.2	45.3	0.3	100,0
Denmark	41.1	–	30.0	25.1	3.5	0.2	100,0
Germany	43.9	–	9.3	14.0	28.7	4.0	100,0
EL	43.0	–	16.1	30.3	–	10.6	100,0
Spain	24.1	0.7	41.8	10.2	17.1	6.1	100,0
France	29.8	–	16.7	9.5	43.8	0.3	100,0
Ireland	26.8	–	14.4	0.2	55.0	3.7	100,0
Italy	26.1	0.3	52.1	0.8	11.9	8.8	100,0
Luxembourg	:	:	:	:	:	:	:
Netherland	8.8	0.0	7.2	49.6	34.3	–	100,0
Austria	54.6	0.1	18.1	15.1	11.3	0.8	100,0
Poland	55.4	0.1	15.3	4.5	20.5	4.2	100,0
Finland	47.7	7.3	15.6	12.5	15.3	1.6	100,0
Slovakia	44.7	1.7	15.4	32.3	2.5	3.3	100,0
United Kingdom	51.6	–	8.3	25.9	13.6	0.7	100,0
EU-15	34.5	0.8	18.8	15.6	27.4	3.0	100,0
Norway	17.2	0.0	5.3	77.0	–	0.5	100,0
2001							
Belgium	18.0	13.5	15.5	12.5	40.1	0.3	100,0
Denmark	39.7	–	32.9	27.2	0.2	0.0	100,0
Germany	46.4	–	10.6	15.6	23.0	4.4	100,0
EL	9.3	–	70.9	16.9	–	2.8	100,0
Spain	22.8	0.6	39.1	12.8	16.8	7.8	100,0
France	27.1	–	15.8	10.3	46.5	0.3	100,0
Ireland	29.0	–	13.1	0.3	50.9	6.7	100,0
Italy	16.1	0.2	60.9	0.7	8.9	13.2	100,0
Luxembourg	:	:	:	:	:	:	100,0
Netherland	9.3	0.0	6.3	49.4	34.9	–	100,0
Austria	53.8	0.0	20.2	16.2	9.0	0.8	100,0
Poland	45.1	0.0	16.4	17.6	17.7	3.2	100,0
Finland	44.9	8.6	16.7	13.9	14.4	1.5	100,0
Slovakia	44.5	1.8	15.7	34.7	0.2	3.1	100,0
United Kingdom	32.3	–	22.6	30.0	14.2	0.8	100,0
EU-15	32.5	0.9	21.4	16.5	25.0	3.8	100,0
Norway	14.4	0.0	5.0	80.1	–	0.5	100,0
2002							
Belgium	20.4	–	18.2	12.9	48.1	0.5	100,0
Denmark	36.9	–	32.1	30.9	0.1	–	100,0
Germany	50.8	0.0	11.0	15.5	17.6	5.1	100,0
EL	50.2	–	22.8	11.6	–	15.4	100,0
Spain	21.2	0.7	42.3	10.2	16.9	8.6	100,0
France	32.6	–	12.3	9.9	44.8	0.4	100,0
Ireland	35.1	–	24.0	–	41.0	–	100,0
Italy	33.6	0.0	56.2	0.6	5.6	4.0	100,0
Latvia	:	:	:	:	:	:	100,0
Netherland	15.2	0.0	4.8	50.0	30.0	–	100,0
Austria	58.8	0.0	14.0	16.7	9.7	0.9	100,0
Poland	40.2	0.0	39.7	10.2	9.0	0.9	100,0
Finland	47.3	7.0	15.1	14.8	14.4	1.5	100,0
Slovakia	47.3	0.8	14.6	34.1	–	3.2	100,0
United Kingdom	77.9	–	6.5	12.2	3.2	0.3	100,0
EU-15	39.6	0.2	20.3	15.6	21.4	3.0	100,0
Norway	10.3	0.0	5.2	84.5	–	–	100,0

Note: Data are taken from Eurostat (2000, 2001, 2002) and follow Eurostat's classification of ALMPs. Category 1, which comprises measures of job search assistance, has been left out, since data are not comparable across countries.

Table 27. Expenditures on labor market policy by category; 2000 to 2002; % of GDP

	(2)	(3)	(4)	(5)	(6)	(7)	(2–7)	(8)	(9)	(8–9)
	Training	Job rotation and job sharing	Employment incentives	Integration of the disabled	Direct job creation	Start-up incentives	Total	Out-of-work income maintenance and support	Early retirement	Total
2000										
Belgium	0.156	0.116	0.149	0.122	0.451	0.003	0.997	1.692	0.486	2.177
Denmark	0.675	–	0.493	0.412	0.057	0.003	1.641	1.581	0.798	2.379
Germany	0.402	–	0.086	0.129	0.263	0.037	0.917	1.910	0.014	1.924
EL	0.109	–	0.041	0.077	–	0.027	0.253	0.449	–	0.449
Spain	0.153	0.004	0.264	0.064	0.108	0.039	0.632	1.370	0.023	1.393
France	0.277	–	0.155	0.088	0.407	0.003	0.931	1.218	0.183	1.401
Ireland	0.249	–	0.134	0.002	0.511	0.034	0.930	0.710	0.077	0.786
Italy	0.114	0.001	0.227	0.003	0.052	0.038	0.436	0.504	0.108	0.611
Luxembourg	:	–	0.041	0.014	:	0.000	:	0.185	0.255	0.440
Netherland	0.081	0.000	0.067	0.457	0.316	–	0.920	1.890	–	1.890
Austria	0.199	0.000	0.066	0.055	0.041	0.003	0.365	1.139	0.065	1.204
Poland	0.141	0.000	0.039	0.012	0.052	0.011	0.254	0.708	0.168	0.875
Finland	0.354	0.054	0.116	0.093	0.114	0.012	0.742	1.620	0.473	2.093
Slovakia	0674	0.026	0.233	0.486	0.038	0.050	1.507	1.348	0.061	1.410
United Kingdom	0.046	–	0.007	0.023	0.012	0.001	0.089	0.434	–	0.434
EU-15	0.235	0.005	0.128	0.106	0.187	0.020	0.681	1.187	0.095	1.282
Norway	0.088	0.000	0.027	0.393	–	0.003	0.511	0.519	–	0.519
2001										
Belgium	0.172	0.129	0.148	0.119	0.382	0.003	0.952	1.780	0.466	2.246
Denmark	0.644	–	0.534	0.442	0.003	0.000	1.624	1.511	0.775	2.286
Germany	0.411		0.094	0.138	0.204	0.039	0.887	1.938	0.025	1.963
EL	0.025	–	0.187	0.045	–	0.007	0.264	0.397	–	0.397
Spain	0.151	0.004	0.259	0.085	0.111	0.052	0.663	1.405	0.021	1.426
France	0.236	–	0.138	0.090	0.406	0.003	0.873	1.243	0.188	1.431
Ireland	0.206	–	0.093	0.002	0.361	0.048	0.710	0.629	0.072	0.701
Italy	0.083	0.001	0.312	0.004	0.046	0.068	0.512	0.530	0.080	0.609
Luxembourg	:	–	0.039	0.016	0.015	0.000	:	0.206	0.250	0.457
Netherland	0.086	0.000	0.058	0.454	0.321	–	0.920	1.673	–	1.673
Austria	0.228	0.000	0.085	0.069	0.038	0.003	0.423	1.113	0.084	1.197
Poland	0.112	0.000	0.041	0.044	0.044	0.008	0.248	0.703	0.306	1.008
Finland	0.307	0.059	0.114	0.095	0.098	0.010	0.683	1.595	0.501	2.095
Slovakia	0.597	0.024	0.211	0.466	0.003	0.041	1.341	1.039	0.034	1.073
United Kingdom	0.024	–	0.017	0.022	0.010	0.001	0.073	0.395	–	0.395
EU-15	0.216	0.006	0.142	0.110	0.166	0.025	0.664	1.174	0.095	1.269
Norway	0.075	0.000	0.026	0.420	–	0.003	0.524	0.549	–	0.549
2002										
Belgium	0.185	–	0.165	0.117	0.435	0.005	0.906	1.944	0.454	2.397
Denmark	0.616	–	0.534	0.515	0.002	–	1.667	1.561	0.761	2.322
Germany	0.477	0.000	0.103	0.145	0.165	0.048	0.939	2.141	0.032	2.173
EL	0.111	–	0.050	0.026	–	0.034	0.221	0.368	–	0.368
Spain	0.125	0.004	0.249	0.060	0.100	0.051	0.588	1.520	0.021	1.540
France	0.299	–	0.112	0.091	0.411	0.004	0.916	1.474	0.133	1.606
Ireland	0.223	–	0.153	–	0.261	–	0.637	0.723	0.067	0.791
Italy	0.216	0.000	0.362	0.004	0.036	0.026	0.643	0.560	0.099	0.659
Latvia	:	–	0.047	0.026	0.031	0.000	:	0.316	0.221	0.537
Netherland	0.142	0.000	0.045	0.467	0.280	–	0.934	1.716	–	1.716
Austria	0.247	0.000	0.059	0.070	0.041	0.004	0.421	1.108	0.154	1.262
Poland	0.180	0.000	0.178	0.046	0.040	0.004	0.448	0.848	0.357	1.205
Finland	0.341	0.050	0.109	0.106	0.104	0.011	0.722	1.630	0.531	2.162
Slovakia	0.656	0.011	0.202	0.473	–	0.044	1.385	1.037	0.012	1.049
United Kingdom	0.126	–	0.010	0.020	0.005	0.000	0.161	0.367	–	0.367
EU-15	0.282	0.001	0.145	0.111	0.152	0.021	0.713	1.274	0.091	1.265
Norway	0.059	0.000	0.030	0.482	–	–	0.571	0.666	–	0.666

Note: Data are taken from Eurostat (2000, 2001, 2002) and follow Eurostat's classification of ALMPs. Categories 2–7 comprise active, categories 8–9 passive labor market policies. Category 1, which comprises measures of job search assistance, has been left out, since data are not comparable across countries.

Table 28. Microeconomic evaluations of European ALMP

Study	Type of program	Target group	Design	Observation period	Outcome(s)	Identification strategy	Results	Notes/Comments [# observations for meta-data]
Austria								
Zweimüller, Winter-Ebmer (1996)	Training programs	Unemployed adults	Non-experimental	1986–1987	Employment stability	Bivariate probit model for repeated unemployment and selection into training. Earnings replacement ratio of UI benefits used as instrument	+ Positive effects for men.Disadvantaged and less motivated unemployed are given priority in program enrollment. Programs improve employment stability.	[1]
Winter-Ebmer (2001)	Training programs with job search counseling	Workers laid off in steel industry	Non-experimental	1987	Employment stability, wage growth	IV	+ Positive effects for men and overall. Wage gains for a period of 5 years. Improved employment prospects. 0 no effect for women.	Favorable factors: long term orientation of occupational reorientation, interaction of training and job-counseling, cooperative and financial structure of the foundation [1]
Weber, Hofer (2003)	1) Training programs 2) Job search programs	Unemployed adults	Non-experimental	1999, 2000	Unemployment durations	Multivariate hazard model, timing-of-events method	Training programs increase unemployment durations: – for men.– overall, 0 for women. Job search programs shorten unemployment, + for men. + for women.+ overall.	[2]
Weber, Hofer (2004)	Job search programs	Unemployed adults	Non-experimental	1999, 2000	Unemployment durations: effects depending on timing of program entry	Multivariate hazard model, timing-of-events method	+ Men and women: Positive program effects for entry into job search during first 12 months of unemployment, no effects for long-term unemployed.	[0: results contained in Weber and Hofer 2003]
Belgium								
Cockx, Göbel (2004)	Subsidized employment	Young unemployed	Non-experimental	1998–2000	Transition rate from employment to unemployment	Mixed proportional hazard (MPH) model	+ Positive effects for women – Positive effects for men only in the first year, negative in the second. Simulated increase of employment duration for women 8.7 months, for men 3.1 months	[1]
Cockx (2003)	Vocational training	Unemployed	Non-experimental	1989–1993	Transition rate from unemployment	Control function estimator	+ Positive effect on the transition rate Simulated decrease of unemployment duration 4 to 6 month	[1]
Denmark								
Kyhl (2001)	Several programs pooled, i.e. program type not explicitly included in the analysis	UI benefit recipients, 25–59 years of age	Non-experimental	1995–1998	Unemployment duration	Comparison of results for different years with different timing of ALMP	+ Evidence of threat effects	Results not directly generalizable, but adds to evidence on threat effects [0; specific program type not identifiable]

Table 28. Microeconomic evaluations of European ALMP (to be continued)

Study	Type of program	Target group	Design	Observation period	Outcome(s)	Identification strategy	Results	Notes/Comments [# observations for meta-data]
Geerdsen (2003)	Several programs pooled, i.e. program type not explicitly included in the analysis	UI benefit recipients, 17–67 years of age	Quasi-experimental	1994–1998	Unemployment duration	Legislative changes in time limit for participation in ALMP	+ Evidence of threat effects	Results not directly generalizable, but adds to evidence on threat effects [0; specific program type not identifiable]
Geerdsen and Holm (2004)	Several programs pooled, i.e. program type not explicitly included in the analysis	UI benefit recipients (analysis only on males, 25–47 years of age in 1994)	Quasi-experimental	1995–1998	Unemployment duration	Legislative changes in time limit for participation in ALMP, combined with modeling individual probability of participation in ALMP	+ Evidence of threat effects	Results not directly generalizable, but adds to evidence on threat effects [0; specific program type not identifiable]
Rosholm and Svarer (2004)	Private sector employment programs, public sector employment program, training program, other programs	UI benefit recipients (analysis only on males, 25–59 years of age)	Non-experimental	1998–2002	Unemployment duration	Timing-of-events and functional form specification of hazard rate out of unemployment	+ Strong threat effects, + private sector employment programs reduce unemployment duration, - all other program types increase unemployment duration	Informative about different types of effects of ALMPs, attempts to estimate the effects of an active labor market policy regime compared to the counterfactual situation of a passive regime [4]
Jensen, Rosholm and Svarer (2003)	Specially designed vocational education programs	Unemployed youths (receiving UI benefits, <25 years, no formal educ. beyond 2ndary school)	Experimental (quasi)	1996	Unemployment duration	Random assignment due to capacity constraints	0 No significant threat effect, + increased transition rate to schooling, 0 weaker effect on transition rate to employment	The findings regarding the combination of benefits, incentives and sanctions could be relevant for other countries (as part of labor market reform) [1]
Bolvig, Jensen and Rosholm (2003)	Employment programs, training program, other programs	Welfare benefit recipients	Non-experimental	1997–1999	Unemployment duration, subsequent employment duration	Timing-of-events	+ Employment programs have positive effects, - training and other programs have negative effects	[2]
Graversen (2004)	Private sector employment programs, public sector employment program, training program, other programs	Welfare benefit recipients (analysis only on males, above 25 years of age)	Non-experimental	1994–1998	Unemployment duration	Timing-of-events and intended timing by municipalities	+ Modest threat effects, + private sector employment programs reduce unemployment duration, - all other program types increase unemployment duration	Informative about different types of effects of ALMPs [3]

Appendix 195

Table 28. Microeconomic evaluations of European ALMP (to be continued)

Study	Type of program	Target group	Design	Observation period	Outcome(s)	Identification strategy	Results	Notes/Comments [# observations for meta-data]
Graversen and Jensen (2004)	Private sector employment programs, public sector employment program, training programs, other programs	Welfare benefit recipients (analysis only on males, 18-59 years of age)	Non-experimental	1994–1998	Employment rates 12 months after participation	Common factor structure (plus instrument for selection)	0 No significant mean effects of private sector employment programs compared to all other program types	Authors suggest improvement in allocation to programs [0; results contained in Graversen 2004]
Hogelund and Holm (2005)	Vocational education	Disabled: long-term "sick-listed" workers	Non-experimental	1995–1999	Re-employment rates	Competing risk duration model	0 No significant effect of educational measures on the return to work of the sick-listed	[1]
Estonia								
Leetmaa, Võrk (2004)	Training	Unemployed adults	Non-experimental	2000–2002	Employment rates	Propensity Score Matching	+ Training has positive effects	Evidence of cream skimming: case workers seem to select more promising candidates to labor market training. Training programs could be expanded, but this should be done hand in hand with careful evaluations.[1]
Finland								
Nätti, Aho, Halme (2000)	1) Labor market training. 2) Start-up grants. 3) Public sector subsidized employment	Registered unemployed	Non-experimental	1990–1995	Employment rates	Regression (Cross-section)	+ Labor market training, + Start-up grants- Subsidized employment in municipal and state sector	[3]
Malmberg-Heimonen, Vuori (2005)	Financial incentives and job-search training	Unemployed	Experimental	1998–2000	Re-employment	–	0 No significant overall impact + Positive for individuals with financial incentives – No positive effects for more disadvantaged	[1]
Hämäläinen, Ollikainen (2004)	Labor market training (LMT), empl. subsidy in private and public sector (SEM), youth practical training (YPT)	Young unemployed	Non-experimental	1988–2000	Six different outcomes	Propensity score matching	+ Increased employment and earnings for LMT + Increased employment and earnings for SEM – Slightly negative impact on all outcomes for YPT	[3]
Hämäläinen (2002)	Labor market training	Unemployed	Non-experimental	1989–1994	Employment probability	Bivariate probit model	+ Positive impact, which is negatively related to overall unemployment	[1]

Table 28. Microeconomic evaluations of European ALMP (to be continued)

Study	Type of program	Target group	Design	Observation period	Outcome(s)	Identification strategy	Results	Notes/Comments [# observations for meta-data]
France								
Cavaco, Fougère, Pouget (2005)	Retraining for displaced workers	Unemployed	Non-experimental	1995–1998	Unemployment duration and employment probability	Dependent competing risks duration model	+ Positive effect, increased employment probability by 8 points Higher benefits for high skilled and high educated workers	[1]
Crépon, Dejemeppe, Gurgand (2005)	Counseling and job-assistance schemes	Unemployed	Non-experimental	2001–2004	Transition to employment and unemployment recurrence	Duration models	+ Positive and significant impact on transition to employment (increase 1 percentage point) and on unemployment recurrence (decrease more than 6 percentage points)	[1]
Fougère, Pradel, Roger (2005)	Public Job Search Assistance	Unemployed workers	Non-experimental	1986–1988	Exit rate from unemployment	Structural partial equilibrium search model	+ Increased exit rate from unemployment through public employment services, especially for low-educated and unskilled workers	[1]
Brodaty, Crepon, Fougere (2002)	Workplace training programs (private sector), workfare programs (public sector) and other programs (e.g. training)	Young unemployed	Non-experimental	1986–1988, 1995–1998	Transition to employment	Propensity score matching	+ Positive effects for all programs in the first cohort, higher effects for workplace training programs (for short-term unemployed), "other programs" more effective for long-term unemployed – Negative effects for all programs for the cohort 95–98	[5: 2 for first cohort, 3 for second cohort]
Germany								
Eichler, Lechner (2002)	Job Creation Scheme	Long-term unemployed and other hard to place persons	Non-experimental	1992–1997	i) Unemployment rates ii) Employment rates,both observed up to ca. 5 years after participation started	Partial propensity score matching (with nearest neighbor) combined with DiD	+ Significant and substantial reduction in unemployment rate; for men this is due to higher employment rate; 0 for women this is due to higher non-participation rates	Location: Federal state of Sachsen-Anhalt, East Germany. Rather small sample sizes. [1]
Bergemann (2005)	Job Creation Scheme	Long-term unemployed and other hard to place persons	Non-experimental	1990–1999	i) reemployment probabilities (hazard) ii) probability to remain employed (hazard), observed up to three years after participation started	Propensity score matching combined with CDiDHR	0 No significant effect for men; + significantly positive effects on women's reemployment probability;+ Significantly positive effects on men's and women's probability to remain employed	Location: East Germany. [1]

Table 28. Microeconomic evaluations of European ALMP (to be continued)

Study	Type of program	Target group	Design	Observation period	Outcome(s)	Identification strategy	Results	Notes/Comments [# observations for meta-data]
Bergemann, Fitzenberger, Schultz, Speckesser (2000)	1) Job Creation Scheme 2) Training	Long-term unemployed and other hard to place persons	Non-experimental	1990–1998	Employment rates	Propensity score matching combined with DiD in a repeated participation framework	–0 First treatment: significant negative effect on employment; 2nd treatment: no significant effect –0 First treatment: sign. negative effect on employment; 2nd treatment: no significant effect. except for women (+ sign. positive)	Location: Federal state of Sachsen-Anhalt, East Germany. Small sample size (min. treatment group n=146). Study covers period after unification, therefore not generalizable. [2]
Caliendo, Hujer, Thomsen (2005a, b,c)	Job Creation Scheme	Long-term unemployed and other hard to place persons	Non-experimental	2000–2002	employment rates) of socio-demographic groups observed for up to 3 years after treatment startedii) in specific sectors, iii) in regions	Propensity score matching (Nearest neighbor)	(1) Locking-in effects in all subgroups2) 0 West Germany: no sign. effects for men: + positive mid-term effects for women;i3) – East: negative medium-term effects; i4) Evidence for effect heterogeneity: + Positive effects in West for women over 50, long- term unemployed, hard-to-place women; in East: - female long-term unemployedii)–0 Negative or insignificant effects in all sectorsiii) – Sign. negative effects in all regions; negative effects stronger in regions with above average labor market performance	i) Policy implication: labor agencies should target JCS betterii) might be interpreted as evidence for stigma effects of JC[1]
Fitzenberger, Speckesser (2005)	Training	Unemployed and those threatened by unemployment	Non-experimental	1993–1997	Employment rates observed up to three years after participation started	Propensity score matching (stratification)	+ West Germany: Lock-in effect in the short run and sign. positive effect on employment rates in the long run. 0 East Germany: lock-in effect in the short run and less significantly positive effect	[1]
Hujer, Thomsen, Zeiss (2004)	Training, i) short-term (1–3 months) ii) medium term (6 months) iii) long-term (12 months)	Unemployed and those threatened by unemployment	Non-experimental	1999–2002	Duration of unemployment and locking-in effect	Multivariate duration model (simultaneous model of duration until treatment and duration until transition into employment)	0 No significant evidence, neither on locking-in nor on effect on unemployment duration0 significant locking-in, no significant effect on U duration- significant locking-in, significantly rises U duration	Location: East Germany. Evidence of locking-in effects for programs of 6 and 12 months. Acc. to the authors, one has to take severe shortage of labor demand in East Germany into account when interpreting the results. [1]
Hujer, Wellner (2000)	Training	Unemployed and those threatened by unemployment	Non-experimental	1985-1992 West1990-199 2 East	duration of unemployment after treatment (hazard rate of transition from U o E)	Propensity score matching (West: oversampling)	+ West: treatment significantly reduces unemployment duration, 0 East: no significant effect; Short-term programs perform better than long-term programs	Rather small sample size (treatment group West Germany: n=87). Moreover, results for East Germany refer to peculiar period shortly after unification. [1]
Klose, Bender (2000)	Training	Unemployed and those threatened by unemployment	Non-experimental	1986–1990	i) Unemployment durationii) employment stabilityboth observed up to 3 years after completing the measure	Hierarchical covariate matching	0 No significant effect of training on unemployment duration- training significantly reduces job stability	Location: West Germany. [1]

Table 28. Microeconomic evaluations of European ALMP (to be continued)

Study	Type of program	Target group	Design	Observation period	Outcome(s)	Identification strategy	Results	Notes/Comments [# observations for meta-data]
Lechner (2000)	Training	Unemployed and those threatened by unemployment	Non-experimental	1990–1994	Unemployment rate observed up to 3 years after completing the training measure	Partial propensity score matching (with varying caliper)	–/0 In the short run, training significantly increases unemployment rates in the long run (3 years), no significant effects	Location: East Germany. Negative results might be due to short period of observation (see Lechner/ Miquel/Wunsch (2005)). Rather small sample size (max n= 116). Study covers period shortly after unification, therefore rather not generalizable. [1]
Lechner, Miquel, Wunsch (2004)	Training in West Germany	Unemployed and those threatened by unemployment	Non-experimental	1993–2002	i) Employment ii) unemployment iii) monthly earnings all outcomes observed up to seven years after participation started	Propensity score matching (Nearest neighbour matching with weighted oversampling) in a multiple treatment framework	i) + Short training: significantly positive effect on employment in short and long run +/0 Long training: significantly positive effect on employment in short run, no significant effect in the long run+ Retraining: sign. negative effect in the short run, sign. positive effect in the long run0 Practice firm: no significant effects ii)0 No significant positive effect on unemployment for all programs iii) + Significantly positive effects on monthly earnings for short and long training	Examination of compensation of locking-in effects after 7 years in terms of total time in employment:- positive gain in total time employed for short training (6 months) and long training (3 months) – no sign. result for practice firms – loss in total time employed for retraining; similar results for time of benefit receipt. Study gives insights on long-term effects of training programs & stresses need for long-term perspective. [1]
Lechner, Miquel, Wunsch (2005)	Training in East Germany	Unemployed and those threatened by unemployment	Non-experimental	1993–2002	i) Employment ii) unemployment iii) monthly earnings all outcomes observed up to eight years after participation started	propensity score matching (Nearest neighbour matching with weighted oversampling) in a multiple treatment framework	i) + Short training: sign. negative effect in the very short run and positive effect in the long run on employment 0 Long training: sign. negative effect in the short run and insignificant effect in the long run on employment + Retraining: sign. negative effect in the short run and sign. positive effect on the long run on employment ii) in the short run vice versa to i) and in the long run zero iii) + increase in 100 to 200 EUR in the long run for all programs, except practice firms	Locking-in effects are over compensated in the long run (after one to three years). Some peculiarities in the allocation of training measures after unification need special attention, especially men being extensively re-trained in the construction sector before the sector collapsed. The study stresses the need for a long-term perspective when effects of training measures are examined.[1]
Hujer, Caliendo, Thomsen, (2005)	Placement Assistance, Job Search Assistance	Unemployed	Non-experimental	2001-2002	Employment rates observed up to 21 months after participation started	Propensity score matching (nearest neighbour without replacement)	+ Significant positive effect of placement assistance for men and women; significant positive effect of job search assistance for women in southern region; – significant negative effect of job search assistance for men	Location: Federal state of Hessen, West Germany.[1]
Hujer, Caliendo, Radi (2004)	Wage subsidies (EGZ, ABM, SAM)	Unemployed (hard-to-place)	Non-experimental	1995–1999	Firm's employment development	Propensity score matching combined with CDiD	0 No significant employment effect	Location: West Germany. Unit of observation is firm; Degree of homogeneity of pooled measures unclear. [1]

Table 28. Microeconomic evaluations of European ALMP (to be continued)

Study	Type of program	Target group	Design	Observation period	Outcome(s)	Identification strategy	Results	Notes/Comments [# observations for meta-data]
Jaenichen (2002)	Wage subsidies (EGZ)	Unemployed, hard-to-place	Non-experimental	1999–2001	Being registered as unemployed observed up to 23 months after participation started	Propensity score matching (nearest neighbor)	+ Treatment significantly reduces unemployment rates	[1]
Hungary								
Micklewright and Nagy (2003)	Monitoring	Unemploy-ment benefits recipients	Experimental	2003	Re-employment rates	Duration model	0 overall+ Only positive and significant effect on women over age 30	Results modestly generalizable due to special character of the Hungarian unemployment benefit system. [1]
Italy								
Paggiaro, Rettore, Trivellato (2005)	Italian Mobility List	Workers in the List	Non-experimental	1995–1999	Probability of transition to a new job	Propensity score matching	+ positive impact for men eligible for the active component only. 0 no significant effect for females.	[1]
Caroleo, Pastore (2002)	The various ALMP targeted to the youth long term unemployed	Young unemployed	Non-experimental	March to June 2000	Probability of transition to a different labor market status (unemployed, formal, informal sector, apprenticeship contract, etc...)	Multinomial logit model	0 no significant impact of the policy variables.	[1]
Netherlands								
Abbring, Van den Berg, Van Ours (2005)	Sanctions	Unemploy-ment insurance recipients	Non-experimental	1992–1993	Re-employment rates	Bivariate duration model	+ Substantial and significant increase in re-employment rates	Policy in its current content is successful. Results appear generalizable. [1]
De Jong, Lindeboom, Van der Klaauw (2005)	Screening of eligibility criteria	Potential disability insurance applicants	Experimental	2001–2003	Sickness absenteeism and disability insurance inflow rates	Difference-in difference	+ Stricter screening reduces sickness absenteeism and number of disability insurance applications	Screening reduces moral hazard of benefits programs. Authors recommend introduction of policy also in control regions. [1]
Gorter and Kalb (1996)	1) counseling, 2) monitoring	Unemploy-ment insurance recipients	Experimental	1989–1990	Re-employment rates	Duration model	0 mixed, pointing towards an insignificant effect. – for temporary contract workers	Large agreements with international literature on similar policies. [1]
Van den Berg, Van der Klaauw (2006)	1) counseling, 2) monitoring	Unemploy-ment insurance recipients with relatively good labor market prospects	Experimental	1998–1999	Re-employment rates	Duration models	0 Small and insignificant positive effect	Large agreements with international literature on similar policies. Policy might be more successful for other target populations. [1]

Table 28. Microeconomic evaluations of European ALMP (to be continued)

Study	Type of program	Target group	Design	Observation period	Outcome(s)	Identification strategy	Results	Notes/Comments [# observations for meta-data]
Van den Berg, Van der Klaauw, Van Ours (2004)	Sanctions	Welfare recipients	Non-experimental	1994–1996	Re-employment rates	Bivariate duration model	+ Substantial and significant increase in re-employment rates	Policy in its current content is successful. Results appear generalizable. [1]
Norway								
Lorentzen, Dahl (2005)	Employment programs and training programs	Social assistance recipients	Non-experimental	1992–1999	Annual gross earnings	Propensity score matching	– Negative and non-significant effects for employment programs, at least positive gains for individuals with medium chances + Positive but modest effects for training	[2]
Røed, Raaum (2003)	1) Training 2) Temporary public employment 3) wage subsidies 4) work practice schemes	Unemployed	Non-experimental	1989–2002	Unemployment duration and transition to employment	Dependent risk hazard rate model	0 Average net effect is around zero + Substantial positive effects for individuals with poor prospects Benefits do not exceed the costs except for male immigrants	The various types of programs are pooled together in the empirical analysis. 0; program type not distinguishable
Zhang (2003)	Training, wage subsidies, employment programs	Unemployed	Non-experimental	1990–2000	Transition to employment	Mixed proportional hazard rate (MPH) model	+ Positive effects for training + Positive effects for wage subsidies 0 No overall effects for employment programs, but some benefits for youth	[3]
Aakvik (2003), Aakvik and Dahl (2006)	Educational programs	Disabled	Non-experimental	1995–1998	Transition to employment	Selection models	0 No significant effect	[2]
Raaum, Torp, Zhang (2002)	Training	Unemployed	Non-experimental	1992–1997	Earnings	Propensity score matching	+ Positive effects for participants with recent-labor market experience 0 Lower or insignificant effects for labor market entrants Cost-beneficial for experienced women Benefits for experienced men close to direct costs and lower for labor market entrants	[1]
Hardoy (2001)	Employment, vocational, training programs and combination programs	Young unemployed	Non-experimental	1989–1993	Employment probability and education level	Maximum likelihood method	0 Overall, no positive effects on employment or education- Negative effects for (classroom) training – Negative effects for vocational programs Increased employment probability for employment and combination programs for womenNo effects for men of any program	[2]

Table 28. Microeconomic evaluations of European ALMP (to be continued)

Study	Type of program	Target group	Design	Observation period	Outcome(s)	Identification strategy	Results	Notes/Comments [# observations for meta-data]
Poland								
Kluve, Lehmann, Schmidt (2005)	1) Training, 2) Wage subsidies	Unemployed adults	Non-experimental	1992-1996	Employment rates	Exact Covariate Matching	+ Training has positive effects, – wage subsidies negative effects, particularly for men	Evidence of "benefit churning": In wage subsidy scheme, individuals participate to restore eligibility.[2]
Portugal								
Centeno, Centeno, Novo (2004)	Job search assistance and small basic skills courses	(Young) unemployed	Non-experimental	1997-2001	Unemployment duration and wages	Propensity score matching and difference-in-difference estimators	0 Small, insignificant impact on unemployment duration – Negative but insignificant effect on wages, large negative impact for men, no impact for women	[2]
Spain								
Arellano (2005)	Training	Unemployed	Non-experimental	2000-2001		Mixed proportional hazard rate (MPH) model	+ Positive effects, higher for women than for men	[1]
Sweden								
Albrecht, van den Berg, Vroman (2005)	Adult Education Initiative	25-55 old unemployed adults	Non-experimental	1990–2000	Earnings, employment probability	Fixed effects, conditional difference-in-differences, conditional probit	+ Positive employment effects for young men, 0 no average income effects for men and no significant effects for women at all	[1]
Andrén, Andrén (2002)	Labor market training	Unemployed	Non-experimental	1993–1997	Employment probability	Latent index sample selection model	+ Small positive effects for Swedish-born, –/+ Negative effects for Foreign-born in the first year, positive afterwards	[1]
Andrén, Gustafsson (2002)	Labor market training	Unemployed	Non-experimental	1984/1985 1987/1988 1990/1991	Earnings	Switching regression model	+ Positive effects for Swedish-born and Foreign-born for the first two cohorts; –/0 Negative effects for Foreign-born and no effects for Swedish-born for the last cohort; –/0 Negative or low pay-off for young adults and individuals with primary education: Better pay-off for males than for women	[3]
Carling, Gustafson (1999)	1) Self-employment grants 2) employment subsidies	Inflow during the period June 1995 to Dec. 1996	Non-experimental	1995-1999	Employment duration	IV, hazard regression model	+ Employment duration is higher for participants in self-employment grants relative to subsidized employment participants.	[0: effectiveness relative to non-participation unclear]
Forslund, Johansson, Lindqvist (2004)	Employment subsidies in the private sector	Unemployed	Non-experimental	1998-2002	Unemployment duration	Exact matching, instrumental variable (IV) methods	+ Positive effect, decreased duration by 8 months. – indications for large dead-weight and substitution effects.	[1]

Table 28. Microeconomic evaluations of European ALMP (to be continued)

Study	Type of program	Target group	Design	Observation period	Outcome(s)	Identification strategy	Results	Notes/Comments [# observations for meta-data]
Fredriksson, Johansson (2003)	Job creation programs, training	Unemployed	Non-experimental	1993-1997	Outflow to employment	Propensity score matching	- Reduced outflow to employment by around 40 percent for both programs, - long-run effects more negative for job creation schemes.	[2]
Harkman, Jansson, Tamás (1996)	Labor market training		Non-experimental	1993	Regular employment and wages after 6 months and 2.5 years		+/0 Positive effect for long-term employment and earnings, no short-term effect for employment	[1]
Larsson (2002)	1) Youth practice, 2) labor market training	20-24 years old youth	Non-experimental	1985-1995	(i)Earnings, (ii)employment probability, (iii) probability of entering studies	OLS, Probit, Matching	- Negative effects on earnings and employment probability.	[2]
Richardson, van den Berg (2001)	Vocational employment-training program	Unemployed	Non-experimental	1993-2000	Transition rate from unemployment to employment	Bivariate duration models	0/+ Net effect on unemployment duration about zero (taking time spent within the program in account), Significantly higher transition rate from unemployment to employment after participation	[1]
Sacklén (2002)	Employment subsidy in the public sector	Unemployed	Non-experimental	1991-1997	Re-employment probability	Multiple equation model and maximum likelihood estimation method	+ Increased (long-term) employment probability by 5 to 10 percentage points.	[1]
Stenberg (2003)	1) Adult Education Initiative 2) vocational part of Labor Market Training	Unemployed	Non-experimental	1996-2000	Earnings, mobility between branches	OLS, IV, Logit	- Negative effect on wage and mobility compared to LMT vocational part	[0; effectiveness relative to non-participation unclear]
Stenberg (2005)	1) Adult Education Initiative 2) Labor Market Training	Unemployed	Non-experimental	1997-2002	Incidence of Unemployment, Unemployment duration	Bivariate probit model, Powell IV	0 Decreased incidence of unemployment, but increased unemployment duration compared to LMT	[0; effectiveness relative to non-participation unclear]
Switzerland								
Steiger (2005)	9 different programs incl. training, employment programs and interim jobs	Unemployed	Non-experimental	1996–1999	8 different outcomes	Propensity score matching	Results sensitive to the definition of nonparticipation. - Negative results for most programs compared to nonparticipation. + Positive results for most programs compared to a delayed participation	[0; program types not distinguishable]

Table 28. Microeconomic evaluations of European ALMP (to be continued)

Study	Type of program	Target group	Design	Observation period	Outcome(s)	Identification strategy	Results	Notes/Comments [# observations for meta-data]
Lalive, Van Ours and Zweimuller (2005)	Sanctions	Unemployment insurance recipients	Non-experimental	1997–1999	Re-employment rates	Bivariate duration model	+ Substantial and significant efect of both sanctions and warnings	Authors conclude that having a benefit system with sanctions is as important as actually imposing sanctions. [1]
UK								
Blundell, Costas Dias, Meghir, van Reenen (2004)	Job search assistance and wage subsidies	Young unemployed	Non-experimental	1982–1999	Outflow to employment	Various difference-in-differences approaches	+ Positive effects for men within the first 4 month, increased outflow to employment of around 5 percentage points (at least 1 percentage point due to job search assistance + Positive effects for women, which are smaller and less precise	[2]
Van Reenen (2003)	Job search assistance and wage subsidies	Young unemployed	Non-experimental	1982–1999	Outflow to employment	Differenc-in-differences approach	+ Social benefits outweigh its social costs, job search assistance more cost effective	[0: results contained in Blundell et al. 2004]
Dolton, O'Neill (2002)	Monitoring and job search assistance	Young unemployed	Experimental	1982–1994	Unemployment rate	–	+ Unemployment rate six percentage points lower for men after 5 years, 0 No significant long- term benefit for women Cost-effective to reduce LTU	[1]

Notes: Columns are self-explaining. The column "Results" includes "+", " ", "–", and "0" signs to indicate qualitatively positive, negative, or zero effects, respectively. The last column contains – in addition to Notes/Comments where applicable – in [brackets] the number of observations that the study contributes to the data for the meta analysis. In general, multiple observations arise if the study discusses several programs. If program types are not sufficiently distinguishable, results usually could not be included in the meta data.

List of figures

List of tables

References

Aakvik, A. (2002), "Estimating the employment effects of education for disabled workers in Norway", Empirical Economics 28(3), 515-533.

Aakvik, A. and S.Å. Dahl (2006), "Transitions to Employment from Labour Market Enterprises in Norway", International Journal of Social Welfare 15, 121–130.

Abbring, J.H., G.J. van den Berg and J.C. van Ours (2005), "The effect of unemployment insurance sanctions on the transition rate from unemployment to employment", Economic Journal 115, 602-630.

Aho, S. and S. Kuntuu (2001), "Työvoimapoliittisten toimenpiteiden vaikuttavuuden tutkiminen rekisteriaineistojen avulla", Työpoliittisia tutkimuksia 233.

Albrecht, J., G.J. van den Berg and S. Vroman (2005), "The Knowledge Lift: The Swedish Adult Education Program That Aimed to Eliminate Low Worker Skill Levels", IZA Discussion Paper 1503, Bonn.

Alonso-Borrego, C., A. Arellano, J.J. Dolado and J.F. Jimeno (2004), "Eficacia del gasto en algunas políticas activas en el mercado laboral espanol", documento de trabajo 53/2004, Fundación Alternativas.

Altavilla, C. and E. Caroleo (2004), "Evaluating asimmetries in Active Labor Policies: the case of Italy", CELPE Discussion Papers, n.84.

Andrén, D. and T. Andrén (2002), "Assessing the Employment Effects of Labor Market Training Programs in Sweden", Working Papers in Economics 70, Göteborg.

Andrén, T. and B. Gustafsson (2004), „Income Effects from Labor Market Training Programs in Sweden During the 80's and 90's", International Journal of Manpower vol. 25, no. 8.

Ardy, B. and G. Umbach (2004), „The European Employment Strategy and employment policy in the UK and Germany", CIBS Working Papers 4-04.

Arellano, F.A. (2005a), „Do training programmes get the unemployed back to work? A look at the Spanish experience", Working Paper 05-25, Economics Series 15, Departamento de Economía, Universidad Carlos III de Madrid.

Arellano, F.A. (2005b), „The effect of outplacement as an active labour market measure: creade case", mimeo, Universidad Carlos III de Madrid, February 2005.

Arellano, F.A. (2005c), „Evaluating the effects of labour market reforms „at the margin" on unemployment and employment stability: the Spanish case", Working Paper 05-12, Economics Series 05, Departamento de Economía, Universidad Carlos III de Madrid.

Arnold, C.U. (2001), „The European Employment Strategy: Composite Factors leading to its Evaluation", mimeo.

Arnold, C.U. and D.R. Cameron (2001), „Why the EU Developed the European Employment Strategy: Unemployment, Public Opinion, and Member State Preferences", mimeo.

Ashenfelter, O. (1978), „Estimating the Effect of Training Programs on Earnings", Review of Economics and Statistics 60, 47-57.

Ballester, R. (2005), „European Employment Strategy and Spanish Labour Market Policies", Working Papers, Department of Economics, University of Girona, Num. 14.

Battistin, E., A. Gavosto and E. Rettore (2002), „Why do subsidised firms survive longer? An evaluation of a program promoting youth entrepreneurship in Italy", in M. Lechner and F. Pfeifer (eds.), Econometric Evaluation of Active Labor Market Politics in Europe, Heidelberg: Physica-Verlag.

Bechterman, G., K. Olivas and A. Dar (2004), „Impacts of Active Labor Market Programs: New Evidence from Evaluations with Particular Attention to Developing and Transition Countries", Social Protection Discussion Paper Series 0402, World Bank.

Bender, S., A. Bergemann, B. Fitzenberger, M. Lechner, R. Miquel, S. Speckesser and C. Wunsch (2005), „Über die Wirksamkeit von FuU-Maßnahmen, Ein Evaluationsversuch mit prozessproduzierten Daten aus dem IAB", Beiträge zur Arbeitsmarkt- und Berufsforschung, Nürnberg.

Bergemann, A. (2005), „Do Job Creation Schemes Initiate Positive Dynamic Employment Effects?", Department of Economics, Free University Amsterdam, unpublished manuscript.

Bergemann, A., B. Fitzenberger and S. Speckesser (2004), „Evaluating the Dynamic Employment Effects of Training Programs in East Germany Using Conditional Difference-in-Differences", ZEW dp No. 04-41.

Bergemann, A., B. Fitzenberger, B. Schultz and S. Speckesser (2000), „Multiple Active Labor Market Policy Participation in East Germany: An Assessment of Outcomes", Konjunkturpolitik, Beiheft Nr. 1, S. 195-243.

Bertelsmann Stiftung (ed.) (2004), International Reform Monitor – Social Policy, Labor Market Policy, Industrial Relations, Issue 9, 2004, Verlag Bertelsmann Stiftung, Gütersloh.

Blien, U., E. Maierhofer, D. Vollkommer and K. Wolf (2003), „Einflussfaktoren der Entwicklung ostdeutscher Regionen – Theorie, Daten, Deskriptionen und quantitative Analysen", in: U. Blien (ed.), Die Entwicklung der ostdeutschen Regionen, Beiträge zur Arbeitsmarkt- und Berufsforschung, Vol. 267, 67-254.

Blundell, R. and C. Meghir (2001), „Active Labour Market Policy vs. Employment Tax Credits: Lessens from Recent UK Reforms", Swedish Economic Policy Review, 8, 239-66.

Blundell, R., M. Costa Dias, C. Meghir, and J. Van Reenen (2004), „Evaluating the Employment Impact of a Mandatory Job Search Program", Journal of the European Economic Association, 2, 569-606.

BMWA Bundesministerium für Wirtschaft und Arbeit (2004), „Arbeitsmarktpolitik in Österreich im Jahre 2003", Vienna.

Bobrowicz, B., W. Durka, B. Klepajczuk, B. Piotrowski and M. Walewski (2004), „Raport z badania Ankietowego, dotyczącego realizacji projektów w ramach działania 1.2 i 1.3 Sektorowego Programu Operacyjnego Rozwój Zasobów Ludzkich", Ministry of Economy and Labor and CASE Foundation, Warsaw [In Polish].

Bolvig, I., P. Jensen and M. Rosholm (2003), „The employment effects of active social policy", IZA Discussion Paper 736, Bonn.

Bonnal, L., D. Fougère and A. Sérandon (1997), „Evaluating the Impact of French Employment Policies on Individual Labour Market Histories", Review of Economic Studies 64, 683-713.

Boone, J. and J. van Ours (2004), „Effective Active Labour Market Policies", IZA Discussion Paper 1335, Bonn.

Boone, J., P. Frederiksson, B. Holmlund and J. van Ours (2002), „Optimal unemployment insurance with monitoring and sanctions", IFAU Working Paper 2002:21, Uppsala.

Bowden, R.J. and D.A. Turkington (1984), Instrumental Variables, Cambridge: Cambridge University Press.

Brodaty, T., B. Crepon and D. Fougere (2002), „Do Long-Term Unemployed Workers Benefit from Active Labor Market Programs? Evidence from France, 1986-1998", mimeo.

Bukowski, M., P. Lewandowski, I. Magda, and J. Zawistowski (2005), „Praca i wzrost", in Zatrudnienie w Polsce 2005, Ministry of Economy and Labor, Warsaw.

Caliendo, M., R. Hujer and S.L. Thomsen (2003), „The Employment Effects of Job Creation Schemes in Germany: A Microeconometric Evaluation", IZA dp No. 1512.

Caliendo, M., R. Hujer and S.L. Thomsen (2004), „Evaluation der Eingliederungseffekte von Arbeitsbeschaffungsmaßnahmen in reguläre Beschäftigung für Teilnehmer in Deutschland", Zeitschrift für Arbeitsmarktforschung, 3/2004, S. 211-237.

Caliendo, M., R. Hujer and S.L. Thomsen (2005a), „Identifying Effect Heterogeneity to Improve the Efficiency of Job Creation Schemes in Germany", IAB discussion paper No. 8/2005.

Caliendo, M., R. Hujer and S.L. Thomsen (2005b), „Indiviudal Employment Effects of Job Creation Schemes in Germany with Respect to Sectoral Heterogeneity", mimeo, Department of Economics, Goethe-University, Frankfurt am Main.

Caliendo, M., R. Hujer and S.L. Thomsen (2005c), „Evaluation individueller Netto-Effekte von ABM in Deutschland – Ein Matching-Ansatz mit Berücksichtigung von regionalen und individuellen Unterschieden", IAB-Werkstattbericht, 2/10.3.2003.

Calmfors, L. (1994), „Active labour market policy and unemployment – a framework for the analysis of crucial design features", OECD Economic Studies 22.

Calmfors, L., A. Forslund and M. Hemström (2002), „Does Active Labour Market Policy work? Lessons from the Swedish Experiences", CESifo Working Paper 675 (4), Munich.

Carling, K. and K. Richardson (2001), „The relative efficiency of labor market programs: Swedish experience from the 1990s", IFAU Working Paper 2001:2, Uppsala.

Carling, K. and L. Gustafson (1999), „Self-employment grants vs. subsidized employment: Is there a difference in the re-unemployment risk?" IFAU Working Paper 1999:6, Uppsala.

Caroleo, E. and F. Pastore (2001), „How fine targeted is ALMP to the youth long term unemployed in Italy", CELPE Discussion Papers 62.

Cavaco, S., D. Fougère and J. Pouget (2005), „Estimating the Effect of a Retraining Program for Displaced Workers on Their Transition to Permanent Jobs", IZA Discussion Paper 1513, Bonn.

Centeno, L., M. Centeno and A.A. Novo (2005), „Evaluating the impact of a mandatory job search program: evidence from a large longitudinal data set", mimeo.

Cockx, B. (2003), „Vocational Training of Unemployed Workers in Belgium", IZA Discussion Paper 682, Bonn.

Cockx, B. and C. Göbel (2004), „Subsidized employment for young long-term unemployed workers – an evaluation", mimeo.

Consejo Económico y Social (2005), „Desequilibrios ocupacionales y políticas activas de empleo", Sesión ordinaria del Pleno de 26 de enero de 2005, CES Departamento de Publicaciones, Colección Informes, Número 1/2005.

Council of the European Union (2003a), „Council decision of 22 July 2003 on guidelines for the employment policies of the Member States", Official Journal of the European Union L 197/13-21.

Council of the European Union (2003b), „Council recommendation of 22 July 2003 on the implementation of Member States' employment policies", Official Journal of the European Union L 205/21-27.

Council of the European Union (2005), „Council decision of 12 July 2005 on Guidelines for the employment policies of the Member States", Official Journal of the European Union L 205/21-27.

Crépon, B., M. Dejemeppe and M. Gurgand (2005), „Counseling the unemployed: does it lower unemployment duration and recurrence?", mimeo.

Cueto, B. (2003), „A microeconometric evaluation of employment programmes in Asturias (Spain)", paper presented at the II Mediterranean Summer School in Theoretical and Applied Economics in Palma de Mallorca, Spain July 14-18, 2003.

Dahlberg, M. and A. Forslund (1999), „Direct Displacement Effects of Labour Market Programmes: The Case of Sweden", Uppsala University Working Paper 1999:22, Uppsala.

Danish Economic Council (2002), „Danish Economy, Autumn 2002", Copenhagen.

Dar, A., Z. Tzannatos (1999), „Active Labor Market Programs: A Review of the Evidence from Evaluations", World Bank.

Davia, M.A., C. García-Serrano, V. Hernanz, M.A. Malo and L.T. Cortes (2001), „Do active labour market policies matter in Spain?", in J. de Koning and H. Mosley (ed.), Labour market policy and unemployment: impact and process evaluations in selected European countries, Cheltenham, Edward Elgar.

De Jong, Ph., M. Lindeboom and B. van der Klaauw (2005), Stricter screening of disability insurance applications, Mimeo Tinbergen Institute, Amsterdam.

De la Porte, C. and P. Pochet (2003), „A two fold assessment of employment policy coordination in light of economic policy coordination", in D. Foden and L. Magnusson (eds.), Five years' experience of the Luxembourg employment strategy.

Dicks, M.J. and N. Hatch (1989), „The relationship between employment and unemployment", Bank of England Discussion Paper No. 39.

Disney, R., L. Bellmann, A. Carruth, W. Franz, R. Jackman, R. Layard, H. Lehmann, and J. Philpott (1991), „Helping the Unemployed: Active Labour Market Policies in Britain and Germany", London, Anglo-German Foundation.

Dolado J.J., C.C. Serrano and J.F. Jimeno (2002), „Drawing lessons from the boom of temporary jobs in Spain", The Economic Journal, 112 (June), F270-F195.

Dolado J.J., F. Felgueroso and J.F. Jimeno (1999), „Los problemas del mercado de trabajo juvenil en España: Empleo, formación y salarios mínimos", Ekonomiaz 43, pp.136-157.

Dolado, J.J. and F. Felgueroso (1997), Los Efectos del Salario Mínimo: Evidencia Empírica para el Caso Espanol, Moneda y Crédito, 204, 213-61.

Dolton, P. and D. O'Neill (1995), „The Impact of Restart on Reservation Wages and Long-Term Unemployment", Oxford Bulletin of Economics and Statistics, 57, 451-470.

Dolton, P. and D. O'Neill (2002), „The Long-Run Effects of Unemployment Monitoring and Work Search Programmes", Journal of Labor Economics Vol. 20, no. 2 (2002).

Dolton, P. and D. O'Neill (1996), „Unemployment duration and the Restart effect: Some experimental evidence", Economic Journal 106, 387-400.

Donner, Allan, N. Birkett, and C. Buck (1981), „Randomization By Cluster: Sample Size Requirements and Analysis", American Journal of Epidemiology 114, 906-914.

Dorsett, R. (2004), „The New Deal for Young People: effect of the options on the labour market status of young men", mimeo, Policy Studies Institute.

Edin, P.A., A. Harkman, B. Holmlund and H. Söderberg (1998), „Escaping long-term unemployment", mimeo.

Eichler, M. and M. Lechner (2002), „An Evaluation of Public Employment Programs in the East German State of Sachsen-Anhalt", Labour economics, Bd. 9 (2002) 2, S. 143-186.

European Commission (2002a), Impact evaluation of the European Employment Strategy, COM (2002) 416 final of 17.7.2002.

European Commission (2002b), Communication from the Commission to the Council, the European Parliament, the Economic and Social Committee and the Committee of the Regions, COM (2002) 416 final.

Eurostat (2001), European social statistics: Labour market policy – Expenditure and participants – Data 1998, Office for Official Publications of the European Communities: Luxembourg.

Eurostat (2002a), European social statistics: Labour market policy – Expenditure and participants-Data 1999, Office for Official Publications of the European Communities: Luxembourg.

Eurostat (2002b), European social statistics: Labour market policy – Expenditure and participants – Data 2000, Office for Official Publications of the European Communities: Luxembourg.

Eurostat (2003), European social statistics: Labour market policy – Expenditure and participants – Data 2001, Office for Official Publications of the European Communities: Luxembourg.

Eurostat (2004), European social statistics: Labour market policy – Expenditure and participants – Data 2002, Office for Official Publications of the European Communities: Luxembourg.

Eurostat (2005), European social statistics: Labour market policy – Expenditure and participants – Data 2003, Office for Official Publications of the European Communities: Luxembourg.

Fertig, M. and J. Kluve (2004), „A Conceptual Framework for the Evaluation of Comprehensive Labor Market Policy Reforms in Germany", Applied Economics Quarterly Supplement 55, 83-112.

Fertig, M., C.M. Schmidt and H. Schneider (2002), „Active Labor Market Policy in Germany – Is There a Successful Policy Strategy?", IZA Discussion Paper 576, Bonn, forthcoming (2006), Regional Science and Urban Economics.

Fertig, M., J. Kluve, C.M. Schmidt, W. Friedrich, H. Apel, and H. Hägele (2004), Die Hartz-Gesetze zur Arbeitsmarktpolitik – Ein umfassendes Evaluationskonzept ["The Hartz reforms of labor market policy – a comprehensive evaluation concept"], RWI Schriften 74, Berlin: Duncker & Humblot.

Filges, T. and B. Larsen (2001), „Stick, Carrot and Skill Acquisition", mimeo.

Fischer, G. and K. Pichelmann (1991), „Temporary layoff unemployment in Austria: empirical evidence from adiministrative data", Applied Economics 23, 1447-1452.

Fitzenberger B. and S. Speckesser (2005), „Employment Effects of the Provision of Specific Professional Skills and Techniques in Germany", mimeo, Department of Economics, Goethe-University, Frankfurt am Main.

Fitzenberger, B. and S. Speckesser (2000), „Zur wissenschaftlichen Evaluation der Aktiven Arbeitsmarktpolitik in Deutschland: Ein Überblick", Mitteilungen aus der Arbeitsmarkt- und Berufsforschung 33, 357-370.

Fitzenberger, B. und H. Prey (1998), „Beschäftigungs- und Verdienstmöglichkeiten von Weiterbildungsteilnehmern im ostdeutschen Transformationsprozeß: Eine Methodenkritik", in F. Pfeiffer and W. Pohlmeier (Eds.), Qualifikation, Weiterbildung und Arbeitsmarkterfolg, Volume ZEW Wirtschaftsanalysen Bd. 31 (S. 39-96). Baden-Baden: Nomos Verlagsgesellschaft.

Forslund, A., P. Johansson and L. Lindqvist (2004), „Employment subsidies – A fast lane from unemployment to work?", IFAU Working Paper 2004:18, Uppsala.

Fougère, D., J. Pradel and M. Roger (2005), „Does Job Search Assistance Affect Search Effort and Outcomes? – A Microeconometric Analysis of Public versus Private Search Methods", IZA Discussion Paper 1825, Bonn, Germany.

Frederiksson, P. and P. Johansson (2003), „Employment, mobility, and active labor market programs", IFAU Working Paper 2003:3, Uppsala.

Geerdsen, L. and A. Holm (2004), „Job-search Incentives From Labor Market Programs – an Empirical Analysis", Working Paper 2004-03, Centre for Applied Microeconometrics, Institute of Economics, University of Copenhagen, Denmark.

Geerdsen, L.P. (2003), „Marginalisation processes in the Danish labor market", PhD thesis, The Danish National Institute of Social Research, Report 03:24.

Goetschy, J. (1999), „The European Employment Strategy: Genesis and Development", European Journal of Industrial Relations vol. 5 no. 2, 117 – 137.

Góra, M. (1997a), „Central and Eastern European labor markets in transition", in S. Zecchini, (eds), Lessons from the economic transition, Dordrecht, Boston, London: Kluwer Academic Publishers.

Góra, M. (1997b), „Employment Policies and Programs in Poland", in Employment Policies and Programs in Eastern and Central Europe (ed. M. Godfrey and P. Richards), Geneva: International Labor Office, pp. 115-134.

Góra, M. (2005), „Trwale wysokie bezrobocie w Polsce. Wyjaśnienia i propozycje", Ekonomista, No.1, pp. 27-48 [In Polish].

Góra, M. and M. Rutkowski (1990), „The Demand for Labor and the Disguised Unemployment in Poland in the 1980s", Communist Economies No.3 pp. 325-334.

Góra, M. and M. Walewski (2002), „Bezrobocie równowagi w Polsce – wstępna analiza i próba oszacowania", Polska Gospodarka, No.4, pp. 36-40 [In Polish].

Góra, M., M. Socha and U. Sztanderska (1995), „Analiza polskiego rynku pracy w latach 1990-1994: Kierunki zmian i rola polityk rynku pracy", Central Statistical Orfice, Warsaw [In Polish].

Gorter, C. and G.R.J. Kalb (1996), „Estimating the effect of counseling and monitoring the unemployed using a job search model", Journal of Human Resources 31, 590–610.

Government Offices of Sweden (2003), „A Report on Education and training in Sweden and the shared European goals", http://www.sweden.gov.se/sb/d/574/a/20479, 21.07.2005.

Graversen, B. (2004), „Employment effects of active labor market programs: Do the programs help welfare benefit recipients to find jobs?", PhD thesis 2004-2, Department of Economics, University of Aarhus, Denmark.

Graversen, B. and P. Jensen (2004), „A reappraisal of the virtues of private sector employment programs", Chapter 3 in Graversen (2004).

Grubb, D. (1999), „Making work pay: the role of eligibility criteria for unemployment benefits", Mimeo OECD, Paris.

Hagen, T. (2003), „Three Approaches to the Evaluation of Active Labor Market Policy in East Germany Using Regional Data", ZEW dp. No. 03-27.

Hämäläinen, K. (1999), „Aktiivinen työvoimapolitiikka ja työllistyminen avoimille työmarkkinoille", Elinkeinoelämän tutkimuslaitos 151.

Hämäläinen, K. (2002), „The Effectiveness of Labour Market Training in Different Eras of Unemployment", in S. Ilmakunnas and E. ja Koskela (eds.), „Towards

Higher Employment. The Role of Labour Market Institutions", VATT Publication 32.

Hämäläinen, K. and V. Ollikainen (2004), „Differential Effects of Active Labour Market Programmes in the Early Stages of Young People's Unemployment", VATT Research Reports 115, Helsinki.

Hardoy, I. (2001), „Impact of Multiple Labour Market Programmes on Multiple Outcomes: The Case of Norwegian Youth Programmes", mimeo.

Harkman, A., F. Jansson and A. Tamás (1996), „Effects, defects and prospects — An evaluation of Labour Market Training in Sweden", Arbetsmarknadsstyrelsen (Swedish National Labour Market Board: Research Unit), Working Paper 1996:5.

Heckman, J.J. (1979), „Sample Selection Bias As A Specification Error", Econometrica.

Heckman, J.J. (1996), „Randomization as an Instrumental Variable", Review of Economics and Statistics 77, 336-341.

Heckman, J.J., R.J. LaLonde and J.A. Smith (1999), „The economics and econometrics of active labour market programs", in O. Ashenfelter and D. Card (eds.), Handbook of Labor Economics 3, Elsevier, Amsterdam.

Høglund, J. and A. Holm (2002), „Returning Long-Term Sick-Listed to Work – The effects of education in a competing risk model with time varying covariates and unobserved heterogeneity", mimeo.

Hübler, O. (1997), Evaluation beschäftigungspolitischer Maßnahmen in Ostdeutschland, Jahrbücher für Nationalökonomie und Statistik, 216, 21-44.

Hujer, R. and C. Zeiss (2003), „Macroeconomic Impacts of ALMP on the Matching Process in West Germany", IZA Discussion Paper 915, Bonn.

Hujer, R. and M. Wellner (2000), „Berufliche Weiterbildung und individuelle Arbeitslosigkeitsdauer in West- und Ostdeutschland: Eine mikroökonometrische Analyse", Mitteilungen aus der Arbeitsmarkt- und Berufsforschung, 33(3), 405-420.

Hujer, R., K.O. Maurer and M. Wellner (1998), „Kurz- und langfristige Effekte von Weiterbildungsmaßnahmen auf die Arbeitslosigkeitsdauer in Westdeutschland", in F. Pfeiffer und W. Pohlmeier (Eds..), Qualifikation, Weiterbildung und Arbeitsmarkterfolg, ZEW Wirtschaftsanalysen Bd. 31 (S. 197-222). Baden-Baden: Nomos Verlagsgesellschaft.

Hujer, R., M. Caliendo and C. Zeiss (2004), „Macroeconometric Evaluation of Active Labor Market Policy – A case study for Germany", in P. Descy and M. Tessaring (ed.), Impact of education and training, Report on vocational training research in Europe: Background report, Luxembourg.

Hujer, R., M. Caliendo and D. Radi (2004), „Estimating the effects of wage subsidies on the labor demand in West Germany using the IAB establishment panel", in: Statistisches Bundesamt (Ed.), MIKAS – Mikroanalysen und amtliche Statistik, Wiesbaden: Statistisches Bundesamt, S. 249-283.

Hujer, R., M. Caliendo and S. Thomsen (2005), „Mikroökonometrische Evaluation des Integrationserfolges", in P. Schaade (Ed.): Evaluation des hessischen Modells der Stellenmarktoffensive, Beiträge zur Arbeitsmarkt- und Berufsforschung, 291, Nürnberg.

Hujer, R., M. Caliendo, and S.L. Thomsen (2004), „New evidence on the effects of job creation schemes in Germany – a matching approach with threefold heterogeneity", Research in economics: an international review of economics, Bd. 58 (2004), 4, p. 257-302.

Hujer, R., S.L. Thomsen and C. Zeiss (2004), „The Effects of Vocational Training Programs on the Duration of Unemployment in Germany", IZA DP No. 1117.

Hujer, R., U. Blien, M. Caliendo and C. Zeiss (2002), „Macroeconomic Evaluation of Active Labour Market Policies in Germany – A Dynamic Panel Approach Using Regional Data", IZA Discussion Paper 616, Bonn.

Jacobi, L. and J. Kluve (2006), "Before and After the Hartz Reforms: The Performance of Activ Labour Market Policy in Germany", RWI Essen, Discussion Paper 41.

Jaenichen, U. (2002), „Lohnkostenzuschüsse und individuelle Arbeitslosigkeit. Analysen auf der Grundlage kombinierter Erhebungs- und Prozessdaten unter Anwendung von Prospensity Score Matching", Mitteilungen aus der Arbeitsmarkt- und Berufsforschung, 35/2002, 327-351.

Jensen, P., M. Rosholm and M. Svarer (2003), „The response of youth unemployment to benefits, incentives, and sanctions", European Journal of Political Economy, vol. 19, pp. 301-316.

Jespersen, S., J. Munch and L. Skipper (2004), „Costs and benefits of Danish active labor market programs", Working Paper 2004:1, Danish Economic Council, Copenhagen.

Johansson K. (2001), „Do labor market programs affect labor force participation?", Swedish Economic Policy Review 8 (2), 215-234.

Jongen, E.L.W., E. van Gameren and J.J. Graafland (2003), „Exploring the Macroeconomic Impact of Subsidized Employment", De Economist 151(1), 81-118.

Kallaste, E. (2003), National Social Dialogue on formulation, implementation and monitoring of employment policies, Country Study, PRAXIS Center for Policy Studies.

Kangasharju, A. and T. Venetoklis (2003), „Do wage-subsidies increase employment in firms?", VATT Discussion Paper 304, Helsinki.

Klose, C. and S. Bender (2000), „Berufliche Weiterbildung für Arbeitslose – Ein Weg zurück in Beschäftigung? Analyse einer Abgängerkohorte des Jahres 1986 aus Maßnahmen zur Fortbildung und Umschulung mit einer ergänzten IAB-Beschäftigungsstichprobe 1975-1990", Mitteilungen aus der Arbeitsmarkt- und Berufsforschung, 24(3), 421-444.

Kluve, J. and C.M. Schmidt (2002), „Can training and employment subsidies combat European unemployment?", Economic Policy 35, 409-448.

Kluve, J., H. Lehmann and C.M. Schmidt (1999), „Active Labour Market Policies in Poland: Human Capital Enhancement, Stigmatization, or Benefit Churning", Journal of Comparative Economics 27, 61-89.

Kluve, J., H. Lehmann and Ch. Schmidt (2005), „Disentangling Treatment Effects of Active Labor Market Policies: The role of labor force status sequences", mimeo, revised version of IZA Discussion Paper, No.355.

Kokkulepe palga alammäära muutmise põhimõtete kohta (2001), „Agreement on changing the minimum wage principles".

Korpi, T. (1994), „Escaping Unemployment", Working Paper, SOFI, Stockholm.

Kuddo, A., R. Leetmaa, L. Leppik, M. Luuk and A Võrk (2002), Sotsiaaltoetuste efektiivsus ja mõju tööjõupakkumisele (Social Benefits in Estonia: efficiency and impact on work incentives), PRAXIS Center for Policy Studies.

Kugler, A., J.F. Jimeno and V. Hernanz (2003), „Emplyoment Consequences of Re-strictive Employment Policies: Evidence from Spanish Labour Market Reforms", FEDEA, working paper 2003-14.

Kyhl, T. (2001), „Does the right and obligation to participate in „activation programs" motivate the unemployed to look for work?" (In Danish), Nationaløkonomisk tidsskrift, vol. 139, no. 3.

Lalive, R., J.C. van Ours and J. Zweimüller (2004), „How changes in financial incentives affect the duration of unemployment", IZA Discussion Paper 1363, Bonn.

Lalive, R., J.C. Van Ours and J. Zweimüller (2005), „The Effect of Benefit Sanctions on the Duration of Unemployment", Journal of the European Economic Association forthcoming.

LaLonde, R.J. (1995), „The Promise of Public Sector-Sponsored Training Programs", Journal of Economic Perspectives 9, 149-168.

Larsson, L. (2002), „Evaluating social programs: active labor market policies and social insurance", IFAU Dissertation Series 2002:1, Uppsala.

Lechner, M. (1998), Training the East German Labor Force, Microeconometric Evalu-ations of Continuous Vocational Training after Unification, Heidelberg: Physica-Verlag.

Lechner, M. (1999), „Earnings and Employment Effects of Continuous Off-the-Job Training in East Germany after Unification", Journal of Business and Economic Statistics, 17(1), 74-90.

Lechner, M. (2000), „An Evaluation of Public Sector Sponsored Continuous Voca-tional Training Programs in East Germany", Journal of Human Ressources, 35, 347-375.

Lechner, M., R. Miquel and C. Wunsch (2004), „Long-Run Effects of Public Sector Sponsored Training in West Germany", IZA DP No. 1443.

Lechner, M., R. Miquel and C. Wunsch (2005), „The Curse and Blessing of Training the Unemployed in a Changing Economy – The Case of East Germany After Unifi-cation", IAB Discussion Paper, 14/2005.

Leetmaa, R. and A. Võrk (2004), „Evaluation of Active Labour Market Programmes in Estonia", mimeo.

Leetmaa, R., A. Võrk, R. Eamets and K. Sõstra (2003), „Aktiivse tööpoliitika tulemuslikkuse analüüs Eestis (Evaluation of the Active Labor Market Policies in Estonia)", PRAXIS Center for Policy Studies.

Lissenburgh, S. (2005), „New deal option effects on employment entry and unem-ployment exit: An evaluation using propensity score matching", International Journal of Manpower Vol.25 No.5, 411-430.

Lorentzen, T. and E. Dahl (2005), „Active labour market programmes in Norway: are they helpful for social assistance recipients?", International Journal of Social Welfare 14 (2), 86-98.

Malmberg-Heimonen, I. and J. Vuori (2004a), „Financial Incentives and Job Search Training – Methods to Increase Labour Market Integration in Contemporary Welfare States?", Social Policy and Administration 39, 247-259.

Malmberg-Heimonen, I. and J. Vuori (2004b), „Activation or Discouragement -Enforced Participation Modifying the Success of Job-search Training", European Journal of Social Work volume 8, in press.

Manski, Ch. F. (1995), Identification Problems in the Social Sciences, Cambridge, Mass. et al.: Harvard University Press.

Martin, J. (2000), What Works among Labor Market Policies: Evidence from OECD Countries' Experiences, OECD Economic Studies, No.30.

Martin, J.P. and D. Grubb (2001), „What works and for whom: a review of OECD countries' experiences with active labour market policies", IFAU Working Paper 2001:14.

Mato, F.J. (2002), La formación para el empleo: una evalucación cuasi-experimental, Madrid, consejería de Trabajo y Promoción de Empleo del Principado de Asturias and Civitas Ediciones.

Micklewright, J. and G. Nagy (2005), Job search monitoring and unemployment duration in Hungary: evidence from a randomised control trial, Mimeo, University of Southampton.

Munch, J. and L. Skipper (2004), „The consequences of active labor market program participation in Denmark", Working Paper.

Newell, A. and F. Pastore (2000), „Regional Unemployment and Industrial Restructuring in Poland", Centro di Economia del Lavoro e dei Politica Economica, Discussion Paper No.51.

OECD (1997), OECD Economic Surveys Austria 1996 – 1997, Paris.

OECD (2001), Labor Market Policies and the Public Employment Service, OECD Paris.

OECD (2003), Statistics on the Member Countries, OECD Observer 2003/Supplement 1, Paris.

OECD (2004), Employment Outlook, OECD: Paris.

Paas, T., R. Eamets, J. Masso and M. Rõõm (2003), „Labor Market Flexibility and Migration in the Baltic States: Macro Evidences", Working Paper Series, Number 16/2003, University of Tartu.

Paggiaro A., E. Rettore and U. Trivellato (2005), „The impact of the Italian „Mobility List" on employment chances: new evidence from linked administrative archives", mimeo.

Pannenberg, M. (1995), Weiterbildungsaktivitäten und Erwerbsbiographie, Eine empirische Analyse für Deutschland, Frankfurt am Main, New York: Campus.

Pannenberg, M. and J. Schwarze (1996), „Unemployment, Labor Market Training Programs and Regional Wages: An Extended Wage Curve Approach", DIW-Diskussionspapiere, 139.

Puhani, P. (2002), „Advantage Through Training in Poland? A Microeconometric Evaluation of the Employment Effects of Training and Job Subsidy Programs", Labor, Vol. 16, No. 3, pp. 569.

Puhani, P. (2003), „Active Labor Market Policy and Employment Flows: Evidence from Polish Regional Data“, International Journal of Manpower, Vol. 24, No. 8, pp. 897-915.

Raaum, O., H. Torp and T. Zhang (2002), „Do individual programme effects exceed the costs? Norwegian evidence on long run effects of labour market training“, Memorandum 15, Department of Economics, University of Oslo.

Regnér, H. (2002), „A nonexperimental evaluation of training programs for the unemployed in Sweden“, Labour Economics 9, 187-206.

Reinowski, E., B. Schultz and J. Wiemers (2003), „Evaluation von Maßnahmen der aktiven Arbeitsmarktpolitik mit Hilfe eines iterativen Matching-Algorithmus – Eine Fallstudie über langzeitarbeitslose Maßnahmeteilnehmer in Sachsen“, IWH DP, Nr. 173.

Reinowski, E., B. Schultz and J. Wiemers (2004), „Evaluation of Further Training Programs with an Optimal Matching Algorithm“, mimeo, IWH.

Richardson, K. and G.J. van den Berg (2001), „The effect of vocational employment training on the individual transition rate from unemployment to work“, Swedish Economic Policy Review 8 (2001), 175-213.

Riley, R. and G. Young (2001a), „Does welfare-to-work policy increase employment? Evidence form the UK New Deal for Young Unemployed“, National Institute for Economic and Social Research Working Paper No. 183.

Riley, R. and G. Young (2001b), „The macroeconomic impact of the New Deal for Young People“, National Institute for Economic and Social Research Working Paper No. 185.

Røed, K. and O. Raaum (2003), „The Effect of Programme Participation on the Transition Rate from Unemployment to Employment“, Memorandum 13, Department of Economics, University of Oslo.

Rosenbaum, P.R. (1995), Observational Studies, New York: Springer Series in Statistics.

Rosholm, M. and M. Svarer (2004), „Estimating the Threat Effect of Active Labor Market Programs“, Working Paper 2004-06, Department of Economics, University of Aarhus, Denmark.

Rubin, D.B. (1974), „Estimating Causal Effects of Treatments in Randomized and Nonrandomized Studies“, Journal of Educational Psychology 66, 688-701.

Rubin, D.B. (1986), „Which Ifs Have Causal Answers?“, Journal of the American Statistical Association 81, 961-962.

RWI Essen (2005), Study on the effectiveness of ALMPs, Project for the European Commission, DG Employment and Social Affairs, Inception report, February.

Sacklén, H. (2002), „An evaluation of the Swedish trainee replacement schemes“, IFAU Working Paper 2002:7.

Schernhammer, B and U. Adam (2002), „Evaluierung von Jobcoaching 2000“, AMS Report 31, Vienna.

Schmid G., S. Speckesser and C. Hilbert (2001), „Does Active Labor Market Policy Matter? An Aggregate Analysis for Germany“, in J. de Koning and H. Mosley

(Eds.), Labor Market Policy and Unemployment – Impact and Process Evaluations in Selected European Countries, Cheltenham (Elgar), 77-114.

Sianesi, B. (2002), „Differential effects of Swedish active labour market programmes for unemployed adults during the 1990s", IFAU Working Paper 2002:5, Uppsala.

Sianesi, B. (2004), „An Evaluation of the Swedish System of Active Labour Market Programs in the 1990s", Review of Economics and Statistics 86 (1), 133-155.

Statistical Office of Estonia (2005), Statistical Yearbook of Estonia, Tallinn.

Statistical Office of Estonia, Labor Force Surveys 1995-2004.

Steiner, V., E. Wolf, J. Engeln, M. Almus, H. Schrumpf and P. Feldotto (1998), „Strukturanalyse der Arbeitsmarktentwicklung in den neuen Bundesländern", ZEW Wirtschaftsanalysen, Volume 30, Nomos, Baden-Baden.

Stenberg, A. (2002), „Short Run Effects on Wage Earnings of the Adult Education Initiative in Sweden", Umeå Economics Studies 593, Umeå.

Stenberg, A. (2003), „The Adult Education Initiative in Sweden – Second year Effects on Wage Earnings and the Influence on Branch Mobility", Umeå Economics Studies 593, Umeå.

Stenberg, A. (2005), „Comprehensive Education for the Unemployed – Evaluating the Effects on Unemployment of the Adult Education Initiative in Sweden", Labour 19(1), 123-146.

Stenberg, A. and O. Westerlund (2004), „Does Comprehensive Education Work for the Long-term Unemployed?", Umeå Economic Studies 641, Umeå.

Stiglbauer, A., F. Stahl, R. Winter-Ebmer and J. Zweimüller (2003), „Job Creation and Job Destruction in a Regulated Labor Market: The Case of Austria", Empirica 30, 127 – 148.

Swedish Institute (2005a), „Swedish Labor market Policy", http://www.sweden.se/templates/cs/FactSheet____12149.aspx, 20.07.2005.

Swedish Institute (2005b), „The Swedish economy", http://www.sweden.se/templates/cs/Print_BasicFactSheet____2636.aspx, 20.07.2005.

Sweeney, K. and D. McMahon (1998), „The effects of Job Seekers' Allowance on the claimant count", Labour Market Trends, 195-202.

Tanguy, S. (2004), „Job search: between Insurance and Incentive", mimeo.

Trabert, L and A. Rhode (2005), „Kosten und Nutzen/Wirksamkeit der Maßnahmen", in P. Schaade (Ed.): Evaluation des hessischen Modells der Stellenmarktoffensive, Beiträge zur Arbeitsmarkt- und Berufsforschung 291, Nürnberg.

Tuomala, J. (2002), „Työnhakukoulutuksen vaikutusten arviointi", Työpoliittisia tutkimuksia 222.

Van den Berg, G.J. and B. van der Klaauw (2006), „Counseling and monitoring of unemployed workers: theory and evidence from a controlled social experiment", International Economic Review, forthcoming.

Van den Berg, G.J., B. van der Klaauw and J.C. van Ours (2004), „Punitive sanctions and the transition rate from welfare to work", Journal of Labor Economics 22, 211-241.

Van der Linden, B. (2005), „Equilibrium Evaluation of Active Labor Market Programmes Enhancing Matching Effectiveness", IZA Discussion Paper 1526, Bonn.

Van Ours, J.C. and J. Boone (2004), „Effective Active Labor Market Policies", IZA Discussion Paper 1335, Bonn.

Van Reenen, J. (2003), „Active Labour Market Policies and the British New Deal for the Young Unemployed in Context", NBER Working Paper Series 9576.

Vella, F. (1998), „Estimating Models with Sample Selection Bias: A Survey", Journal of Human Resources 33, 127-172.

Vollkommer, D. (2004), „Regionalisierung der aktiven Arbeitsmarktpolitik", Beiträge zur Arbeitsmarkt- und Berufsforschung, Nr. 287, Nürnberg.

Weber, A. and H. Hofer (2003), „Active job-search programs a promising tool? A microeconometric evaluation for Austria", IHS working paper, Economic Series 131, Vienna.

Weber, A. and H. Hofer (2004), „Employment effects of early interventions on job search programs", IZA Discussion Paper 1076, Bonn.

Winter-Ebmer, R. (2001), „Evaluating an Innovative Redundancy-Retraining Project: The Austrian Steel Foundation", IZA Discussion paper 277, Bonn.

Zhang, T. (2003), „Identifying treatment effects of active labour market programmes for Norwegian adults", Memorandum 26, Department of Economics, University of Oslo.

Zweimüller, J. and R. Winter-Ebmer (1996), „Manpower training programs and employment stability", Economica 63, 113-130.